HarperCollins *practical gardener*

FLOWERS

HarperCollins *practical gardener*

FLOWERS

ALAN TOOGOOD

HarperResource

An Imprint of HarperCollinsPublishers

First published in Great Britain in 2003 by HarperCollins*Publishers* Ltd.

HARPERCOLLINS PRACTICAL GARDENER: FLOWERS. Text by Alan Toogood;
copyright © 2003, 2004 HarperCollins*Publishers*.
Artworks and design copyright © 2003, 2004 HarperCollins*Publishers*.

The majority of the photographs in this book were taken by
Tim Sandall. For a detailed breakdown of photographic credits, see page 160.

Photographic props: Coolings Nurseries, Rushmore Hill, Knockholt, Kent,
TN14 7NN, UK, www.coolings.co.uk

Design and Editorial: Focus Publishing, Sevenoaks, Kent, UK
Project Editor: Guy Croton
Editor: Vanessa Townsend
Project Coordinator: Caroline Watson
Designer: Philip Clucas
Illustration: David Etherington

For HarperCollins*Publishers*
Managing Editor: Angela Newton
Art Direction: Luke Griffin
Editor: Alastair Laing

ISBN 0-06-073339-X

Color reproduction by Colourscan
Printed and bound in Hong Kong by Printing Express Ltd.

Contents

Introduction

The dictionary definition of a flower is a plant that is grown or is especially notable for its flowers, which are the reproductive organs of a plant. Gardeners use the term flowers to mean nonwoody blooming plants—that is, plants other than trees, shrubs, roses, and woody climbers. It is the nonwoody blooming plants that form the subject of this book.

Perennials Among the best-known and most widely planted flowers are the perennials—plants that live for a number of years. A few are fairly short-lived, performing only for a few years before they start to deteriorate, such as campions or lychnis, and mulleins or verbascums, some of which die after they have flowered and set seeds. The majority, though, have a very long life and some, including peonies, perform well for decades.

Hardy perennials are those kinds that can be grown outdoors year-round in frost-prone climates. Many are herbaceous: the top growth dies down in the fall, the plants lie dormant over winter, and come into growth again in the spring. Other hardy perennials, such as bergenias, are evergreen, retaining their leaves year-round, although they are still winter dormant.

Tender perennials, such as geraniums or pelargoniums, are sensitive to frost and cannot be grown outside year-round in cool and cold climates. Some are herbaceous, others evergreen. Many tender perennials are used as summer bedding plants in frost-prone climates.

Many of the popular rock plants or alpines are hardy perennials, but because of their dwarf or prostrate habit they are ideally suited to rock gardens.

Aquatic plants are mainly hardy perennials, the only difference being that they live in water. The most popular flowering aquatics are waterlilies (Nymphaea), which no self-respecting garden pool should be without.

Bulbs, corms, and tubers Bulbs form another large group of flowers and are to be seen in most gardens. They are storage organs, containing a supply of

Iris bucharica

Paeonia 'Bowl of Beauty'

water and food that keeps the plant alive while it is dormant. Bulbs, such as daffodils (Narcissus), are composed of fleshy modified leaves enclosing an embryo flower—so when you buy a bulb you can almost guarantee that it will flower. Gardeners also loosely describe corms and tubers as bulbs. These are also storage organs. Some corms and tubers, such as crocuses and cyclamen respectively, are modified, swollen stems, with the new growth coming from buds at the top. However, the tubers of other plants, such as dahlias, are swollen roots—the tuber itself being unable to produce new growth.

As with perennials, bulbs, corms, and tubers are either hardy, being able to survive year-round in frost-prone climates, or tender, liable to be damaged or killed by frost.

Annuals and biennials A large group of flowers, the annuals and biennials, live for only a short time. Annuals grow from seed, flower, produce seeds, and then die within one season or year. Once again there are hardy and tender kinds, such as pot marigolds (*Calendula officinalis*) and French marigolds (*Tagetes patula*) respectively.

Most of the biennials that are grown in gardens are hardy, such as the common foxglove (*Digitalis purpurea*). These plants grow from seed one year, flower and set seeds the next, and then die.

How to Use This Book

This book is divided into three parts. The opening chapters guide you through all areas of garden practice, from assessing your site, through planting and general care, to propagation techniques. A comprehensive plant directory follows, with individual entries on over 200 of the most commonly available flowers, listed in alphabetical order.

All the most colorful and popular flowers are included, covering many different styles of gardening and uses. The final section of the book covers plant problems. Troubleshooting pages allow you to diagnose the likely cause of any problems, and a directory of pests and diseases offers advice on how to solve them.

latin name of the plant genus, followed by its **common name**.

detailed descriptions give specific advice on care for each plant, including planting and pests and diseases.

alphabetical tabs on the side of the page, color-coded to help you quickly find the plant you want.

a key at the bottom of the page explains what each symbol means.

variety charts list recommended varieties for most genera of flowers or the best individual species. These display key information to help you choose your ideal plant, showing:

• when the plant is in flower during the year
• the time to plant for the best results
• the height and spread of the flowers in feet/inches
• the minimum temperature the plant will withstand
• the plant's watering and light/shade requirements
• a rough approximation of the flower color
• additional comments from the author

Assessing Your Garden

To be a successful flower gardener, first assess the conditions in your garden. This should ideally take place over a complete year, and will require attention to various features.

Aspect

Find out, by observation through the year, which are the sunny parts of the garden and which are in shade for most of the day, and then choose suitable plants for each condition. Plants that like plenty of sun will not perform well in shade, and shade-loving plants will be scorched and generally fail to thrive in a hot, sunny spot. Sun and shade are not problems, though—there are plenty of plants suited to both sets of conditions.

Shade below trees also needs to be considered when choosing plants. Evergreen trees cast heavy shade year-round and provide a suitable home only for plants that tolerate continuous, dense shade. However, deciduous trees allow sun through during late fall, winter, and early spring when devoid of leaves, allowing such plants as dwarf spring bulbs and woodland-garden perennials to be grown beneath them.

Wind

Wind not only damages plants by whipping them around and tearing their leaves, but constant wind can also result in stunted and deformed growth. Therefore, try to overcome the problem as much as possible. Some gardens are windier than others, especially those in open, exposed places and coastal areas.

If your garden seems to have more than its fair share of wind, then grow only those plants that are able to survive it. For example, opt mainly for shorter-growing plants rather than tall kinds, and those that move with the wind rather than resist it, such as ornamental grasses and other more open kinds.

Create shelter from the wind. Do not try to stop it in its tracks with a solid object such as a wall or close-boarded fence, as it will simply rush over the top, resulting in damaging turbulence on the other side. Rather, slow the wind down by filtering it with a semi-permeable screen. For example, plant a hedge of wind-resistant plants such as *Crataegus monogyna* (hawthorn), *Ligustrum ovalifolium* (oval-leafed privet), *Pyracantha rogersiana* (firethorn), *Rosa rugosa* (Ramanas rose), or *Taxus baccata* (yew).

Soil

It really pays to improve the soil in your garden as much as you possibly can before you start sowing or planting flowers. Few gardens are blessed with the ideal soil—a fertile, medium loam that is well drained yet retains sufficient moisture during dry weather. However, there are plenty of things you can do to improve it (see below).

Drainage

If the soil becomes very wet or waterlogged in the winter, it will need to be improved to make it drain more freely, as most plants will not tolerate such conditions—their roots will suffocate and rot. Conditions can usually be

Digging organic matter into your garden soil will help enrich it.

improved by incorporating copious amounts of horticultural grit or coarse sand, plus bulky organic matter, during digging, to open up the soil and allow water to pass through more easily. Clay soils are the most likely to become waterlogged.

At the other extreme are very free-draining soils such as sandy and chalky types that are unable to hold on to much rainwater and become very dry during rainless periods. The way to improve these soils is to add copious amounts of bulky organic matter during digging.

Choose plants suited to your soil conditions. For instance, moisture-loving plants will be happy in the moister clay soils, while plants that tolerate dry or drought conditions are a better bet for free-draining sandy and chalky soils. Loam soils will grow almost anything.

Specific Conditions

Each garden is different, with its own specific, prevailing conditions to take into account. The illustration below is a representation of a "typical" garden, comprising a number of different elements which often feature in most gardens.

Of course, your own garden may look very different from the one illustrated here, but you will almost certainly need to take the same factors into account when assessing the suitability of your garden for the cultivation of flowers. Remember that it is always easier to work with conditions as you find them. Don't try too hard to fight nature, because nature usually wins in the end. That said, with a few slight changes to your garden, you can improve considerably your plants' chances of growing without too much effort and expense.

KEY

This symbol denotes the shadiest parts of the garden, typically to be found wherever a tree or building casts a shadow.

The yellow line denotes sunshine in the garden. On one side the sun will shine in the morning, on the other, in the afternoon.

This blue arrow denotes the direction of wind. In this case, the wind swirls over the fence and across the border beneath.

This green arrow denotes a gradient in the garden floor. In this case, the garden slopes from one end to another.

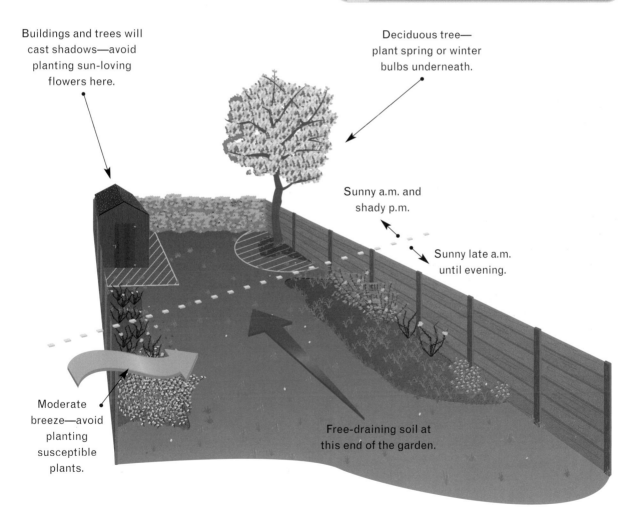

Buildings and trees will cast shadows—avoid planting sun-loving flowers here.

Deciduous tree— plant spring or winter bulbs underneath.

Sunny a.m. and shady p.m.

Sunny late a.m. until evening.

Moderate breeze—avoid planting susceptible plants.

Free-draining soil at this end of the garden.

Choosing & Buying Plants

Plants can be bought at many stages of growth, from dormant seed to flowering plant. Each type offers its own set of benefits.

Seeds

Seeds represent the cheapest way for gardeners to obtain new plants. A packet of seeds, promising several dozen or even hundreds of new plants, often costs at least fifty per cent less than a single plant ready for

planting out. Not only that, but there is a wider choice of plants and varieties available as seeds. Then there is the excitement of raising your own plants. There is nothing quite like waiting expectantly for seeds to germinate, and then the sheer sense of achievement when the seedlings at last emerge through the soil.

Seeds can be bought from retail mail order seed companies. Each year, generally during the fall, they publish catalogs, usually very well illustrated, so you can sit by the fire on a cold, damp fall or winter's day and choose your seeds at leisure.

From fall onward most garden centers are also well stocked with seeds from various seed companies, but the ranges are usually more limited.

Tiny "sprinkling" seeds Many plants have small or very tiny seeds, which are sown by sprinkling them thinly over the soil surface in containers. Seedlings from sprinkled seeds need to be transplanted, which is rather time-consuming.

Larger seeds Other plants have larger seeds, which are easier to handle. Examples include sunflowers

(Helianthus), marigolds (Tagetes), and sweet peas (Lathyrus). And there are many plants with medium-sized seeds, such as Ageratum, which are fairly easy to handle. Large and medium seeds can be space-sown so there is no need for thinning out.

> **TIP**
>
> Seed tapes can make outdoor seed sowing easy. Seeds, usually tiny ones, are pre-sown on a length of biodegradable tape. The tape is simply laid in a shallow drill or furrow and covered with soil. Seedlings should then come up at the correct spacing, so there is no need to thin them out.

Pelleted seeds Some tiny seeds are available as pelleted seeds to make them easier to handle. Each seed is coated with a substance, such as clay, and resembles a small pill. Pelleted seeds can be sown at the correct spacing so there is no need to transplant or thin out seedlings.

Bulbs

Bulbs, such as daffodils and tulips, are extremely easy to plant and they almost guarantee a display of flowers, provided there are no pest or disease attacks. The term "bulb" is used rather loosely by gardeners to include not only true bulbs, but also bulb-like plants such as corms (crocuses and gladioli are good examples) and tubers such as dahlias and cyclamen.

The majority of bulbs are bought and planted in fall to flower in winter or the following spring, but summer-flowering bulbs are purchased and planted in spring. Those that flower in the fall are usually planted in late summer.

A tray full of healthy young Viola plants.

but they are easy. On purchase plants need only potting up and growing on in a greenhouse until large enough for planting out.

When buying young plants, make sure they are sturdy and short-jointed, not thin and spindly. The leaves should be a good shade of medium or deep green, not pale or a sickly-looking yellow-green. Plants must be free from pests and diseases.

Seedlings Pots of seedlings of summer bedding plants are available from garden centers in early spring. They need pricking out, or transplanting, into trays and growing in a greenhouse until large enough for planting out, but they work out cheaper than plugs.

Bulbs can be bought from mail order bulb specialists, most of whom supply well-illustrated catalogs. Garden centers sell a more limited range of bulbs, available from fall onward. At least in garden centers, though, you can see immediately what you are buying in terms of quality and size.

Generally speaking, top-sized bulbs will perform best and produce the most flowers. When buying, make sure the bulbs are very firm and do not have any soft spots, an indication that they are starting to rot. Ensure that they do not have any white or gray fungal growth on them. Remember that bulbs should not be starting into growth at the time of purchase.

Most bulbs are bought in the dry, dormant state. Garden center bulbs may be supplied in net bags or some form of display packaging, complete with a picture of the particular bulb.

It is possible to buy bulbs already growing in pots, maybe at the point of flowering, but this is an expensive way to buy them. They are available from garden centers.

Plants

Buying small, young plants for growing on at home is a popular way of obtaining bedding plants and other summer-display plants. They are more expensive than seeds, the choice of plants and varieties is more limited,

Plugs Plugs represent a very popular way of buying bedding plants. They are small plants produced commercially in module trays (trays that contain a varying number of "cells"). The plants are potted up when received and grown in a greenhouse until large enough for planting out.

Young plants Larger bedding plants, ready for planting out and almost ready to flower, are widely available. They may be offered in large-cell module trays, or in flexible plastic or rigid polystyrene strips.

Mature plants Large potted bedding plants that are coming into flower are available from garden centers, local stores, and supermarkets. Of course, these provide an instant effect, but they also represent the most expensive way of buying bedding plants. They should have plenty of flower buds and must not have outgrown their pots. Sturdy, short-jointed plants are best.

Prepacked plants Dormant hardy perennials are sold in prepacks in winter and spring. Widely available, they come in display packaging complete with a picture of the plant.

Sowing & Planting

As so many flowers are grown from seed, it is important to learn how to prepare soil, sow seeds, and plant correctly in order to give your flowers the best possible start.

Soil preparation

Soil is initially prepared for flower-growing by digging, which allows grit or sand and organic matter to be added and helps to aerate it and prevent compaction. Digging is not needed every year for permanent hardy perennials and bulbs, only before initial planting. Thereafter beds or borders are renovated (dug and replanted) only every three to four years. Beds devoted to temporary bedding plants and annuals are usually dug over in the fall to revitalize them and bury annual weeds, say between removing summer bedding plants and the planting of spring bedding.

Soil being initially prepared for planting must first be cleared of perennial weeds, as otherwise they will forever be a problem. This is most effectively achieved by spraying the weeds while they are in full growth with a weed-killer containing glyphosate.

When weeds are dead the ground can be dug, the best time generally being in the fall ready for spring planting. Usually it is only necessary to dig to the depth of the spade blade, but if there is a bad drainage problem or the lower soil is very compacted, then digging to two depths of the spade blade is advised.

Before planting, scatter a general-purpose fertilizer over the dug soil and lightly fork it in, at the same time breaking down any lumps of soil. Firm the soil by treading systematically with your heels and then use a fork or rake to create a smooth, level surface.

Seed sowing

Seeds of many flowering plants are sown in the open ground. Hardy annuals are sown in beds and borders in spring (or in the fall for some) where they are to flower. Many of the easier hardy perennials such as lupines, delphiniums, and columbines (Aquilegia) can be sown in a nursery bed in early summer and later transplanted to their flowering positions. Hardy biennials such as wallflowers (Erysimum), double daisies (Bellis), foxgloves (Digitalis), and forget-me-nots (Myosotis) are raised in the same way. Seeds of slow-germinating hardy bulbs, alpines, and various hardy perennials are sown in pots outdoors or in a cold frame as soon as they are ripe.

Seed-bed preparation For seed sowing outdoors the soil surface needs to be smooth and level. Carry out all preparatory work only when the soil is dry or only slightly moist on the surface, never when wet.

Starting with a site that has been previously dug, first break down any lumps of soil with a fork. Then firm the soil by systematically treading over the site with the weight on your heels. Using a steel garden rake, lightly rake the soil surface until it is level and has a shallow layer of fine soil in which to sow the seeds, with no lumps, debris, or stones. While the soil surface is being prepared, a general-purpose fertilizer should be spread over the surface [A] and then thoroughly raked in [B]. Apply at the rate recommended on the container.

Sowing in rows The usual and easiest way to sow seeds outdoors is in straight rows, in shallow furrows known as drills. It makes subsequent care of seedlings, such as thinning and weeding, much easier. This is certainly the best technique when sowing seeds of plants such as hardy biennials and perennials in nursery beds.

Hardy annuals, being sown in their flowering positions, can also be sown in rows. Generally, each annual is grown in a bold, informal group in a border. Before sowing, the groups can be marked out with a trickle of dry sand. Within each group the seeds are sown in straight drills, spaced according to the size of the particular plant, but in the region of 6–12in (15–30cm) apart. As the plants grow and close up, it will become less and less obvious that they have been sown in straight rows.

To make drills you will need a garden line (at its simplest, a length of string with each end tied to a

A

B

Using seed tapes Seed tapes are laid along slightly wider drills, following the information on the packet regarding depth. Before covering with fine soil as above, moisten the tape using a watering can fitted with a fine rose.

Broadcast sowing Another way of sowing seeds is to broadcast them, or scatter them thinly over the soil surface. This technique is not often used for flowers, but is the normal method of sowing lawn grass seed and wildflower meadows. Broadcast sowing can be used for hardy annuals, but bear in mind that thinning and weeding will be more difficult. First the soil surface should be prepared by raking shallowly in one direction to create a series of closely spaced mini furrows. Then scatter the seeds thinly and evenly all over the surface and cover them by gently raking across the furrows to fill them in.

Thinning seedlings Even if seeds have been sown very thinly, seedlings will still need to be thinned out to the correct distance apart. To avoid overcrowding, which results in weak, spindly, drawn-up seedlings, thin out as soon as seedlings are large enough to handle. This can be done in two stages if desired, an initial thinning to provide seedlings with a bit more room to grow, and a second thinning to the correct distance apart when they are a bit larger.

The soil should be moist at the time of thinning. Most people prefer to use their fingers to remove surplus seedlings, but some gardeners use an onion hoe to chop them out. Place a finger on the soil surface on each side of the seedling that is to remain to prevent it being pulled out, then gently pull out surplus seedlings on either side. Work along the row in this way.

When thinning seedlings also pull out any weeds. After thinning, hoe between the rows to kill off any remaining weeds.

short cane), a draw hoe or short-handled onion hoe, or a pointed stick. First stretch the line tightly where you want to take out the drill. Then, using it as a guide, use the corner of the hoe or the pointed stick to create a shallow furrow [C]. The depth will depend on the size of the seeds, but bear in mind that seeds should be sown to about twice their own depth. On average drills are about ¼in (6mm) deep.

Sow seeds straight from the packet, or take a pinch of seeds between finger and thumb. Sprinkle them thinly and evenly along the drill [D]. Cover them by gently raking fine soil into the drill [E]. Water the seed bed if the soil is dry, using a garden sprinkler or watering can fitted with a fine rose. Thereafter, keep the soil moist to encourage germination.

C

D

E

Sowing in pots outdoors Seeds of hardy bulbs, alpines, and slow-germinating hardy perennials such as hellebores, anemones, spurges (Euphorbia), and primulas, are usually sown in pots as soon as they are ripe and placed outdoors or in an open cold frame. After a cold period during the following winter they should germinate in the spring.

Use a soil-based seed starting mix and cover the seeds with a thin layer of the mix followed by a thin layer of coarse sand or fine grit to prevent disturbance from rain and to deter the growth of moss and liverwort. Sink the pots up to their rims in a bed of grit or coarse sand to prevent drying out and excessive freezing.

Planting techniques

Plants that you have carefully raised in the greenhouse or in an outdoor nursery bed, and those that you have purchased from seed companies and the local garden center, will eventually need to be planted out in their flowering positions. This needs to be done with a great amount of care, as the correct planting technique makes all the difference to subsequent growth and flowering. Poorly planted specimens may never become properly established and will fail to perform well.

Hardening off Young plants that have been raised and grown on in a heated greenhouse, such as summer bedding plants, and including all those purchased plugs, and larger young plants, must be gradually acclimatized to outdoor conditions before they are planted out. If they are not allowed to do this, they will receive a severe check to growth. This technique, known as hardening off, is carried out in a cold frame.

Hardening off needs to start at least three weeks before planting out. Remember that frost-tender plants must not be planted out until the danger of frost is over.

After putting the young plants in the cold frame, give them a little ventilation for the first few days by opening the covers slightly during the day. Close the frame at night. Then over the next few weeks open the frame daily, gradually increasing the ventilation over this period by opening the covers more widely until fully open. Continue to close the frame at night. A few days before planting

out, the covers should be left fully open at night also, provided that there is no risk of frost. Following this procedure will give the plants in the cold frame the best chance of survival and success in the future.

Planting out When plants are fully hardened off they can be safely planted out. Let us first consider young plants in pots, seed trays, large-cell module trays, and flexible-plastic or rigid polystyrene strips. The plants should be watered the evening before planting so that the compost is moist when they are planted out.

There are various techniques for removing plants from their containers, but it must always be done carefully to avoid root disturbance as much as possible. Plants can be removed from pots by inverting the pot, placing one hand over the compost surface and tapping the pot rim on a hard surface, such as the edge of a bench. The rootball should slide out.

To remove plants from an ordinary seed tray, first tap the lower ends and sides on a hard surface to loosen the soil and, holding the tray close to the ground,

gently throw the contents out. The soil should remain intact. Then the plants can be gently teased apart with your fingers. There will be some root disturbance, but this is inevitable. You can do the same with plants growing in strips.

Plants can be removed from module trays by pushing a pencil through the drainage hole in the base. This will loosen the plant, which can then be lifted out.

TIP Lightweight soilless potting mix is favored for filling containers such as patio tubs, window boxes, and hanging baskets. Firm it only very lightly. Heavier soil-based potting mixes are better for larger, permanent plants in patio tubs such as hardy perennials, shrubs, and trees. Regularly replace the potting mix in patio tubs and window boxes.

Plant immediately after removing plants from their containers to prevent the roots from drying out. Arrange the plants as required in the bed or border. Planting holes can be made with a hand trowel. Each hole should be large enough to take the rootball without squashing it, and should be of such a depth that after planting the surface of the potting mix is only slightly below soil level. Fill in around the plant with fine soil, making sure it is in close contact with the rootball and there are no air pockets, and firm it well with your fingers. To check whether it is firm enough, lightly tug the top of the plant—it should remain firm in the soil. The top of the rootball should be lightly covered with soil.

After planting, "tickle" the soil with a fork to remove any footprints, and water in the plants if the soil is dry, ideally with a garden sprinkler or a watering can fitted with a rose.

Larger plants, such as herbaceous perennials bought in 5–6in (12.5–15cm) pots from the local garden center, are planted in the same way as smaller potted plants. Some gardeners like to carefully tease out the outer roots before planting to help them establish quickly in the new soil. Just carefully pull out the roots with your fingers so that they are not growing in a circle around the soil ball. Again, set the plants so that the top of the rootball is only just below soil level.

You may also have larger plants of your own to plant, such as divisions of hardy perennials—large clumps of plants that you have divided or split into smaller portions for replanting. It is important to dig deep enough holes for these so that the roots are able to hang straight down without turning up at the ends. Work fine soil between and around the roots and firm it well with your fingers.

It is equally important to plant them at the same depth that they were positioned in originally—that is, with the crown of the plant, where the growth buds are situated, at soil level. The buds must not be covered with soil, otherwise the crown may rot. If you are planting divisions of bearded irises, which produce thick rhizomes (swollen stems that grow above the soil), the rhizomes should sit on the soil surface, but the fibrous roots below should, of course, be under the soil.

Transplanting seedlings Seedlings raised in a nursery bed, such as hardy biennials and perennials, need to be transplanted to another nursery bed to grow on to a larger size before they are planted in their flowering positions.

As soon as they are about 2–3in (5–8cm) high and easily handled, carefully lift them with a hand fork, a few at a time to prevent the roots from drying out. They are replanted in rows spaced about 12in (30cm) apart, setting the plants about 6in (15cm) apart within the rows. Dig deep enough holes to allow the roots to dangle straight down, then return fine soil around them and firm it with your fingers. Plant them to the same depth that they were positioned in originally. After planting, water them in thoroughly with a garden sprinkler or watering can fitted with a rose.

By the fall of the same year you will have sizeable young plants for setting out in their flowering positions. The biennials will flower in the following spring or summer, and some of the perennials may also flower then, but others may need to grow a bit larger before they bloom. Lift and plant in the same way as seedlings, setting the plants at the appropriate distance apart.

For perennials and alpines raised in pots there are two options. Either pot up the seedlings individually as soon as they are large enough to handle and grow them on outdoors or in an open cold frame, or line them out in nursery beds to grow on, as for biennials (above). If potting, start them off in 3in (8cm) pots and use a well-drained, gritty, soil-based potting mix.

Leave seedling bulbs in their pots for another year to grow larger before transplanting them. Then, in the second year, and while they are dormant, pot them to twice their own depth—say six to eight per 5in (12.5cm)

Carefully nurtured bulbs will ultimately reward with stunning displays.

pot—using a gritty soil-based potting mix [A & B]. Place in a sheltered spot outside or in an open cold frame and grow on for another year [C] before planting out when dormant.

Planting bulbs

Bulbs, corms, and tubers are generally planted when dormant, but if bought in pots when in growth they should be planted immediately and in the same way as pot-grown perennials. Do not disturb the roots. Bulbs that are bought "in the green" after flowering, such as snowdrops (Galanthus), should be planted immediately on purchase. If they have been lifted from the open ground, plant them to the depth that they were growing originally (soil level is indicated by the change from white to green at the base of the leaves). The planting of dormant bulbs, corms, and tubers (all referred to as bulbs here) is discussed below.

The time of planting depends on the flowering period of the bulb. Winter- and spring-flowering bulbs are planted in the fall. Summer-flowering kinds are planted in the spring. Those that flower in the fall, such as colchicums and some crocuses, are planted in late summer.

There is confusion among gardeners about how deep to plant bulbs. The correct depth is governed by the size of the bulb. A good guide is to plant a bulb two to three times deeper than its length (measured from its tip to its base). In other words, the bulb should be covered with a depth of soil equal to two or three times its own depth. Planting should be deeper in light soils, such as sandy types, than in heavy soils, such as clay. Space between bulbs should equal two to three times their own width.

In mixed borders Bulbs are generally planted in informal groups or drifts in mixed borders, so they look more natural. There are two ways to plant them, the easiest is to plant them in a large, flat-bottomed hole of the appropriate depth made with a spade. Space the bulbs at random in the hole, as again this makes for a more natural appearance when they grow. After setting them all out, cover them with fine soil. Use your hands for this to avoid disturbing the bulbs. Then firm the soil moderately by pressing it down with the back of a rake.

You can also plant the bulbs individually, using a trowel or bulb planter to make the hole. A bulb planter takes out a core of soil, which is then replaced over the bulb when it has been planted. You may need to remove some soil from the top of the core. When planting in individual holes make sure that the base of the bulb is in close contact with the soil in the bottom of the hole. If there is an air pocket, the bulb will not produce roots and consequently will not grow.

In spring bedding schemes Bulbs such as tulips are often planted among other plants, such as wallflowers (Erysimum) and forget-me-nots (Myosotis) in spring bedding schemes. There are two ways to do this, the easiest being to plant the bulbs first, followed by the other plants. This does not harm the bulbs as the other plants are planted to a more shallow depth (tulips need deep planting). If you are unhappy about this, plant the other plants first, then plant the bulbs between them. Use a trowel for planting both. Plants and bulbs should be spaced out evenly in bedding schemes.

In grass Generally, bulbs are planted in very informal drifts in grass to create a natural appearance. The best way to do this is to scatter handfuls of bulbs over the area and to plant them where they fall. But if there are any large gaps, you can fill them with some more bulbs.

The easiest way to plant bulbs in grass, especially small kinds, is to remove the turf where you want to plant them. This can be done with a spade, lifting the turf with about 1in (2.5cm) of soil attached. Scatter the bulbs and plant them with a trowel. Then return the

turf and firm it. Alternatively, you can plant bulbs individually in the turf, using a bulb planter as above, especially for large ones.

Planting aquatics

Aquatic or water plants, such as waterlilies (Nymphaea), are planted in special plastic aquatic baskets. Spring is the usual planting time. Line the basket with burlap to retain the soil, then fill with heavy loam or commercial aquatic mix. Set a plant in the center, firm well, then cover the soil surface with a layer of grit or pea gravel to prevent disturbance by fish.

Place the basket in the pool at the correct depth for the plant. Since waterlily leaves float on the surface, these plants prefer to be in shallow water when first planted, and gradually lowered as they grow until they are at the correct depth. To do this, stand the basket on bricks and gradually remove them as the plant grows.

Scatter-plant bulbs in grass to achieve wonderful springtime effects.

Planting in containers

Growing flowering plants in containers, such as patio tubs, window boxes, and hanging baskets, has never been more popular. They easily add color to paved areas and the walls of the building.

Patio tubs and pots Use large containers to avoid rapid drying out and to enable effective displays. Ideally, the depth of containers should ideally be no less than 12in (30cm), and the width from 12–24in (30–60cm). Shape is not important.

Cover drainage holes with broken clay pots [A] and add a 1–2in (2.5–5cm) layer of gravel for drainage. There are two methods of planting: either fill the tub with potting mix and make planting holes, or partially fill the container [B], stand the plants on the potting mix, and then fill in around them with more potting mix [C]. If you are planting bulbs with other plants, the latter technique is the best to use. Always fill the container with potting mix to within 1in (2.5cm) of the top, to allow room for watering.

Plants are generally set close together in containers (almost touching) for effect, so ignore the usual plant spacings. They need to be arranged attractively and to make best use of the limited space. Generally, a tall plant should be set in the center of the container to create height. Then the main plants should be arranged around this. Trailing plants can be set around the edge of the container [D].

Window boxes Window boxes are prepared and planted in the same way as patio containers. It is best to use soilless potting compost to reduce the amount of weight in the window box. Do make sure that window boxes are firmly secured to the windowsills with metal brackets—never rely on weight alone to hold them in position.

There are various ways of arranging the plants. For instance, try a triangular arrangement, with tall plants in the center of the box, shorter plants on either side, then some still shorter subjects out toward the edges of the box. Trailing plants can be set at the ends of the window box and along the front edge.

Alternatively, you could position some tall plants at one end, grading down the length of the window box to shorter plants at the other end. Again, make use of trailing plants to add variety to the arrangement—they hang down over the sides of the window box, enhancing the display.

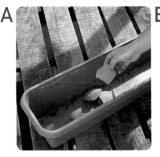

TIP

Before putting the planting medium into the container, place a layer of coarse grit over the crocks in a trough for herbs or alpines, which need good drainage. Also use grit in the base of pots containing bulbs to be left outside throughout the winter, as bulbs will rot if they are left in wet soil.

When you plant up containers, ensure that the arrangement is well balanced.

Hanging baskets Hanging baskets are invaluable for adding color to the walls of the house, especially around the patio or the front door. Always use the largest baskets available, as the bigger they are the less rapidly they dry out. Traditional wire baskets are still popular and allow for better plant arrangements, although some people prefer the modern molded-plastic versions, which do not need liners and do not dry out as quickly (some have a water reservoir in the base). Wire baskets need a liner of some sort to hold the compost. Sphagnum moss is the traditional material used for this purpose, although some people prefer not to use it for environmental reasons. Coir fiber (coconut fiber) is a good alternative. Other choices include compressed paper in the shape of the basket, and sheets of recycled cotton fiber.

To plant a wire hanging basket, line the entire basket firmly with a generous layer of sphagnum moss [A]. Next, pour a layer of lightweight soilless potting mix into the bottom of the basket and lightly firm it [B]. Then arrange a circle of plants in the side of the basket (trailing or semi-trailing kinds are suitable) by pushing the roots through the liner from the outside and laying them on the potting mix surface [C]. Cover the roots of the plants with a layer of potting mix and then add another circle of plants and cover their roots with potting mix. Of course, you will have to make holes in the liner to insert the plants. Then add plants at the top by standing them on the potting mix and filling in around them with more potting mix, leaving space at the top for watering [D].

Hanging baskets provide instant, portable bundles of flowers for any situation.

A 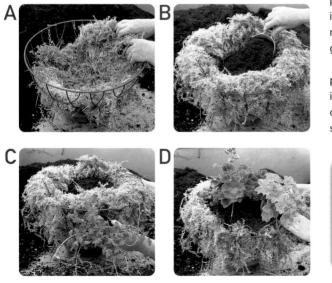 B

C D

As a general rule for your hanging basket planting arrangements, place a tall plant in the center, shorter plants around it, and trailing plants at the edge. Plants in the side and around the edge should be alternated as much as possible (not placed one above the other) to give them space to grow.

Of course, if you are planting up a solid, molded-plastic basket you can only plant in the top of it, and not in the sides. Arrange the plants as you would for the top of a wire basket, trying to create a good balance of shapes and sizes and a pleasing arrangement of colors.

TIP

If you are using a traditional wire basket and moss, as shown, ensure that the moss is well soaked before putting it in the basket. Place a plastic pot saucer on the moss in the bottom of the basket to act as a reservoir. Alternatively, use a circle of black plastic. Add another ring of moss to build up the sides of the basket, then fill this with potting mix.

Care & Maintenance

All plants need a little care and attention if they are to thrive. Simple maintenance will help to ensure a fantastic garden year-round.

Feeding

Plants need to be given regular applications of fertilizer to encourage them to grow and flower well. For plants in beds and borders, apply a base dressing of general-purpose granular fertilizer a few days before planting. For permanent plants, use another application of

A well-fed and watered border will give handsome rewards.

fertilizer as an annual top-dressing in spring. This should be sufficient for most border plants, although some vigorous kinds that bloom prolifically, such as dahlias, may benefit from booster feeds of liquid fertilizer during the growing period, especially from the time they start flowering.

Hardy bulbs are treated slightly differently. As soon as flowering is over, liquid feed with a general-purpose fertilizer once a week for two or three weeks to build up the bulbs, thus ensuring optimum flowering the following year.

Plants in containers such as patio tubs and hanging baskets need frequent feeding as plant foods are quickly leached out of containers due to frequent watering. Foods are supplied for the first six weeks or so by the new potting mix, but once plants are established they will need to be fed weekly or every two weeks during the growing season with liquid fertilizer. Or you could insert fertilizer tablets when plants are established.

There are many organic gardeners these days, so you have a choice of organic or chemical fertilizers.

Granular fertilizers As the name suggests, these fertilizers are supplied as granules, which are easily sprinkled over the soil surface. Always lightly fork them into the soil, whether you are applying a base dressing or a top-dressing. For flowers, widely available general-purpose fertilizers are suitable (some of these are available in organic forms), or a special flower-garden fertilizer can be used.

Slow-release tablets
These are ideal for hanging baskets or window boxes as they save a lot of time. Once buried in the soil surface, they release plant foods steadily over the entire growing season. After about six weeks, when the supply of plant foods is diminishing from the new potting mix, insert tablets as directed on the carton. For permanent plants in containers, insert tablets in spring, at the start of the growing season.

Liquid feeds There are numerous liquid fertilizers available; some of the most popular are seaweed-based. There are general-purpose types as well as fertilizers for specific plants or groups of plants. They are all first

Measure and dilute liquid feeds with water.

diluted with water according to the manufacturer's instructions, then watered around the plants with a watering can.

Watering

Never allow plants to become stressed due to lack of water, as they will not grow and flower well. Aim to keep the soil, or container potting mix, steadily moist. Do not allow it to completely dry out and then apply water—by this time plants will be suffering.

Plants need watering as soon as they are planted, particularly if the soil is dry. Check beds and borders several times a week during the growing season. Containers such as tubs, window boxes, and hanging baskets should be checked daily for water requirements from spring to fall. Apply water as soon as the soil or potting mix has become dry on the surface.

Always apply sufficient water each time to soak the soil to a good depth. For example, to moisten the soil to a depth of 6in (15cm) you need to apply the equivalent of about 1in (2.5cm) of rain. This is about 4.8 gal per sq yd (18 liters per sq m). With containers, fill the gap between the potting mix surface and the rim of the container (usually about 1in) with water to ensure that the full depth of potting mix is moistened. It should run out of the bottom of the container.

When using a hosepipe connected to the water supply, install a back-siphonage protection device to prevent contamination of the water supply.

Hand watering Using a watering can is the most time-consuming method of watering, but is recommended for small numbers of plants. Water plants individually, applying water to the soil around the stems rather than sprinkling the plants from above. A rose fitted to the watering can will give a slower delivery rate and will thus ensure that most of the water penetrates the soil instead of running off. A watering can is also the best method for watering a small number of containers.

Watering systems Automatic watering of beds, borders, and containers saves a great deal of time. A watering system attached to a faucet needs only the turn of a tap when water is required. But to be fully automatic, timing devices that switch the water on and off are available from most garden centers.

A seep hose watering system is ideal for beds and borders. This is a porous pipe that releases water steadily but gently through its pores. The pipe is laid among plants just below the soil surface, or it can be covered with mulching material. Alternatively, you can use a portable garden sprinkler.

Large numbers of containers, such as patio tubs, window boxes, and hanging baskets, can be watered by means of a drip or trickle watering system, consisting of thin tubes sprouting from the main pipe. Each container is supplied with one or more tubes.

Mulching

Mulching beds and borders of permanent plants (as opposed to temporary bedding) is strongly recommended to prevent the soil from drying out rapidly

Mulch permanent plants to help the soil retain moisture.

and to suppress weed growth. A mulch consists of a 2–3in (5–8cm) layer of organic matter spread over the soil surface between plants (but not right up to the stems). Apply in spring after a top-dressing of fertilizer to moist, weed-free soil. Suitable materials include well-rotted garden compost, chipped or shredded bark (including composted bark), and spent mushroom compost. Top up as necessary in subsequent years.

Control annual weeds with regular hoeing.

To apply top-dresssings of fertilizer, the mulch will have to be scraped away to expose the soil surface.

Weeding

If the ground was cleared of perennial weeds before planting, there should be little subsequent weeding, apart from dealing with annual weeds—and not even these where the ground is mulched. In beds and borders without

Use a glyphosate-based weed killer to kill perennial weeds.

mulch, control annual weeds by hoeing when they are in the seedling stage. Choose a warm, sunny day when the soil is dry on the surface so that they die quickly.

If the occasional perennial weed appears among plants, treat it with glyphosate. This is available in gel form as a spot weed-killer, as a ready mixed solution in a spray bottle, or as concentrated liquid for mixing in a watering can. Take care to avoid cultivated plants. Alternatively, dig out the weeds, complete with roots.

Any annual weeds that appear in containers can be pulled out by hand.

Supporting plants

Fortunately, the majority of perennials and other plants are self-supporting, but there are some with weak or thin stems, or with heavy flowers, that will need artificial supports to keep them from being flattened by wind and rain. Climbing plants must also have supports.

Thin or weak-stemmed hardy perennials, especially if they are tall such as some cultivars of bellflower (Campanula), can be supported with twiggy hazel or

birch sticks pushed in around them as they are starting to grow. Tall multistemmed annuals can be supported in the same way. Alternatively, metal plant supports that link together around the plant, forming the size required, are very effective.

Single bamboo canes can be used for tall annuals with single stems, such as sunflowers (Helianthus). Heavy plants such as dahlias are best supported with a single wooden stake, about 1in (2.5cm) square, tying each stem to it as it grows. Support each stem of a delphinium with a single bamboo cane.

Make sure all supports are shorter than the flowering height of the plants, and tie in stems loosely with soft garden string.

Climbing annuals such as sweet peas can be grown up a wigwam formed of bamboo canes. Alternatively, use an obelisk. Various kinds are available, including metal versions or more rustic ones made from willow or hazel. Some are suitable for patio tubs. Climbers can be supported on walls or fences with trellis panels fixed to the structure. Annual climbers can also be grown through larger plants, like shrubs.

General care

With some additional care, various plants can be made to flower for longer, some tender kinds can be kept for a number of years, and hardy kinds can be encouraged to remain young and vigorous. It is also important to ensure that borders and beds remain neat and tidy at all times.

Deadheading The removal of dead flower heads helps to ensure a neat and tidy appearance, and also encourages some plants to flower for a longer period. This applies especially to annuals and tender perennials, but also to some hardy perennials—for example, delphiniums and lupines may produce a second flush of flowers later in the summer if dead blooms are removed.

Dead flower heads are usually cut off with some of the flower stem attached, using pruners or flower

A well-supported *Thunbergia alata* (Black-eyed Susan vine) growing up a pyramid.

down completely, as this will adversely affect the development of the bulbs, resulting in poor flowering the following year. For the same reason do not bunch up the leaves and tie them in a knot for the sake of neatness. Once the foliage is dead, cut it off at ground level.

Wintering plants Many tender plants in containers used for summer bedding can be kept from year to year by rescuing them before the frosts start in the fall. For example, tender perennials such as pelargoniums, fuchsias, and osteospermums are propagated from cuttings in late summer or early fall, and the resultant young plants are wintered in a cool but frost-free greenhouse. The parent plants are lifted and discarded because they will probably be too big to store under glass, and in any case young plants are best for replanting. Tender winter-dormant tubers such as dahlias, cannas, and tuberous begonias are lifted, cut down, and stored in boxes of peat substitute in a cool, frost-free place over winter.

Annuals, whether tender or hardy, are pulled up and discarded when frosts start in the fall, as they cannot be kept

scissors. With others, such as marigolds (Tagetes) and pelargoniums, the dead blooms are easily snapped off between finger and thumb, thus speeding up the process. You may be able to use garden shears for plants that produce masses of very small flowers.

Remember that the dead flower heads of some hardy perennials look attractive over winter and can therefore be left until they become untidy in early spring. Examples are the flat-headed stonecrops (sedums) and achilleas, and ornamental grasses including Miscanthus.

Cutting down Hardy herbaceous perennials should be cut down almost to ground level when they have died down. This can be done in the fall, although some gardeners prefer to wait until early spring. Cut down the stems with pruners, to just above the crown of the plant where the growth buds are located.

Evergreen perennials, such as bergenias, only need to have dead leaves removed whenever necessary. The foliage of bulbs must not be removed before it has died

from year to year, although you may be able to save the seeds for sowing in spring.

Renovating borders Borders or beds where perennials are grown need renovating every three to four years. This allows for improvement of the soil by digging and manuring, and if necessary the removal of any perennial weeds that have become established.

Border renovation also enables plants to be rejuvenated. The plants are lifted and heeled in on a spare piece of ground while the border is being dug. Then the large clumps of plants are split or divided into smaller portions, using the younger, more vigorous parts around the outside edge for replanting. The older center part, which is declining in vigor, should be discarded.

Borders and beds can be dug in the fall and the plants split and replanted in early spring of the following year, or the whole operation can be undertaken in early spring, if that is more convenient.

Propagation

Increasing your stock (propagation) is both rewarding and economical. Whether raising seeds indoors or taking cuttings, you will be able to add new stock to your garden year after year.

Raising seeds indoors

In frost-prone climates, seeds of tender plants—such as tender perennials and annuals to be used for summer bedding and container display—are raised indoors. Ideally this will be in a frost-free greenhouse, although plants can also be raised on a windowsill in a warm room

of seeds, in which case 3½–5in (9–13cm) pots or half pots are more suitable.

To save time pricking out or transplanting seedlings, any seeds that are easily handled can be sown individually in 60-cell module trays. Very small seeds that cannot be handled individually are best sown in a pot or half pot and the resultant seedlings pricked out.

Most gardeners use soilless seed starting mixes for all their sowings, traditionally made from peat but increasingly of peat substitutes, such as coir, as peat is being phased out. You could also use a multipurpose potting mix. Traditionalists may prefer a soil-based seed starting mix.

Sowing Sowing techniques differ according to the type of container you are using, but filling containers with seed starting mix is much the same whether you are using pots or trays. Filling is especially easy with soilless mixes as they need very little firming. Overfirming will affect drainage and the mix may remain too wet. Fill the container to overflowing with the mix, tapping it on the bench to get rid of any air pockets, then scrape off the surplus with a straight piece of wood to give you a smooth, level surface. Now tap the container firmly on the bench several times to firm it—the level should be slightly below the top of the container. If using a soil-based starting mix, fill the container as above, scrape

in the house, provided that there is really good light to prevent them from becoming weak and spindly. Seeds of various hardy perennials can also be raised indoors early in the year if desired. (In which case they may flower in the same year.) Other kinds, however, germinate better indoors rather than in the open ground (read the instructions on the seed packets before sowing).

Containers and seed starting mixes Various containers can be used for sowing seeds. Standard or half-size seed trays are suitable for large quantities. However, most gardeners will be sowing small amounts

> **TIP**
>
> To make very fine or dust-like seeds such as Begonia and Lobelia easier to handle when sowing, first mix them thoroughly with some very fine, completely dry silver sand. A good proportion would be two to three parts sand to one part seed. Mix thoroughly and then sow from a sheet of folded paper. You could also sow the mixture from the seed packet.

Use a dibber to press large seeds into starting mix.

off any surplus mix, then firm moderately with your fingers. Create a smooth, level surface with a wooden presser of a size that fits the container.

To sow seeds in seed trays or pots, take a pinch of seeds in the palm of one hand. Hold it about three inches above the surface of the seed starting mix at an angle, and move your hand gently backward and forward over the container so that the seeds scatter evenly across the surface [A].

Sow as evenly as possible and very thinly. Seeds should not be touching each other. If seed is sown too thickly, you will have a dense crop of seedlings that will become drawn and spindly and difficult to prick out.

To sow in 60-cell module trays make a shallow hole in the starting mix surface of each cell using a dibber and drop in a seed.

Most seeds need to be covered with a layer of starting mix, the depth equaling twice the diameter of the seed. The covering should be as even as possible. Sift starting mix over the seeds using a small mesh sieve (some kitchen sieves are ideal for this). Very fine or dust-like seeds such as begonias should not be covered. Lightly press these into the surface of the starting mix with a flat piece of wood. Seeds sown in module trays can be covered individually with a pinch of starting mix.

Fine-grade vermiculite can be used instead of starting mix for covering seeds, and is ideal for rapidly germinating subjects. It holds the seeds in contact with the starting mix while allowing air to easily reach them, reducing the risk of damping off. To do this, cover seeds with a ¼in (5mm) layer of vermiculite [B].

After sowing, containers with covered seeds should be watered [C], ideally with a watering can fitted with a fine rose. Otherwise, trickle the water very gently. For very fine seeds sown on the surface, stand the container almost up to its rim in water until the starting mix surface becomes moist, then remove, and allow to drain.

Germination conditions Most seeds will germinate in a temperature range of 60–70°F (15.5–21°C), so stand the containers in a place that provides these conditions. Ideally seeds are germinated in a propagating case with bottom heat. An unheated propagating case is also suitable provided that it is in a warm place, such as a windowsill in a warm room. If there is no propagating case, the container should be covered to prevent the starting mix from rapidly drying out. Use a sheet of plastic bubble wrap, Saran wrap, or ordinary clear plastic film, tucking the edges under the container. Or you could use a sheet of glass. Remove the cover as soon as seeds germinate. Shade seeds and seedlings from strong sunshine and never allow the mix to dry out.

Transplanting Seedlings raised in ordinary seed trays or pots will need pricking out or transplanting as soon as they are large enough to handle, to give them more room to grow. Plants that are intended for planting out later, such as summer bedding plants and hardy perennials, can be pricked out into module trays with large cells, such as 24-cell trays, one seedling per cell. The plants suffer no root disturbance when planted out from these. Alternatively, use plastic growing strips which, like module trays, are inserted into standard-size seed trays.

The more traditional method for bedding plants is to prick out into standard-size seed trays (see below), say 40–54 seedlings per tray, or for small quantities use a half-size seed tray. Plants that are to be grown as pot plants can be pricked out individually into 3in (8cm) pots.

Containers for pricking out can be filled with a soilless or soil-based mix (whichever was used for sowing). Use a potting or multipurpose mix and fill containers in the same way as for seed sowing.

Seedlings to be pricked out should be lifted, a few at a time to prevent drying out, with a dibber or old table fork [A]. Always hold seedlings by the seed leaves, never by the stems, since these are easily damaged. Carefully separate them and make a hole for each seedling with a dibber, of such a depth that the roots are able to dangle straight down without turning up at the ends. Hold the seedling in the hole so that the seed leaves are just above the surface of the potting mix, then with the dibber gently push potting mix around it to cover the roots and lightly firm [B].

Ensure that the seedlings are evenly spaced within the tray so that each of them has plenty of space in which to grow [C].

After pricking out, water in the seedlings with a watering can with a narrow nozzle or fine rose [D], and place in suitable growing conditions.

Seedlings raised in small-cell module trays, such as 60-cell trays (known as plugs at this stage), generally need potting before they are finally planted out to give them more room to grow. Use 3–3½in (8–9cm) pots and soilless or soil-based potting mix. Partially fill the pot, lightly firm the potting mix, stand the plug in the center, and fill up with more potting mix, firming lightly. Water in with a rosed can.

If any plants seem to be outgrowing larger-cell trays before planting time, these should also be potted on to give them more room. Large, vigorous plants like pelargoniums or dahlias, for instance, may require 5in (13cm) pots.

Growing on The seedlings and young plants should be grown on in warm conditions, such as on a bench in a heated greenhouse, or on a windowsill indoors. In the latter instance, remember to turn the plants regularly so that they grow straight and are not angled toward the light. They must be shaded from strong sunshine otherwise leaves may be scorched, and they should receive adequate ventilation. Water regularly, as seedlings soon succumb to drying out.

Plants intended for planting out when frosts are over are hardened off in a cold frame over several weeks prior to planting (see page 14).

Division

A major method of propagating hardy perennials that form clumps or mats is division, which involves splitting the clump or mat into a number of smaller portions for replanting. Many alpines with the same

A

B

C

D

habit of growth can also be divided. Bulbs can be propagated by removing the small bulbs or offsets that develop around the parents.

Perennials Most hardy perennials can be divided, except for those which do not form clumps but produce a single crown, or maybe a single, thick taproot. Examples include Anchusa, pinks and carnations, lupines, mulleins (verbascums), and oriental poppies (*Papaver orientale*).

A good time to lift and divide is early to mid-spring, as the soil is warming up and plants are just awakening from winter dormancy, though you could also divide in the fall. Early-flowering (spring or early summer) perennials are best divided as soon as flowering is over, examples being doronicums, epimediums, rhizomatous irises, lily-of-the-valley (Convallaria), primulas, and pyrethrums (Tanacetum).

Lift large, established clumps with a fork and shake off most of the soil. The clump can be split by inserting two garden or hand forks through it back to back and levering them apart. Or you could pull clumps apart with your hands, cutting through any thick, tough crown

Harden off young plants in a cold frame before planting them out.

Dividing a clump of hardy perennials with forks.

SAVING SEEDS

Seeds can be saved from many garden plants, provided that they are species and not hybrids, which do not breed true.

In summer and early fall keep an eye on plants and, as soon as the seed pods and capsules turn from green to brown (but before they split open), cut off the entire seed heads and place in paper-lined seed trays, with a label containing the name of the plant.

Stand the trays in a warm, dry, airy place for a week or two to allow the seeds to dry. During this time many of the pods or capsules may split open to shed the seeds, but if not, then gently crush them with your fingers. In this case you will have a mixture of seeds and chaff, or debris, which must be separated. Place the mixture of seeds and chaff on a sheet of newspaper and gently blow over it—the lighter chaff should then be blown clear of the seeds.

Place the cleaned seeds in paper envelopes (you may find a kitchen funnel helpful) and label them with the plant name.

Store the seeds in a cool, dry place until sowing time arrives once more in the spring.

---

with a knife if necessary. The center part of a clump should be discarded as it is old and declining in vigor. Use only divisions from the edge of a clump, as these are young and vigorous. They should be roughly palm-sized. Replant immediately to prevent roots from drying out.

Rhizomatous iris divisions consist of a portion of rhizome (swollen stem) with a fan of leaves attached and some fibrous roots. The leaves can be cut down by half. Replant so that the rhizome is only half buried, with the top above soil level.

Carpeting plants that form mats of underground rhizomes, such as lily-of-the valley (Convallaria) and epimediums, can simply be pulled apart into suitable-sized portions and replanted.

Alpines Clump- and mat-forming alpines are propagated as before. Many alpines form offsets or rosettes (young plants) around themselves, a good example being various saxifrages such as London pride (*Saxifraga* x *urbium*).

Rooted offsets can be removed in spring without disturbing the parent plant. Ease them out of the soil with a hand fork and cut them away from the parent plant—they are attached by a short stem.

As rooted rosettes are quite small, you may prefer to pot them individually into 3in (8cm) pots and grow them on for a year before planting out. Use a soil-based potting mix with added grit. Place in a sunny spot but in the fall transfer to a well-ventilated cold frame to protect from cold, harsh winter rains.

Bulbs Remove smaller bulbs or offsets from around the parent bulbs while they are dormant (during summer for most hardy bulbs). Dry off and store in a cool, dry place until planting time in the fall. Tiny bulbs are planted more shallowly than mature bulbs (about half the usual depth), ideally in a nursery bed to grow to flowering size.

Removing dormant bulblets from parent bulbs.

Cuttings

Many hardy and tender perennials are easily propagated from cuttings. Some are propagated on an annual basis, particularly chrysanthemums and dahlias, and tender perennials used for summer bedding such as zonal pelargoniums.

Basal stem cuttings These are taken in spring from shoots that grow from the crown of the plant. Stock plants started into growth early in the year in a heated greenhouse usually provide the cuttings of dahlias and chrysanthemums. Cuttings of other perennials such as achilleas, delphiniums, and lupines can be taken from plants in the garden.

Shoots are removed close to the crown of the plant, so that each retains a piece of parent tissue or "heel" at the base, when 2–3in (5–8cm) high. Remove lower leaves, insert in pots of cutting mix (equal parts coarse horticultural sand or grit and peat substitute), and root in a temperature of 59–66°F (15–19°C), ideally in a heated propagating case, otherwise on a windowsill indoors, enclosing the pot in a plastic bag supported with split canes. Pot off individually into 3½in (9cm) pots of soilless potting mix when rooted, and harden off in a cold frame before planting out.

Semi-ripe cuttings Tender perennials used for summer bedding, such as diascias, fuchsias, gazanias, osteospermums, and zonal and ivy-leaf pelargoniums, are propagated annually from semi-ripe cuttings in late summer.

Prepare semi-ripe cuttings from shoots that are partially ripe or hardened at the base while the tips are still soft. Use nonflowering side shoots and make the cuttings about 3–4in (8–10cm) long, cutting just below a node or leaf joint at the base. Remove the lower leaves, dip the base in hormone rooting powder, insert in pots of cutting mix and root in a heated propagator at 59°F (15°C) or in a cold frame. Rooting takes longer in the cold frame. Pot up when rooted, using 3½in (9cm) pots and soilless potting mix, and winter in a frost-free greenhouse.

Root cuttings Propagating from pieces of root is a good technique for certain hardy perennials, including those that do not lend themselves to division. Plants that are often propagated from root cuttings include acanthus, globe thistle (Echinops), Japanese anemones,

TIP Bergenias can be propagated from rhizome cuttings in the fall. After washing, cut the thick rhizomes into 2in (5cm) sections and push them horizontally into a tray of moist perlite to half their depth, dormant growth buds uppermost. Root with bottom heat of 70°F (21°C) and high humidity. Pot up when rooted (about 12 weeks) and plant out after hardening off.

A semi-ripe cutting from a fuchsia, with the base and lower leaves removed.

mulleins (verbascums), oriental poppies (*Papaver orientale* cultivars), pasque flower (Pulsatilla), border phlox, drumstick primrose (*Primula denticulata*), and sea holly (Eryngium).

Root cuttings are taken in the fall or winter when the plants are dormant. Lift a plant and remove a few of the thickest roots. Replant the parent immediately to prevent drying out.

The roots are now cut into sections 2–4in (5–10cm) in length, the thinnest root cuttings (such as phlox) being the longest. Thick root cuttings (such as oriental poppies) are prepared by cutting the tops flat and the bases slanting, so that you know the tops from the bottoms and can therefore insert the cuttings the right

way up [A]. The tops are always the part of the root that was nearest to the crown of the plant. It is easier and less confusing to lay a root on a bench the right way up and then cut it up. Thin roots are simply cut into sections without worrying about tops and bottoms.

Insert cuttings in deep trays or pots of cutting mix. Thick root cuttings are inserted vertically— simply push them down into the cutting mix until the tops are just below the surface [B]. Then lightly cover the tops with cutting mix. Thin root cuttings are laid horizontally on the compost surface and covered with a ¼in (6mm) layer of compost.

Heat is not needed for rooting, so place the cuttings in a cold frame. The cuttings should root and produce top growth in the spring, when they can be lifted and lined out in a nursery bed to grow on for a year. Alternatively, plant them in their permanent positions in beds or borders if this is more convenient.

Rhizome cuttings Where large numbers of new plants are required for mass planting—for example, certain perennials such as lily-of-the-valley (Convallaria) and epimediums—try propagating from rhizome cuttings in winter. Rhizomes are horizontal, root-like stems, generally growing underground. Prepare and insert like thin root cuttings, chopping the rhizomes into 3in (8cm) sections and making sure each has some dormant growth buds. Trim back any overlong fibrous roots. They should be rooted in a cold frame, and the young plants then lined out in a nursery bed or in permanent positions in spring when they are well rooted and producing top growth.

A
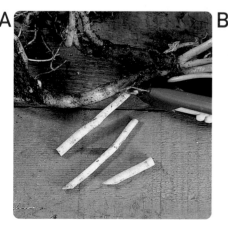

B

Planting Combinations

For the most effective beds and borders, plants should be combined in pleasing ways. You may want to create dramatic or exciting contrasts in flower shape or color, opt for more relaxing harmonious combinations, or even try color themes, such as an all-blue or all-red border, or even a green and white scheme.

The possibilities for effective plant combinations are limited only by your imagination. Go for whatever pleases you. However, bedding schemes and annuals last for only one season, so if you are not happy with combinations of these, try something different next year. Even hardy perennials and bulbs can be moved at the end of the season or the following year if you are not satisfied with their arrangement.

The following examples show how some of the plants included in this book can be combined effectively in various parts of the garden. They are

Good bedding schemes should feature a variety of different plants.

small-scale ideas, based on selecting a major feature plant and then choosing several more plants that flower at the same time to combine with it. Entire borders can be planned in this way, using a range of your favorite feature plants, and of course this is the traditional way of planning spring and summer bedding schemes.

Further ideas can be obtained by visiting public gardens armed with a notebook and pencil and jotting down any plant combinations that appeal to you.

Bedding schemes

These are formal arrangements of plants in geometric beds providing color at various seasons of the year. Summer bedding schemes are perhaps the most popular with home gardeners, but do not neglect the other seasons, as it is easy to provide color year-round by

---

BEDDING SCHEMES

Spring bedding Main plants: Tulips, single late (maroon and orange cultivars). Companions: *Erysimum* x *allionii* (orange); *Myosotis sylvatica* (blue).

Main plant: Tulip, lily-flowered (yellow). Companions: *Myosotis sylvatica* (blue) as a carpet below the tulip.

Main plants: Tulip, Darwin hybrid (cherry red), *Erysimum* x *cheiri* (golden yellow). Companions: *Myosotis sylvatica* (blue) as an edging.

Summer bedding Main plant: Pelargonium, zonal (bright red or orange). Companions: Ageratum (blue) as an edging; heliotrope (blue); petunias (blue or purple).

Main plant: Pelargonium, zonal (pink). Companions: Ageratum (blue); heliotrope (blue); *Verbena* x *hybrida* (blue).

Main plant: Pelargonium, ivy-leafed (pink). Companions: *Lobelia erinus* (blue); petunia (purple); *Salvia farinacea* (blue and white cultivar); *Verbena* x *hybrida* (blue or purple).

Main plant: *Begonia semperflorens* (pink, red, or mixture). Companions: Ageratum (blue); cannas (red) as dot plants; fuchsias (pink and blue or red and blue) as dot plants.

Main plant: *Begonia semperflorens* (pink, red, or mixture). Companions: *Lobelia cardinalis* (red); *Lobularia maritima* (white); *Salvia farinacea* (blue, or blue and white cultivar).

Main plant: *Salvia splendens* (red or scarlet). Companions: Heliotrope (blue); nicotiana (green cultivar); *Nicotiana* x *sanderae* (white cultivar).

Fall bedding Main plant: Chrysanthemum, dwarf, such as Korean or Pompon (any color). Companions: Colchicums (pink) plunged in pots; *Nerine bowdenii* (pink) plunged in pots.

Winter bedding Main plant: Pansies, winter flowering (single or mixed colors). Companions: *Chionodoxa forbesii* (blue and white); *Muscari armeniacum* (blue), *Narcissus cyclamineus* hybrids (yellow); *Scilla siberica* (blue). N.B. These will be flowering in spring, when pansies will still be in bloom.

choosing suitable plants. In planning such a scheme choose a major feature plant, or even two feature plants mixed together, then decide on one or two other plants. These could be used as an edging to the bed or as dot plants scattered randomly over the bed. Or they could be mixed more liberally with the main feature plant.

Mixed borders

One of the main ways of growing plants is in mixed borders containing shrubs, hardy perennials, and bulbs, with perhaps temporary plants such as annuals and tender perennials filling any gaps.

The following examples are combinations of mainly hardy perennials and bulbs. Again a major feature plant is chosen and then a number of other plants that effectively combine with it are considered, all flowering together. However, if desired, companion plants may be chosen to precede or follow that of the feature plant to give an extended period of color and interest, for example, by mixing spring-flowering tulips with early summer-flowering lupines and bearded irises.

Remember that it makes sense to combine your groups of perennials and bulbs with shrubs that have the same season of color or interest. For example, those that flower in the fall can be planted around or in front of shrubs noted for their fall leaf color or berries, such as Rhus, Cotinus, cotoneasters, and Berberis. Winter-flowering perennials and bulbs are effectively

Classic mixed borders need color, height, and varied form to work well.

MIXED BORDERS

Spring Main plant: *Pulmonaria officinalis* (pink and blue). Companions: *Doronicum* 'Frühlingspracht' (yellow); *Euphorbia polychroma* (yellow).

Main plant: *Euphorbia* x *martinii* (yellow-green). Companions: *Ajuga reptans* 'Atropurpurea' (blue); *Narcissus* 'Actaea' (white).

Main plant: *Bergenia* 'Sunningdale' (deep lilac-magenta). Companions: *Erythronium dens-canis* (pink); *Narcissus* 'Jack Snipe' (yellow and white); *Pulmonaria* 'Sissinghurst White' (white).

Summer Main plant: *Kniphofia* 'Royal Standard' (scarlet and yellow). Companions: *Agapanthus* Headbourne Hybrids (blue); *Cortaderia selloana* (silvery); *Miscanthus sinensis* (light gray, flushed purple-brown).

Main plant: *Achillea filipendulina* (yellow). Companions: *Artemisia lactiflora* (cream); delphiniums (blue); *Verbascum chaixii* 'Gainsborough' (yellow).

Main plant: Irises, rhizomatous bearded (various). Companions: Lupines (various); *Papaver orientale* (red, pink, or orange).

Main plant: *Hemerocallis* 'Golden Chimes' (deep yellow). Companions: *Canna* 'Wyoming' (orange; purple leaves); *Gladiolus* 'Jester' (yellow and red).

Fall Main plant: *Aster* x *frikartii* 'Mönch' (lavender blue). Companions: *Rudbeckia fulgida* var. *sullivantii* 'Goldsturm' (golden yellow); *Stipa gigantea* (gold).

Main plant: *Aster novi-belgii* (blue, purple, red, or pink). Companions: *Cortaderia selloana* (silvery); *Nerine bowdenii* (pink); Schizostylis (pink or red); *Sedum* 'Herbstfreude' (deep pink).

Main plant: *Anemone* x *hybrida* (pink cultivar). Companions: *Aster novae-angliae* 'Andenken an Alma Pötschke' (bright salmon pink); *Miscanthus sinensis* 'Silberfeder' (silvery to light pink-brown).

Winter Main plant: *Helleborus* x *hybridus* cultivars (various colors). Companion plants: *Eranthis hyemalis* (brilliant yellow), *Galanthus nivalis* (white).

Main plant: *Bergenia cordifolia* 'Purpurea' (magenta-purple; leaves tinted red). Companions: *Crocus tommasinianus* (lilac to purple); *Galanthus* 'Atkinsii' (white).

---

associated with shrubs such as colored stemmed dogwoods or Cornus, white-stemmed Rubus, and flowering kinds including witch hazels or Hamamelis. In the spring and summer there are many shrubs with colored foliage, as well as flowers, which make good backgrounds for perennials and bulbs.

Containers

Containers such as patio tubs and window boxes are normally filled with combinations of winter or spring bedding plants and bulbs followed by summer bedding plants. Hanging baskets are generally planted with the latter. Very often a tall central foliage plant, which may be a permanent hardy shrub, is used in patio tubs or window boxes to give height to the planting scheme—especially useful for spring bedding.

CONTAINERS

Winter and spring Any of the ideas for winter and spring bedding can also be used in patio tubs or window boxes. Also try the following:

Main plant: Pansies, winter flowering (blue). Companions: Central plant of the hardy *Hebe* x *franciscana* 'Variegata' (cream and green variegated leaves); *Narcissus* 'Tête-à-Tête' (golden yellow).

Summer Main plant: Argyranthemum, as a centerpiece (white, pink, magenta, or yellow). Companions: *Brachyscome iberidifolia* (white, pink, purple, or blue); Felicia (blue); osteospermums (white, pink, or yellow).

Main plant: *Impatiens walleriana* cultivars (red, pink, orange, violet, white). Companions: *Begonia semperflorens* cultivars (pink, red, or white); bush fuchsia as centerpiece (pink and blue or red and blue).

Containers are deal for making quick and easy colorful displays.

Rock gardens provide a good alternative setting for combinations of many different dwarf and low-growing plants.

Rock gardens

The main color in rock gardens is in spring and summer. Popular rock garden plants can be combined with dwarf bulbs for effective displays, together with woody plants such as dwarf shrubs and conifers.

ROCK GARDENS

Spring Main plant: *Aubrieta* 'Doctor Mules' (violet-blue). Companions: *Arabis alpina* subsp. *caucasica* 'Variegata' (white; leaves variegated green and light yellow); *Aurinia saxatilis* (bright yellow); *Muscari armeniacum* (blue).

Summer Main plant: *Helianthemum* 'Fire Dragon' (orange-red). Companions: *Euphorbia myrsinites* (for its blue-gray foliage); *Iberis sempervirens* (white).

Flowers

In most planting schemes, flowers are combined with woody plants such as shrubs, trees, roses, and climbers. They help to create year-round color and interest in gardens and, although it is true that many of them flower in spring and summer, there are many others that provide color in the fall and winter.

By and large, flowers are easily grown. Given suitable conditions in the garden, even beginners should have few problems. Bulbs, corms, and tubers are among the easiest, as they are almost guaranteed to flower, and the hardy kinds can be left alone to flower year after year. In frost-prone climates tender kinds have to be lifted and stored for the winter in a frost-free place.

The same applies to perennials, both the hardy kinds flowering year after year with little attention and the tender sorts needing frost-free conditions over winter in cool and cold climates.

Annuals and biennials are a bit more challenging, since they are raised from seed each year, either outdoors or under glass, though some, such as sunflowers (*Helianthus annuus*), are very easy and germinate readily.

In the past beds and borders were often devoted to one group of plants—gardeners had "shrubberies," rose beds, annual borders, herbaceous borders, and so on—but planting today is mixed, with the typical border containing all kinds of plants. The exceptions to this rule are bedding plants, which are still often grown on their own in formal beds—but the current trend is to mix bedding plants with other kinds.

Patio tubs, window boxes, and hanging baskets also provide a popular way of growing seasonal bedding plants around the house and patio. Do not forget that many hardy perennials and bulbs are also suitable for growing in patio tubs and are useful for those gardeners who do not want to replant containers several times a year.

Whatever you want to achieve—an attractive single container or an impressive border display—the following directory should provide some inspiration.

Acanthus
Bear's breeches

These hardy herbaceous perennials have a distinctive form, earning them the description "architectural plants." The long, deeply lobed leaves, spiny in some species, are particularly attractive. The flowers, carried in bold spikes, appear beneath hood-shaped bracts.

Bear's breeches are ideal for use as specimen plants in a garden to create focal points, but give them plenty of space to show off their form. A good choice for a gravel area or in association with paving or architecture, and excellent as cut flowers. Propagate by division in spring or from root cuttings in winter.

Acanthus spinosus

	SPRING	SUMMER	FALL	WINTER	height (ft)	spread (ft)	min temp (°F)	moisture	sun/shade	colors	
Acanthus mollis	planting	flower			5	3	1°	well drained	sun/shade		Large lobed leaves
A. spinosus	planting flower	flower flower			5	3	1°	well drained	sun/shade		Deeply cut spiny leaves

Achillea
Yarrow

The yarrows are hardy, mainly herbaceous perennials, although a few, especially the mat-forming rock-garden species, are evergreen. The tall border kinds are the most popular, especially those with flat, plate-like heads of flowers. Other species produce clusters of small, button-like flowers.

Achillea 'Coronation Gold'

The gray ferny foliage of some species is attractive, contrasting well with flowers. Yarrows are ideal for mixing with other hardy perennials of contrasting habit, especially spiky plants, such as gayfeather (*Liatris spicata*) and cultivars, and with ornamental grasses. Propagate by division or from basal stem cuttings in spring. Watch out for powdery mildew and aphids.

	SPRING	SUMMER	FALL	WINTER	height (ft)	spread (ft)	min temp (°F)	moisture	sun/shade	colors	
Achillea 'Coronation Gold'	planting	flower flower	flower		3	1½	1°	well drained	sun		Gray leaves
A. filipendulina 'Gold Plate'	planting	flower flower flower			4	1½	1°	well drained	sun		Large flower heads
A. millefolium 'Cerise Queen'	planting	flower flower flower			2	2	1°	well drained	sun		Vigorous habit
A. 'Moonshine'	planting	flower flower	flower		2	2	1°	well drained	sun		Gray leaves
A. ptarmica 'The Pearl'	planting	flower flower flower			2½	2	1°	moist	sun/shade		Double flowers
A. 'Taygetea'	planting	flower flower flower			2	1½	1°	well drained	sun		Gray leaves

planting	flower	well drained	moist	wet

A

Flowers

Agapanthus
African blue lily

Agapanthus Headbourne Hybrids

Herbaceous or evergreen clump-forming perennials, some are hardy while others are half-hardy. African lilies have long, strap-shaped leaves and heads of tubular, lily-like flowers, mainly in shades of blue but also white. Many hybrids have been bred, especially for hardiness.

Plants need plenty of space so that their habit of growth shows to advantage. Grow them in a border with plants of contrasting form, such as spiky kniphofias. They are excellent plants for patio containers. The flowers are good for cutting. Propagate by division in the spring. Watch out for slugs and snails, which are very keen on this plant.

	SPRING	SUMMER	FALL	WINTER	height (ft)	spread (ft)	min temp (°F)	moisture	sun/shade	colors	
Agapanthus 'Bressingham White'					3	2	1°	💧💧	☀		Strap-shaped leaves
A. Headbourne Hybrids					3	2	1°	💧💧	☀		Strap-shaped leaves
A. 'Lilliput'					1½	1½	1°	💧💧	☀		One of the smallest

Ageratum
Floss flower

These half-hardy annuals are dwarf, bushy plants with fluffy flower heads mainly in shades of blue, but also pink hues and white.

Floss flowers are the staples of summer bedding schemes, mixing well with many other plants. They are also extensively used in containers, including hanging baskets, and are good for edging beds and borders. Remove the dead flower heads of Ageratum regularly to ensure continuous flowering throughout the summer. Raise plants from seed in the spring under cover. These plants may suffer from black root rot.

Ageratum 'Blue Danube'

	SPRING	SUMMER	FALL	WINTER	height (in)	spread (in)	min temp (°F)	moisture	sun/shade	colors	
Ageratum houstonianum 'Blue Danube'					6	12	34°	💧💧	☀		Rain-resistant flowers
A. houstonianum 'Blue Mink'					12	12	34°	💧💧	☀		Vigorous, loose habit
A. houstonianum 'Blue Mist'					6	6	34°	💧💧	☀		Neat, compact habit
A. houstonianum 'Hawaii White'					6	6	34°	💧💧	☀		Very compact habit

☀ *sunny* ☼ *semi-shady* ● *shady*

Ajuga
Bugleweed

The bugleweeds are hardy, mat-forming, ground cover perennials, generally with evergreen leaves. Some kinds are very vigorous. The leaves of some cultivars are variegated or multicolored. Stumpy spikes of blue flowers—or white in some species—rise above the carpets in spring.

Ajuga reptans 'Catlin's Giant'

These plants are ideal for moist, shady areas, such as a woodland garden or beneath deciduous shrubs, associating well with dwarf spring bulbs. They also look good drifted among clumps of yellow-green lady's mantle (*Alchemilla mollis*), red or pink astilbes, and candelabra primulas. If plants outgrow their allotted space, simply dig out the excess. Propagate by division, or single, rooted rosettes, in spring. Plants are sometimes affected by powdery mildew.

	SPRING	SUMMER	FALL	WINTER	height (in)	spread (in)	min temp (°F)	moisture	sun/shade	colors	
Ajuga reptans 'Atropurpurea'					6	24	1°				Dark purple foliage
A. reptans 'Catlin's Giant'					6	24	1°				Bronze-purple foliage
A. reptans 'Multicolor'					6	24	1°				Bronze, cream, and pink leaves
A. reptans 'Variegata'					6	24	1°				Cream and green leaves

Alcea
Hollyhock

These short-lived hardy herbaceous perennials are generally tall, sometimes up to 8ft (2.5m), although dwarf cultivars have been bred. All produce sturdy, upright stems bearing fully double or single flowers in various colors, and pale green, hairy, lobed leaves.

Hollyhocks are very popular for cottage garden borders, where they associate well with old-fashioned plants, including old roses, honeysuckles, sweet williams, and peonies. Tall kinds may need staking. Raise from seed in spring or early summer under cover or outdoors; best grown as annuals or biennials. Hollyhock rust may be a problem.

Alcea rosea cultivar

	SPRING	SUMMER	FALL	WINTER	height (ft)	spread (ft)	min temp (°F)	moisture	sun/shade	colors	
Alcea rosea Chater's Double Group					6½	2	1°				Double flowers. Many colors
A. rosea Majorette Group					3	1	1°				Semi-double flowers. Many colors
A. rosea Summer Carnival Group					6½	2	1°				An annual

planting   flower   well drained   moist   wet

Alchemilla
Lady's mantle

These popular hardy herbaceous perennials produce clouds of yellow-green flowers above attractive, light green, hairy, lobed leaves.

Alchemilla mollis

Lady's mantles are used in mixed borders where they combine effectively with many other perennials and shrubs, particularly those with strong or bright red flowers, including roses. Remove dead flower heads if you want to prevent self-seeding. Propagate by division in spring, or transplant self-sown seedlings in spring. The main pests are slugs and snails, which can ruin the appearance of the foliage.

	SPRING	SUMMER	FALL	WINTER	height (in)	spread (in)	min temp (°F)	moisture	sun/shade	colors	
Alchemilla erythropoda					8	8	1°				Blue-green leaves
A. mollis					24	30	1°				Soft hairy leaves

Allium
Ornamental onions

Alliums are hardy bulbs valued for their rounded heads of tubular flowers in shades of blue, purple, pink, or white. They have long leaves, either thin or strap-shaped, which may die down before the flowers appear.

Allium caeruleum

Allium cristophii

Onions are generally grown in a mixed border where they associate well with many perennials, including plants with spikes of flowers like lupines and plate-like heads such as achilleas. Try them also with ornamental grasses. Tall kinds are effective companions for shrub roses. Propagate by removing offsets in the fall.

	SPRING	SUMMER	FALL	WINTER	height (in)	spread (in)	min temp (°F)	moisture	sun/shade	colors	
Allium caeruleum					24	1	25°				Star-shaped flowers
A. cristophii					12	6	25°				Wide, gray-green leaves
A. 'Globemaster'					30	8	1°				Large, globular flower heads
A. hollandicum 'Purple Sensation'					36	3	1°				Large, globular flower heads
A. moly					60	2	1°				Spreads rapidly
A. sphaerocephalon					36	3	1°				Egg-shaped flower heads

☼ *sunny* ☀ *semi-shady* ● *shady*

Alonsoa
Mask flower

Alonsoa warscewiczii

Mask flowers are half-hardy perennials or shrubby plants but are generally grown as annuals. They are dwarf, bushy plants producing a profusion of spurred flowers over a very long period, generally in brilliant colors such as red or orange.

In recent years they have come to the fore as summer bedding and container plants, being especially good for hanging baskets. Combine them with cooler flowers, such as blue or white lobelia or ageratum. Raise plants from seed in spring under cover. Main pests are aphids.

	SPRING	SUMMER	FALL	WINTER	height (ft)	spread (ft)	min temp (°F)	moisture	sun/shade	colors	
A. meridionalis Firestone Jewels Series	planting	flower			1	1	34°	well drained	sun		May grow taller in some situations
A. warscewiczii	planting	flower			1½	1	34°	well drained	sun		Compact and bushy plant

Alstroemeria
Peruvian lily

Peruvian lilies are tuberous, herbaceous perennials and most are frost-hardy. This plant's flowers are trumpet-shaped, somewhat lily-like, in bright or pastel colors. The leaves are generally lance-shaped and in some species are grayish-green.

These plants are used in mixed borders, where they combine well with shrubs, including shrub roses. The flowers are suitable for cutting, often lasting for several weeks in water, and indeed they are among the staple flowers of florists. Plants benefit from a permanent mulch of organic matter to protect roots from frost, and are best left undisturbed for as long as possible. Propagate by division in the fall. Main problems are slugs, snails, and virus.

Alstroemeria ligtu Hybrids

	SPRING	SUMMER	FALL	WINTER	height (ft)	spread (ft)	min temp (°F)	moisture	sun/shade	colors	
Alstroemeria aurea		flower	planting		3	1½	25°	well drained	sun		Easily grown
A. ligtu Hybrids		flower	planting		1½	2½	25°	well drained	sun		Flowers often multicolored

planting   flower   well drained   moist   wet

Amaranthus

Love-lies-bleeding
or Chinese
spinach

Amaranthus cruentus 'Plenitude'

Amaranthus are half-hardy annuals that vary considerably in habit. Some, like A. caudatus (Love-lies-bleeding) have dangling, tassel-like flowers, while others, such as A. cruentus, bear more upright plumes. Flowers are red or green.

A. tricolor (Chinese spinach) is grown for its multicolored foliage. Use amaranthus as dot plants in summer bedding schemes, as container plants, or in subtropical plantings. Flowers are good for cutting and drying. Provide sheltered conditions. Raise from seed in spring under cover. Main pests are aphids.

	SPRING	SUMMER	FALL	WINTER	height (ft)	spread (ft)	min temp (°F)	moisture	sun/shade	colors	
Amaranthus caudatus					3	1½	34°				Bushy habit
A. cruentus 'Plenitude'					6½	1½	34°				Bushy habit
A. tricolor 'Joseph's Coat'					3	1½	34°				Grown for foliage

Anchusa

Alkanet

A group of hardy single-crown herbaceous perennials and frost-hardy annuals. Flowers are mainly blue and the rough, hairy leaves are elliptical or lance-shaped. The perennial A. azurea is ideal for a mixed border, combining with spiky plants like lupines and delphiniums, and Oriental poppies (papaver).

Anchusa azurea 'Loddon Royalist'

The annual *A. capensis* can be used in a similar way, and also combines well with other annuals such as California poppies (eschscholzia). Deadhead annuals, and cut back perennials when flowering is over to encourage vegetative growth. Sow annuals under cover in spring. Propagate perennials from root cuttings in winter. Mildew can be a problem with these plants.

	SPRING	SUMMER	FALL	WINTER	height (in)	spread (in)	min temp (°F)	moisture	sun/shade	colors	
Anchusa azurea 'Loddon Royalist'					36	24	1°				Self-supporting
A. capensis 'Blue Angel'					8	6	25°				Compact habit

☼ *sunny*   ◐ *semi-shady*   ● *shady*

Anemone
Windflower

A large and variable group of hardy herbaceous perennials. The dwarf *A. blanda* grows from tubers and produces blue, pink, or white daisy-like flowers in spring. It is excellent for naturalizing in a woodland garden or among shrubs in a border.

A. coronaria also grows from tubers, and has large single or double flowers in blue, red, or white, ideal for cutting. Grow this windflower in a cutting garden or mixed border and in hard-winter areas provide a permanent mulch of organic matter for frost protection. *A. hupehensis* and *A.* x *hybrida* (Japanese anemone) are taller, clump forming, fibrous-rooted perennials, valued for their late summer and fall flowers in shades of pink and also white. Grow

Anemone coronaria De Caen Group

these in a mixed border with other late-flowering perennials such as golden rod (Solidago) and sedums. *A. nemorosa* (wood anemone) is a dwarf rhizomatous perennial with blue or white spring flowers. Use in the same way as *A. blanda*. Propagate by division in the fall or spring. It is possible to buy *A. blanda* in pots from garden centers in spring. The main problems are leaf spot, powdery mildew, slugs, and snails.

Anemone blanda

Anemone nemorosa

	SPRING	SUMMER	FALL	WINTER	height (in)	spread (in)	min temp (F)	moisture	sun/shade	colors	
Anemone blanda	● ● ●		🌱 🌱 🌱		6	6	1°	💧	☀		Good for naturalizing
A. blanda 'White Splendour'	● ● ●		🌱 🌱 🌱		6	6	1°	💧	☀		Large flowers
A. coronaria De Caen Group	🌱 🌱 ● ●				12	6	1°	💧	☀		Single flowers
A. hupehensis 'Hadspen Abundance'	🌱 🌱 🌱	●			36	15	1°	💧	☀		Provide permanent mulch
A. h. var. *japonica* 'Bressingham Glow'	🌱 🌱 🌱	●			36	15	1°	💧	☀		Provide permanent mulch
A. x *hybrida* 'Honorine Jobert'	🌱 🌱 🌱		● ● ●		48	24	1°	💧	☀		Provide permanent mulch
A. x *hybrida* 'September Charm'	🌱 🌱 🌱		● ● ●		36	24	1°	💧	☀		Provide permanent mulch
A. nemorosa 'Robinsoniana'	● ● ● ●		🌱 🌱 🌱		3	12	1°	💧	☀		Vigorous habit
A. nemorosa 'Vestal'	● ● ● ●		🌱 🌱 🌱		3	12	1°	💧	☀		Double flowers

🌱 *planting*   ● *flower*   💧 *well drained*   💧 *moist*   💧 *wet*

Anthemis
Golden marguerite *or* Ox-eye chamomile

The species listed here, *A. tinctoria*, is a hardy herbaceous perennial that freely produces yellow daisy-like flowers. But it may be short-lived.

The cultivars are indispensable border plants, mixing well with many other perennials, such as blue salvias and delphiniums. Try them also with blue cranesbills (geraniums). They are also a good choice for a gravel garden. When flowering is over, cut plants hard back to encourage vegetative growth. The blooms are suitable for cutting.

Propagate by division or from basal cuttings in spring. Main problems are aphids, powdery mildew, slugs, and snails.

Anthemis tinctoria 'Wargrave Variety'

	SPRING	SUMMER	FALL	WINTER	height (ft)	spread (ft)	min temp (°F)	moisture	sun/shade	colors	
Anthemis tinctoria 'E.C. Buxton'					1½	3	1°	🌢	☼	⬜	Very free-flowering
A. tinctoria 'Wargrave Variety'					3	3	1°	🌢	☼	⬜	Very free-flowering

Antirrhinum
Snapdragon

The *A. majus* cultivars are grown as half-hardy annuals, although in reality they are short-lived perennials. They are bushy plants, producing spikes of two-lipped flowers in a huge range of colors over a long period.

Snapdragons are used for summer bedding and are also good for patio containers. Very tall cultivars are better in a mixed border. Flowers are suitable for cutting, but choose tall varieties for this purpose. Deadhead regularly to ensure continuous flowering. Raise plants from seed in spring under cover. Main problem is rust, so choose rust-resistant cultivars where possible. Also prone to aphids and powdery mildew.

Antirrhinum majus cultivar

	SPRING	SUMMER	FALL	WINTER	height (in)	spread (in)	min temp (°F)	moisture	sun/shade	colors	
Antirrhinum majus Coronette Series					24	18	34°	🌢	☼	◫	Rust-resistant. Many colors
A. majus Madame Butterfly Series					30	18	34°	🌢	☼	◫	Double flowers. Many colors
A. majus Magic Carpet Series					6	12	34°	🌢	☼	◫	Excellent for bedding. Many colors
A. majus 'Peaches and Cream'					8	12	34°	🌢	☼	◫	Excellent for bedding. Many colors
A. majus Sonnet Series					24	18	34°	🌢	☼	◫	Rain-tolerant. Many colors
A. majus Sweetheart Series					12	12	34°	🌢	☼	◫	Double flowers. Many colors

☼ *sunny*   ☀ *semi-shady*   ● *shady*

Aquilegia
Columbine

Columbines are hardy herbaceous perennials that produce spurred flowers in many colors above attractive lobed, sometimes bluish-green foliage.

Grow them in a mixed border with other perennials such as lupines, delphiniums, peonies, and irises. They are a good choice for cottage-garden borders, especially in combination with old roses. Deadhead regularly. Propagate by division in spring—divisions are slow to establish as columbines do not like to be disturbed. Main problems are aphids, caterpillars of various kinds, and powdery mildew.

Aquilegia McKana Group

	SPRING	SUMMER	FALL	WINTER	height (ft)	spread (ft)	min temp (°F)	moisture	sun/shade	colors	
Aquilegia McKana Group	🌱🌱 ●	● ●			2½	2	1°	💧	☀	▮	Vigorous grower
A. vulgaris 'Nora Barlow'	🌱🌱 ●	●			3	1½	1°	💧	☀	▮	Double flowers

Arabis
Rock cress

Arabis subsp. 'Rosabella'

The species listed here, *A. alpina* subsp. *caucasica*, is a hardy, evergreen, mat-forming perennial of very vigorous habit. Cultivars with variegated foliage or double flowers are generally grown and they have white flowers.

Rock cress can be grown on a rock garden with aubrieta, aurinia, and helianthemum, but make sure it does not take over. It is also good for covering dry sunny banks, or edging a mixed border. Trim plants after flowering to keep them compact. Propagate from softwood cuttings as soon as available in spring or early summer. The main problem for Arabis is aphids.

	SPRING	SUMMER	FALL	WINTER	height (in)	spread (in)	min temp (°F)	moisture	sun/shade	colors	
A. alpina subsp. *caucasica* 'Flore Pleno'	🌱🌱 ●	●			6	24	1°	💧	☀	▯	Double flowers
A. alpina subsp. *caucasica* 'Variegata'	🌱🌱 ●	●			6	24	1°	💧	☀	▯	Leaves variegated green and yellow

🌱 *planting*   ● *flower*   💧 *well drained*   💧 *moist*   💧 *wet*

Arctotis
African daisy

Arctotis x hybrida 'Flame'

In frost-prone climates the African daisy is grown as a half-hardy annual, although in warm climates it is a perennial.

Daisy-like flowers in various bright colors including orange and red shades are freely produced. The lobed leaves are silvery green. Ideal for summer bedding or for planting in bold groups at the front of a mixed border or in a gravel area. Suitable for patio containers. Blooms can be cut but do not last for long. Propagate from seed in spring under cover, or from cuttings in late summer. Aphids are the main problem.

	SPRING	SUMMER	FALL	WINTER	height (ft)	spread (ft)	min temp (°F)	moisture	sun/shade	colors	
Arctotis x hybrida 'Flame'					1½	1	41°				Attractive lobed leaves
A. x hybrida 'Harlequin'					1½	1	41°				Multicolored flowers

Argyranthemum

These half-hardy evergreen subshrubs have a bushy or spreading habit and produce single or double daisy-like flowers in shades of pink, yellow, or orange, as well as white.

Argyranthemum 'Butterfly'

Argyranthemum 'Petite Pink'

The foliage is variable, from ferny to lobed, and green to gray-green. Argyranthemums are grown as annual summer bedding plants in frosty climates, and are good for mixed borders, patio tubs, and window boxes. They mix well with other daisy-flowered plants such as brachyscome and gazanias. Pinch out tips of young plants. Propagate from semi-ripe cuttings in late summer. Generally free of problems.

	SPRING	SUMMER	FALL	WINTER	height (ft)	spread (ft)	min temp (°F)	moisture	sun/shade	colors	
Argyranthemum 'Butterfly'					2	1½	34°				Single flowers
A. 'Jamaica Primrose'					3	3	34°				Single flowers
A. 'Petite Pink'					1	1	34°				Single flowers
A. 'Summer Melody'					2	1½	34°				Double flowers
A. 'Vancouver'					3	2½	34°				Double flowers

☼ *sunny*   ◐ *semi-shady*   ● *shady*

Armeria
Sea thrift

The species *A. maritima* is a hardy, dwarf, clump-forming evergreen perennial. Cultivated varieties are normally grown. The rounded heads of tiny flowers, in shades of pink, red, or white, are carried above deep green grassy leaves.

Armeria maritima

Thrift is one of the staples of rock and scree gardens, but is also good for edging a mixed border. It is excellent for seaside gardens and can also be used to create a "lawn," but not for frequent use. This primarily decorative lawn is largely maintenance-free, apart from trimming off the dead flowers once plants have finished blooming. Propagate by division in spring. Generally trouble-free.

	SPRING	SUMMER	FALL	WINTER	height (in)	spread (in)	min temp (°F)	moisture	sun/shade	colors	
Armeria maritima	🌱🌱	● ● ● ●			8	12	1°	💧	☀	▊	Good for poor soil
A. maritima 'Alba'	🌱🌱	● ● ● ●			8	12	1°	💧	☀	☐	White flowers
A. maritima 'Vindictive'	🌱🌱	● ● ● ●			8	12	1°	💧	☀	▩	Good for poor soil

Artemisia
Mugwort

This is a large and varied group of plants but the species listed are hardy, clump-forming herbaceous perennials.

Artemisia ludoviciana

A. lactiflora is grown mainly for its flowers, although its deeply cut green leaves are attractive, while *A. ludoviciana* is more of a foliage plant with its striking silvery leaves. Both act as a foil for strongly colored perennials, such as crocosmias, in mixed borders and combine well with daisy-flowered plants. Flowers are suitable for cutting. Propagate by division in spring. Powdery mildew may be a problem.

	SPRING	SUMMER	FALL	WINTER	height (ft)	spread (ft)	min temp (°F)	moisture	sun/shade	colors	
Artemisia lactiflora	🌱🌱🌱		● ● ●		5	2	1°	💧	☀	☐	Attractive deep green foliage
A. ludoviciana	🌱🌱🌱	● ● ●	● ●		4	2	1°	💧	☀	▩	Woolly flower heads

🌱 *planting* ● *flower* 💧 *well drained* 💧 *moist* 💧 *wet*

Aster

The plants included here are hardy herbaceous perennials. There are both tall and dwarf cultivars, producing single or double daisy-like flower heads in shades of blue, violet, purple, red, and also white.

Some flower in late summer but many are of great value in the fall garden, combining well with other late-flowering perennials such as rudbeckias, helianthus, and anemones, as well as with shrubs noted for fall leaf tints and berries, such as rhus and berberis. As asters dislike drying out, maintain a permanent mulch of organic

Aster novae-angliae 'Harrington's Pink'

matter. Support tall plants with twiggy sticks as they start into growth. Divide *A. novae-angliae* and *A. novi-belgii* cultivars every two or three years to keep them young, vigorous, and free-flowering. Alternatively, *A. novi-belgii* cultivars can be divided annually. Lift the mats of growth and remove single shoots with roots attached (like rooted cuttings) and replant them 2in (5cm) apart in groups. Propagate by division in spring. Powdery mildew can affect *A. novi-belgii* cultivars quite badly. Unfortunately, there are several other problems that affect asters: watch out for aphids, slugs, snails, gray mold, leaf spot, and wilting caused by drought.

Aster x *frikartii* 'Mönch'

	SPRING	SUMMER	FALL	WINTER	height (ft)	spread (ft)	min temp (°F)	moisture	sun/shade	colors	
A. amellus 'King George'			●	● ● ●		1½	1½	1°	◐	☀	■	Large single flowers; late flowering
A. x frikartii			●	●		2½	1½	1°	◐	☀	■	Large single flowers
A. x frikartii 'Mönch'			●	●		2½	1½	1°	◐	☀	□	Large single flowers
A. novae-angliae 'Harrington's Pink'			●	● ●		4	2	1°	◐	☀	□	Semi-double flowers; likes a moist spot
A. novi-belgii 'Fellowship'			●	● ●		3	3	1°	◐	☀	□	Double flowers; likes a moist spot
A. novi-belgii 'Lady in Blue'			●	●		1	1½	1°	◐	☀	□	Single flowers; likes a moist spot
A. novi-belgii 'Marie Ballard'			●	● ●		3	3	1°	◐	☀	□	Double flowers; likes a moist spot
A. novi-belgii 'Winston S. Churchill'			●	● ●		3	3	1°	◐	☀	■	Double flowers; likes a moist spot
A. sedifolius 'Nanus'			●	●		1½	2	1°	◐	☀	■	Single flowers

☼ *sunny*   ☀ *semi-shady*   ● *shady*

Astilbe

These hardy clump-forming herbaceous perennials produce attractive ferny foliage, which is often tinted bronze or red when young, and pink, red, purple or white plume-like flowers.

The dead flower heads can be left for winter interest. Astilbes are ideal for moist parts of the garden, especially around the edge of a pool, in combination with moisture-loving primulas and day lilies (Hemerocallis). Divide regularly (every three years) to keep plants young and vigorous. Propagate by division in spring. Plants may be troubled by leaf spot and powdery mildew.

Astilbe chinensis 'Serenade'

	SPRING	SUMMER	FALL	WINTER	height (ft)	spread (ft)	min temp (°F)	moisture	sun/shade	colors	
Astilbe x *arendsii* 'Bressingham Beauty'	🌱🌱🌱	🌸			3	2	1°	🌢🌢	☀	▧	Leaves flushed with bronze
A. x *arendsii* 'Fanal'	🌱🌱🌱	🌸			2	1½	1°	🌢🌢	☀	■	Deep green leaves
A. chinensis 'Serenade'	🌱🌱🌱	🌸			1½	1½	1°	🌢🌢🌢	☀	▧	Feathery flowers

Astrantia
Masterwort

Masterworts are hardy, clump-forming herbaceous perennials. The flowers, on tall upright stems, are pink, red, or green and surrounded with a collar of colored bracts.

Deeply lobed or hand-shaped leaves make an attractive background for the blooms. Grow in mixed borders and woodland gardens, or drift around shrubs, combining them with foliage perennials such as hostas and the new heucheras or coral flowers with colored foliage. The flower heads can be cut and dried. Deadhead if you do not want plants to self-seed. Propagate in spring by division or by transplanting self-sown seedlings. Watch out for aphids, powdery mildew, slugs, and snails.

Astrantia major 'Sunningdale Variegated'

Astrantia major 'Ruby Wedding'

	SPRING	SUMMER	FALL	WINTER	height (ft)	spread (ft)	min temp (°F)	moisture	sun/shade	colors	
Astrantia major	🌱🌱🌱	🌸🌸🌸			3	1½	1°	🌢🌢	◐	▧	White bracts
A. major 'Ruby Wedding'	🌱🌱🌱	🌸🌸🌸			3	1½	1°	🌢🌢	◐	■	Bracts are a similar color to flowers
A. major 'Hadspen Blood'	🌱🌱🌱	🌸🌸🌸			3	1½	1°	🌢🌢	◐	■	Bracts are a similar color to flowers
A. major 'Sunningdale Variegated'	🌱🌱🌱	🌸🌸🌸			3	1½	1°	🌢🌢	◐	▨	Green and cream variegated foliage

🌱 planting   🌸 flower   🌢 well drained   🌢🌢 moist   🌢🌢🌢 wet

Aubrieta

Aubrieta hybrid

These hardy evergreen carpeting perennials produce masses of small, four-petaled flowers in blue, red-purple, mauve, pink, or white. The small leaves are roughly oval.

Indispensable plants for the rock or scree garden in combination with aurinia, arabis, and helianthemums. When flowering is over cut back plants to ensure a compact habit. Propagate from semi-ripe cuttings in summer. Main pests are aphids.

	SPRING	SUMMER	FALL	WINTER	height (in)	spread (in)	min temp (°F)	moisture	sun/shade	colors	
Aubrieta 'Aureovariegata'	🌱 ● ●				2	24	1°	💧	☼		Gold and green variegated leaves
A. 'Doctor Mules'	🌱 ● ●				2	24	1°	💧	☼		Single flowers
A. 'Red Carpet'	🌱 ● ●				2	24	1°	💧	☼		Single flowers

Aurinia

A hardy dwarf evergreen perennial, Aurinia produces masses of sunshine yellow flowers above mounds of gray-green foliage.

A favorite companion for aubrieta on rock and scree gardens, this plant is also suitable for covering a well-drained, sunny bank. When flowering is over cut back plants to ensure a compact habit. Propagate in early summer from softwood cuttings. Main pests are aphids.

Aurinia saxatilis

	SPRING	SUMMER	FALL	WINTER	height (in)	spread (in)	min temp (°F)	moisture	sun/shade	colors	
Aurinia saxatilis	🌱 🌱 ● ●				8	12	1°	💧	☼		Gray-green leaves
A. saxatilis 'Citrina'	🌱 🌱 ● ●				8	12	1°	💧	☼		Gray-green leaves

Baptisia
False *or* Wild indigo

Baptisia australis

A fully hardy perennial, false indigo has deep blue, pea-shaped flowers and hand-shaped leaves. It is an excellent border plant, particularly for prairie-style borders in combination with ornamental grasses.

Baptisia australis is suitable for a well-drained bank in full sun. It has a gently spreading or erect habit and flowers in early summer. The dark blue flowers are often flecked with white or cream. Propagate by division in spring. No problems from pests or diseases.

☼ sunny   ☼ semi-shady   ● shady

Begonia

This is a huge group of very tender perennials. In frost-prone climates tuberous and fibrous-rooted begonias are used for summer bedding and for containers such as patio tubs, window boxes, and hanging baskets.

They flower profusely, producing blooms in shades of red, pink, orange, yellow, or white. The trailing Pendula tuberous begonias are especially suitable for hanging baskets,

Begonia semperflorens 'Olympia Red'

Begonia Multiflora Nonstop Series

Begonia 'Illumination Rose'

while the tuberous Multiflora and giant-flowered Tuberhybrida begonias are better in tubs and window boxes. The compact, bushy, fibrous-rooted *B. semperflorens* cultivars are generally used for massed summer bedding in combination with other bedding plants such as ageratum, impatiens, and lobelia. The leaves are often flushed with bronze. Deadhead all plants

regularly. The Multiflora and Pendula begonias are generally treated as annuals and raised from seed each year. Tuberhybrida begonias can also be seed-raised or purchased as tubers. Dormant tubers of all types can be stored over winter in frost-free conditions. *B. semperflorens* cultivars are raised from seed and treated as annuals. Propagate from seed in late winter or early spring under cover. Tuberous begonias are prone to attack by vine weevil grubs. Also watch out for aphids, gray mold, and powdery mildew.

	SPRING	SUMMER	FALL	WINTER	height (in)	spread (in)	min temp (°F)	moisture	sun/shade	colors	
Begonia Multiflora Nonstop Series	planting	flower			12	12	41°	well drained	sun		Double flowers
B. Pendula Illumination Series	planting	flower			24	12	41°	well drained	sun		Double flowers
B. Pendula Sensation Series	planting	flower			24	12	41°	well drained	sun		Double flowers
B. Pendula Show Angels Series	planting	flower			24	12	41°	well drained	sun		Double flowers
B. semperflorens Ambassador Series	planting	flower			8	8	41°	well drained	sun		Green leaves
B. semperflorens Olympia Series	planting	flower			8	8	41°	well drained	sun		Green leaves
B. semperflorens President Series	planting	flower			8	8	41°	well drained	sun		Mix of green and bronze leaves
B. semperflorens Senator Series	planting	flower			8	8	41°	well drained	sun		Brown bronze leaves
B. Tuberhybrida 'Giant Double Mixed'	planting	flower			12	12	41°	well drained	sun		Double flowers
B. Tuberhybrida Picotee Series	planting	flower			24	24	41°	well drained	sun		Double flowers

planting   flower   well drained   moist   wet

Bellis
Daisy

Hardy perennials grown as biennials, the cultivars of *B. perennis*, the common daisy, are dwarf, rosette-forming plants with large, double or semi-double flowers in shades of pink, red, or white.

The leaves are somewhat spoon-shaped. Daisies are used in spring bedding schemes, in combination with other spring bedding plants and bulbs such as tulips, hyacinths, forget-me-nots (Myosotis), or wallflowers (Erysimum). Also good for tubs and window boxes. Remove dead flower heads regularly. Propagate from seed outdoors in early summer. Not troubled by pests or diseases.

Bellis perennis 'Tasso Red'

	SPRING	SUMMER	FALL	WINTER	height (in)	spread (in)	min temp (°F)	moisture	sun/shade	colors	
Bellis perennis Carpet Series	● ● ●		🌱 🌱 🌱		6	6	1°	💧💧	☀	▮	Double flowers
B. perennis 'Goliath'	● ● ●		🌱 🌱 🌱		8	8	1°	💧💧	☀	▯	Double flowers
B. perennis Tasso Series	● ● ●		🌱 🌱 🌱		8	8	1°	💧💧	☀	▮	Double flowers

Bergenia
Elephant's ears

Hardy dwarf evergreen perennials, bergenias have large, showy heads of bell-shaped flowers carried on thick stalks, in shades of pink, red, and magenta, as well as white.

Bergenia 'Abendglut'

The large leathery, shiny, rounded or oval leaves may become tinted with red or purple in winter. These are excellent plants for the front of mixed borders, perhaps surrounding shrubs and interplanted with winter and spring bulbs, and for woodland gardens. Bergenias benefit from a permanent mulch of organic matter. Propagate from rhizome cuttings in the fall, or by division after flowering. Watch out for leaf spot, slugs, snails, and vine weevil grubs.

Bergenia 'Bressingham White'

	SPRING	SUMMER	FALL	WINTER	height (ft)	spread (ft)	min temp (°F)	moisture	sun/shade	colors	
Bergenia 'Abendglut'	● 🌱 🌱				1	2	1°	💧💧	◐	▮	Red-purple winter foliage
B. 'Bressingham White'	● 🌱 🌱				1½	2	1°	💧💧	◐	▯	Dark green foliage
B. cordifolia	● 🌱 🌱			●	2	2½	1°	💧💧	◐	▮	Leaves purple flushed in winter
B. cordifolia 'Purpurea'	● 🌱 🌱			●	2	2½	1°	💧💧	◐	▮	Leaves deep red-purple in winter
B. 'Silberlicht'	● 🌱 🌱				1½	2	1°	💧💧	◐	▯	Medium green leaves
B. 'Sunningdale'	● 🌱 🌱				1½	2	1°	💧💧	◐	▮	Leaves turn red in winter

☀ *sunny*   ◐ *semi-shady*   ● *shady*

Bidens

Bidens ferulifolia

This is a short-lived, slender, somewhat spreading, half-hardy perennial. It is grown as an annual in frost-prone climates.

The daisy-like, rich yellow flowers of this plant are produced over a long period, the bright green ferny foliage making a pleasing background. *Bidens ferulifolia* is excellent for providing summer color in patio tubs, window boxes, and hanging baskets. Propagate from seed in spring under cover. Not troubled by pests or diseases.

Brachyscome
Swan River daisy

Cultivars of the half-hardy annual *B. iberidifolia* have daisy-like, blue, purple, pink, or white flowers on bushy plants, and finely divided, gray-green leaves.

B. iberidifolia 'Bravo'

Excellent for summer color in patio tubs and window boxes, and for mixed borders. Grow with other daisy-flowered plants such as osteospermums. Young plants should have growing tips pinched out, as this encourages the plants to become well branched or bushy and therefore to produce many more flowers. Propagate from seed in spring under cover. Watch out for slugs and snails.

	SPRING	SUMMER	FALL	WINTER	height (in)	spread (in)	min temp (°F)	moisture	sun/shade	colors	
Brachyscome iberidifolia 'Blue Star'	🌱🌱🌱	●●●			12	12	34°	💧	☀		Tolerates drought
B. iberidifolia 'Bravo'	🌱🌱🌱	●●●			10	12	34°	💧	☀		Flowers are several different colors
B. iberidifolia Splendour Series	🌱🌱🌱	●●●			12	12	34°	💧	☀		Flowers are several different colors

Bracteantha
Strawflower

Bracteantha bracteata

The strawflower *B. bracteata* is a half-hardy annual with papery, daisy-like flower heads on strong, upright stems.

Cultivars, mainly with double flowers, come in shades of yellow, orange, pink, red, and also white. Grow in a mixed border or cutting garden. Support tall cultivars. Flowers are suitable for cutting and drying. Propagate from seed in spring under cover. Generally trouble-free.

	SPRING	SUMMER	FALL	WINTER	height (in)	spread (in)	min temp (°F)	moisture	sun/shade	colors	
B. bracteata Bright Bikini Series	🌱🌱🌱	●●●	●●		12	12	34°	💧	☀		Large double flowers
B. bracteata Chico Series	🌱🌱🌱	●●●	●●		12	12	34°	💧	☀		Fade-resistant blooms

🌱 *planting*   ● *flower*   💧 *well drained*   💧 *moist*   💧 *wet*

Calceolaria
Pouch flower *or* Slipper flower

The species *C. integrifolia* is a somewhat shrubby, evergreen, half-hardy perennial but is generally grown as an annual in frost-prone climates. Cultivars are usually grown and these have yellow, orange, or red pouched flowers over a long period, and gray-green leaves.

Pouch flowers are good for summer color in containers, including hanging baskets. They can also be used in summer bedding schemes, and look good with *Salvia farinacea* cultivars. Propagate from seed in spring under cover, or from semi-ripe cuttings in late summer. Watch out for aphids, slugs, and snails.

Calceolaria 'Kentish Hero'

	SPRING	SUMMER	FALL	WINTER	height (ft)	spread (ft)	min temp (°F)	moisture	sun/shade	colors	
Calceolaria integrifolia 'Sunshine'					1	1	34°				Rain-resistant blooms
C. 'Kentish Hero'					2	1	34°				Good old cultivar

Calendula
English *or* Pot marigold

The hardy annual English marigold produces double or single daisy-like flowers over a long period. Colors include shades of orange, apricot, yellow, and cream. Flowers have conspicuous darker centers, usually brown or purplish.

The strongly aromatic leaves are generally spoon-shaped. Dwarf and tall cultivars are available. Calendulas are a good choice for cottage-garden borders, plus ordinary mixed borders, and the flowers are suitable for cutting. Blue cornflowers make good companions. Deadhead regularly to ensure continuous flowering. Propagate from seed sown in flowering position in spring or fall. These plants are prone to aphids and powdery mildew.

Calendula officinalis 'Fiesta Gitana'

	SPRING	SUMMER	FALL	WINTER	height (ft)	spread (ft)	min temp (°F)	moisture	sun/shade	colors	
Calendula officinalis 'Art Shades'					2	2	1°				Double flowers
C. officinalis 'Fiesta Gitana'					1	1	1°				Double flowers
C. officinalis Kablouna Series					2	1½	1°				Double, crested flowers
C. officinalis 'Orange King'					1½	1	1°				Double flowers
C. officinalis Pacific Beauty Series					2	1½	1°				Double flowers

☼ *sunny*   ◐ *semi-shady*   ● *shady*

Callistephus
China aster

Cultivars of *C. chinensis* are half-hardy annuals. They make bushy, branching plants and produce heads of single or double flowers reminiscent of chrysanthemums.

Callistephus chinensis Ostrich Plume Series

Colors include pink, crimson, violet-blue, purple, and white. Some are dwarf, others tall. Dwarf kinds make good summer bedding or container plants, while taller cultivars are better grouped in a mixed border. Flowers are excellent for cutting. Deadhead plants regularly. Provide supports for tall cultivars. Propagate from seed in early spring under cover. Watch out for aphids, cutworms, and wilt caused by various diseases (pull up and discard affected plants).

	SPRING	SUMMER	FALL	WINTER	height (in)	spread (in)	min temp (°F)	moisture	sun/shade	colors	
C. chinensis Comet Series	🌱🌱🌱	●●●● ●			10	8	34°	💧	☀	▨	Large double flowers, quilled petals
C. chinensis Duchess Series	🌱🌱🌱	●●●● ●			30	12	34°	💧	☀	▨	Incurved blooms
C. chinensis Milady Series	🌱🌱🌱	●●●● ●			12	10	34°	💧	☀	▨	Double flowers
C. chinensis Ostrich Plume Series	🌱🌱🌱	●●●● ●			24	12	34°	💧	☀	▨	Double, feathery flowers

Caltha
Kingcup *or* Marsh marigold

***Caltha palustris* is a hardy, early flowering aquatic perennial. Bright yellow or white buttercup-like flowers are produced above deep green kidney-shaped leaves. The double-flowered 'Flore Pleno' is the most popular of the various cultivars.**

Caltha palustris

Grow Caltha in very shallow water at the margins of a garden pool, or in boggy soil near the water's edge. This plant is generally grown with other bog- or moisture-loving plants such as the skunk cabbage (*Lysichiton americanus*).

The marsh marigold is also a good subject for a mini pool created in a large watertight tub on the patio, as it is

🌱 *planting*	● *flower*	💧 *well drained*	💧 *moist*	💧 *wet*

Caltha palustris 'Flore Pleno'

small enough not to overwhelm the tub.

Propagate by division as soon as flowering is over. Watch out for powdery mildew. Otherwise, this plant is not troubled by pests and diseases.

	SPRING	SUMMER	FALL	WINTER	height (in)	spread (in)	min temp (°F)	moisture	sun/shade	colors	
Caltha palustris	✎ ● ●				15	18	1°	●●	☼	■	Deep green lobed leaves
C. palustris 'Flore Pleno'	✎ ● ●				10	10	1°	●●	☼	▢	Double flowers
C. palustris var. *alba*	✎ ● ●				8	10	1°	●●	☼	▢	Single flowers

Camassia
Quamash

Camassias are frost-hardy bulbs. The flowers are generally star-shaped, in shades of blue or white, and carried on tall stems. The long narrow upright leaves are bright green.

Excellent for a mixed border, combined with late spring or early summer flowering shrubs. Can also be naturalized in a wild or woodland garden. The flowers are suitable for cutting. In areas with hard winters the plants benefit from a permanent mulch of organic matter to protect bulbs from frost. Propagate by removing offsets when bulbs are dormant. These plants are not troubled by pests or diseases.

Camassia leitchlinii subsp. *suksdorfii*

	SPRING	SUMMER	FALL	WINTER	height (in)	spread (in)	min temp (°F)	moisture	sun/shade	colors	
Camassia cusickii	● ●	● ●	✎ ✎ ✎		36	4	25°	●	☼	■	Avoid very wet soil
C. cusickii 'Zwanenburg'	● ●	● ●	✎ ✎ ✎		36	4	25°	●	☼	■	Deep blue flowers
C. leitchlinii subsp. *suksdorfii*	● ●	● ●	✎ ✎ ✎		36	4	25°	●●	☼	▥	Blue to violet flowers

Campanula
Bellflower

This is a huge group of plants, those listed being hardy herbaceous perennials, although *C. medium* is a hardy biennial and *C. portenschlagiana* is evergreen. Habit is variable, although most have bell-shaped flowers produced over a very long period.

Some species have star-shaped or saucer-shaped blooms. Flower colors are mainly shades of blue, plus pink, purple, and white.

The taller kinds such as *C. glomerata* (clustered bellflower), *C. lactiflora* (milky bellflower) and *C. persicifolia* (peach-leafed

☼ *sunny*   ☼ *semi-shady*   ● *shady*

Campanula carpatica 'Karl Foerster'

Campanula lactiflora 'Loddon Anna'

bellflower) are ideal for mixed borders and combine effectively with many other summer-flowering perennials and shrubs, including shrub roses. Dwarf campanulas such as *C. carpatica*, *C. portenschlagiana* (Dalmation bellflower), and *C. poscharskyana* are suitable for rock or scree gardens. The last two are quite vigorous.

The biennial *C. medium* (Canterbury bells) is a good border plant and an "essential" ingredient of cottage-garden borders. However, do provide supports for tall bellflowers as these can be battered by strong winds. The thin floppy stems can be supported by inserting twiggy sticks around clumps in spring as growth is commencing. Border kinds should be cut back when flowering is over to encourage a second flush of blooms. Propagate by division or basal cuttings in spring, *C. medium* from seed sown in spring in a cold frame. Campanulas are prone to slugs, snails, and powdery mildew, while rust may affect some kinds—check labels for resistance.

Campanula glomerata 'Superba'

	SPRING	SUMMER	FALL	WINTER	height (in)	spread (in)	min temp (°F)	moisture	sun/shade	colors	
Campanula carpatica 'Karl Foerster'	planting	flower flower flower			12	24	1°	moist	sun		Large saucer-shaped blooms
C. glomerata 'Superba'	planting	flower flower flower			24	30	1°	moist	sun/shade		Bell-shaped flowers
C. lactiflora 'Loddon Anna'	planting	flower flower flower flower			60	24	1°	moist	sun		Bell-shaped flowers
C. lactiflora 'Pouffe'	planting	flower flower flower			10	18	1°	moist	sun		Bell-shaped flowers
C. medium 'Bells of Holland'	planting	flower			18	12	1°	moist	sun		Single, bell-shaped flowers
C. persicifolia	planting	flower flower flower			36	12	1°	moist	shade		Bowl-shaped flowers
C. persicifolia 'Alba'	planting	flower flower flower			36	12	1°	moist	shade		Bowl-shaped flowers
C. portenschlagiana	planting	flower flower flower			6	24	1°	moist	shade		Bell-shaped flowers
C. poscharskyana	planting	flower flower flower flower			6	24	1°	moist	shade		Star-shaped flowers
C. poscharskyana 'Stella'	planting	flower flower flower flower			6	24	1°	moist	shade		Star-shaped flowers

planting   ● flower   well drained   moist   wet

Canna
Indian shot

These half-hardy herbaceous perennials grow from thick rhizomes. They have long, broad leaves, purple, bronze, variegated, or blue-green in some cultivars, and lily-like flowers, often in brilliant colors such as red, yellow, and orange.

Cannas give a tropical touch to gardens in frost-prone climates where they are used as dot plants in summer bedding schemes and patio containers. Cut down in the fall and store the dormant rhizomes in slightly moist peat substitute in a frost-free place for the winter. Propagate by dividing rhizomes in spring, each with a growth bud, and start into growth under glass. Watch out for slugs and snails.

Canna 'President'

	SPRING	SUMMER	FALL	WINTER	height (ft)	spread (ft)	min temp (°F)	moisture	sun/shade	colors	
Canna indica 'Purpurea'					6½	2	34°				Purple foliage
C. 'Lucifer'					2	2	34°				Green foliage
C. 'President'					4	2	34°				Glaucous foliage
C. 'Striata'					5	2	34°				Leaves variegated green and yellow
C. 'Wyoming'					6½	2	34°				Purple foliage

Celosia
Cockscomb

Cockscombs are half-hardy perennials grown as annuals in frost-prone climates. The Plumosa Group of *C. argentea* is the most popular, with brightly colored plume-like flower heads.

Celosia spicata Flamingo Series

These plants give an exotic touch to summer bedding schemes, patio tubs, and window boxes, and the flowers are good for cutting. Coleus (solenostemon) are good companions. *C. spicata* Flamingo Series produces spikes of flowers on branching plants. Suitable for a mixed border, the flowers are ideal for cutting and drying. Propagate from seed in spring under cover. Watch out for foot rot and leaf spot.

	SPRING	SUMMER	FALL	WINTER	height (in)	spread (in)	min temp (°F)	moisture	sun/shade	colors	
C. argentea Kimono Series (Plumosa Group)					8	8	34°				Compact habit
C. argentea 'Dwarf Geisha' (Plumosa Group)					8	8	34°				Compact habit
C. spicata Flamingo Series					24	24	34°				Branching habit

☼ *sunny*   ◐ *semi-shady*   ● *shady*

Centaurea
Cornflower *or* Knapweed

The plants described here are hardy annuals and herbaceous perennials. The annual cornflower (*C. cyanus* and cultivars) is ideal for cottage-garden borders and more modern mixed borders. Blue is possibly still the favorite color.

Flowers are good for cutting. Also suitable for mixed borders, associating well with shrub roses, and for prairie-style borders with ornamental grasses, are the perennials *C. dealbata* 'Steenbergii', a clump former, and *C. montana*, which forms mats. Provide supports for both. Propagate in spring, *C. cyanus* from seed sown in flowering position, the perennials by division. Watch out for powdery mildew.

Centaurea cyanus 'Blue Diadem'

	SPRING	SUMMER	FALL	WINTER	height (in)	spread (in)	min temp (°F)	moisture	sun/shade	colors	
Centaurea cyanus 'Blue Diadem'	planting planting	flower flower flower	flower flower			30	6	1°	well drained	sun		Extra-large flowers
C. cyanus 'Polka Dot'	planting planting	flower flower	flower flower			18	12	1°	well drained	sun		Bushy habit
C. dealbata 'Steenbergii'	planting planting planting		flower		24	24	1°	well drained	sun		Deeply cut leaves
C. montana	planting planting	flower flower	flower flower			18	24	1°	moist	sun		Hairy stems
C. montana 'Alba'	planting planting	flower flower	flower flower			18	24	1°	well drained	sun		Hairy stems

Ceratostigma

Ceratostigma willmottianum

These hardy herbaceous perennials and shrubs are valued for their late-season blue flowers. *C. plumbaginoides* is a perennial, woody at the base, while *C. willmottianum* is a true shrub.

The foliage of both these varieties takes on autumnal tints. Ideal for mixed borders, combined with plants for late summer and fall color such as nerines, rudbeckias, Schizostylis, sedums, Rhus, and Berberis. In spring, cut back flowered shoots of shrubs to just above older growth. At the same time, cut down dead herbaceous growth in spring. Propagate from semi-ripe cuttings in summer. Watch out for powdery mildew.

	SPRING	SUMMER	FALL	WINTER	height (ft)	spread (ft)	min temp (°F)	moisture	sun/shade	colors	
Ceratostigma plumbaginoides	planting planting planting		flower			1½	1	1°	well drained	sun		Leaves turn red in the fall
C. willmottianum	planting planting planting		flower flower	flower flower		3	4½	1°	moist	sun		Red foliage in the fall

planting | flower | well drained | moist | wet

Cerinthe
Honeywort

The fine species described here is a frost-hardy annual grown for its tubular flowers amid striking blue bracts, and attractive gray-green foliage.

Cerinthe major 'Purpurascens' is suitable for the front of a sunny, well-drained mixed border and also gravel areas, combining effectively with blue-gray fescue grasses and annuals such as English marigolds (calendula). Plants may need the support of twiggy sticks as stems are rather lax. Pinch out tips of young plants to encourage branching. Propagate from seed in spring under cover, or in flowering position in late spring. Plants often self-sow freely. Generally free from problems.

Cerinthe major 'Purpurascens'

Chionodoxa
Glory of the snow

These hardy dwarf bulbs produce starry, blue, white-centered flowers. Of extremely easy culture, they are ideal for naturalizing in mixed borders, planted, say, around deciduous spring-flowering shrubs such as Forsythia, flowering currants (ribes), and flowering quince (chaenomeles).

Glory of the snow combines well with bergenias and with dwarf yellow daffodils (narcissus). It is an easy task to plant the bulbs among the bergenias. Chionodoxas are also among the best small bulbs for rock

Chionodoxa forbesii 'Pink Giant'

Chionodoxa forbesii

gardens. Propagate from offsets while dormant in summer or early fall. Plants may self-seed freely. Not troubled by pests or diseases.

	SPRING	SUMMER	FALL	WINTER	height (in)	spread (in)	min temp (°F)	moisture	sun/shade	colors
Chionodoxa forbesii (syn. *C. luciliae*)	●		🌱🌱🌱		4	1	1°	💧	☀	▨ Star-shaped flowers
C. forbesii 'Pink Giant'	●		🌱🌱🌱		6	1	1°	💧	☀	▢ Star-shaped flowers

☀ sunny   🌓 semi-shady   ● shady

Chrysanthemum

Annual chrysanthemums such as half-hardy *C. carinatum* and fully hardy *C. coronarium* provide summer color in mixed borders with their single, daisy-like flowers on branching stems. The early flowering or garden chrysanthemums are half-hardy to hardy perennials. These plants really epitomize fall with their wide range of colors.

The hardy Rubellum hybrids are especially good for mixed borders. The early-flowering florists' chrysanthemums, such as the Sprays, are grown in borders as well, but generally are not so hardy. The hardy dwarf

Chrysanthemum 'Brown Eyes'

Chrysanthemum 'Clara Curtis'

kinds, especially the Pompons, are ideal for patio tubs as well as mixed borders. In mixed borders, chrysanthemums combine effectively with fall-flowering anemones, nerines, schizostylis, and rudbeckias. The

flowers of all chrysanthemums are excellent as cut flowers.

Pinch out tips of young plants to encourage branching. Side shoots can also be pinched out. Provide supports for tall chrysanthemums. In mid- or late fall cut stems down to 6in (15cm) and winter crowns in trays of potting mix in a frost-free greenhouse. The hardy Rubellum hybrids can be left in the ground if winters are not too severe. Propagate from basal cuttings in spring; Rubellum hybrids can also be propagated by division in spring. Sow seed of annuals during spring in their final flowering positions.

	SPRING	SUMMER	FALL	WINTER	height (ft)	spread (ft)	min temp (°F)	moisture	sun/shade	colors	
C. 'Brown Eyes' (Florists', Pompon)	⚘ ⚘ ⚘	• •	•		2	2	1°	◐	☼	◼	Small double flowers
C. carinatum 'Court Jesters' (Annual)	⚘ ⚘ ⚘	• • • •	•		2	1	34°	◐	☼	◼	Single, daisy-like flowers
C. 'Clara Curtis' (Rubellum)	⚘ ⚘ ⚘	• •	• •		2½	2	1°	◐	☼	◻	Masses of single flowers
C. 'Emperor of China' (Rubellum)	⚘ ⚘ ⚘	• •	•		4	2	1°	◐	☼	◻	Double flowers
C. 'Enbee Wedding' (Florists', Spray)	⚘ ⚘ ⚘		•		4	2½	1°	◐	☼	◻	Single flowers
C. 'Nancy Perry' (Rubellum)	⚘ ⚘ ⚘	• •			2½	2	1°	◐	☼	◼	Semi-double flowers
C. 'Pompon Pink' (Florists', Pompon)	⚘ ⚘ ⚘	• •			2	2	1°	◑	☼	◻	Small double flowers
C. 'Pompon Purple' (Florists', Pompon)	⚘ ⚘ ⚘	• •			2	2	1°	◐	☼	◼	Small double flowers
C. 'Spartan' cultivars (Florists', Spray)	⚘ ⚘ ⚘		• • •		3	2	1°	◐	☼	◼	Single and semi-double flowers
C. 'Yellow Pennine Oriel' (Florists', Spray)	⚘ ⚘ ⚘		•		4	2½	1°	◐	☼	◻	Anemone-centered flowers

⚘ planting   • flower   ◐ well drained   ◑ moist   ◕ wet

Clarkia

A hardy annual, *C. unguiculata* in its Royal Bouquet Series produces double, rosette-like flowers during the summer.

Grow in a mixed border with other annuals such as *Gypsophila elegans*. Include some in a cutting garden as the flowers last well in water. Flowering is sparse in rich soils. Propagate from seed sown in fall or spring in flowering positions. Watch out for foot and stem rot.

A mixed group of clarkias.

Cleome
Spider flower

C. hassleriana 'Sparkler Lavender'

The spider flower is a tall, frost-tender annual with large heads of spidery flowers with long stamens, in shades of pink and red plus white, and large hand-shaped leaves.

Creating an exotic effect in a mixed or subtropical border, the flowers are suitable for cutting. Deadhead regularly and ensure plenty of water in dry conditions. Propagate from seed in spring under cover. The main pests are aphids.

	SPRING	SUMMER	FALL	WINTER	height (ft)	spread (ft)	min temp (°F)	moisture	sun/shade	colors	
Cleome hassleriana 'Colour Fountain'	🌱🌱🌱	● ● ●			4	1½	41°	💧💧	☀	▨	Large hand-shaped leaves
C. hassleriana 'Helen Campbell'	🌱🌱🌱	● ● ●			4	1½	41°	💧💧	☀	☐	Large hand-shaped leaves
C. hassleriana 'Sparkler Lavender'	🌱🌱🌱	● ● ●			3	1	41°	💧💧	☀	▥	Compact habit

Colchicum
Autumn crocus

Colchicum speciosum

These hardy corms are grown for their large, crocus-like flowers in the fall, in shades of pink or purple, plus white. The large leaves appear in spring and need plenty of space to develop.

Best grown around shrubs in a mixed border or around deciduous trees in a lawn. Can be naturalized in long grass. Propagate by separating corms during summer dormancy. Watch out for gray mold, slugs, and snails.

	SPRING	SUMMER	FALL	WINTER	height (in)	spread (in)	min temp (°F)	moisture	sun/shade	colors	
Colchicum autumnale		🌱🌱🌱	🌱 ● ●		6	4	1°	💧💧	☀	▥	Very vigorous habit
C. speciosum		🌱🌱🌱	🌱 ● ●		6	4	1°	💧💧	☀	▥	Very vigorous habit
C. 'The Giant'		🌱🌱🌱	🌱 ● ●		8	4	1°	💧💧	☀	▰	Very vigorous habit
C. 'Waterlily'		🌱🌱🌱	🌱 ● ●		6	4	1°	💧💧	☀	▥	Double flowers

☀ *sunny*　　◑ *semi-shady*　　● *shady*

Consolida
Larkspur

This hardy annual has spikes of flowers reminiscent of delphiniums but is of much more slender habit with attractive feathery foliage.

A favorite for cottage-garden borders, it is equally at home in modern borders combined with other old-fashioned annuals such as cornflowers (centaurea) and love-in-a-mist (nigella).

The blooms are excellent for cutting, especially those of taller-growing cultivars. The tall ones will need supports of twiggy sticks. For continuous flowering, deadhead regularly. Raise plants from seed in spring, early summer, or fall, sowing in flowering positions. Watch out for powdery mildew, slugs, and snails.

Consolida ajacis

	SPRING	SUMMER	FALL	WINTER	height (in)	spread (in)	min temp (°F)	moisture	sun/shade	colors	
Consolida ajacis Dwarf Hyacinth Series	🌱🌱🌱	🌱 ● ●	🌱🌱🌱		18	12	1°	💧	☀	▦	Double flowers; many different colors
C. ajacis Dwarf Rocket Series	🌱🌱🌱	🌱 ● ●	🌱🌱🌱		18	8	1°	💧	☀	▦	Double flowers; many different colors
C. ajacis Giant Imperial Series	🌱🌱🌱	🌱 ● ●	🌱🌱🌱		36	12	1°	💧	☀	▦	Double flowers; many different colors

Convallaria
Lily-of-the-valley

A well-loved, hardy, carpeting herbaceous perennial spreading vigorously from rhizomes. The tiny bell-shaped flowers are highly scented and are produced through a mass of fresh green oval leaves.

Use as ground cover in moist, shady situations such as around and beneath shrubs or in a woodland garden. Lily-of-the-valley benefits from a permanent mulch of organic matter such as composted bark chips or leaf mold applied in the fall. The flowers are ideal for cutting. Propagate in the fall by teasing the rhizomes apart and replanting. Almost problem-free, but gray mold can make an appearance.

Convallaria majalis

	SPRING	SUMMER	FALL	WINTER	height (in)	spread (in)	min temp (°F)	moisture	sun/shade	colors	
Convallaria majalis	● ● ●		🌱🌱🌱		8	18	1°	💧	◐	☐	Also takes full shade
C. majalis 'Albostriata'	● ● ●		🌱🌱🌱		8	18	1°	💧	◐	☐	Cream-striped leaves
C. majalis 'Fortin's Giant'	● ● ●		🌱🌱🌱		12	18	1°	💧	◐	☐	Large flowers
C. majalis var. *rosea*	● ● ●		🌱🌱🌱		8	18	1°	💧	◐	☐	Also takes full shade

🌱 planting   ● flower   💧 well drained   💧 moist   💧 wet

Convolvulus
Bindweed

Not to be compared with the notorious weeds, ornamental bindweeds are desirable plants. All produce characteristic flaring, trumpet-shaped flowers.

Convolvulus sabatius

Frost-hardy *C. sabatius*, a perennial with trailing stems, is a good rock-garden or container plant. The latter can be moved into an unheated greenhouse if winters are excessively wet and cold. The hardy annual *C. tricolor* has a somewhat spreading habit and is suitable for the front of mixed borders. Good plants for infertile soils. Deadhead annuals. Propagate in spring, *C. sabatius* by division, *C. tricolor* from seed in flowering positions. Generally trouble-free.

	SPRING	SUMMER	FALL	WINTER	height (in)	spread (in)	min temp (°F)	moisture	sun/shade	colors	
Convolvulus sabatius					6	18	25°				Very free-flowering
C. tricolor mixed					12	12	1°				Long succession of flowers
C. tricolor 'Royal Ensign'					12	12	1°				Good in hanging baskets

Coreopsis
Tickseed

Hardy herbaceous perennials include *C.* 'Goldfink', *C. verticillata*, and *C. grandiflora*, although gardeners usually grow the latter as an annual. *C. tinctoria* is a true hardy annual and is very useful for filling gaps in mixed borders.

All have colorful daisy flowers and are ideal for prairie-style borders, combined with ornamental grasses. Ideal, too, for ordinary mixed borders where they associate well with spiky plants such as delphiniums. A good plant for cut flowers. Tall kinds will need some support. Deadhead these flowers regularly. Raise annuals from seed in spring, in flowering positions; perennials under glass in winter. Propagate perennials by division in spring. Watch out for slugs and snails.

Coreopsis verticillata 'Moonbeam'

	SPRING	SUMMER	FALL	WINTER	height (ft)	spread (ft)	min temp (°F)	moisture	sun/shade	colors	
Coreopsis 'Goldfink'					1	1	1°				Dwarf and compact
C. grandiflora 'Early Sunrise'					1½	1½	1°				Semi-double flowers
C. tinctoria					4	1½	1°				Provide supports
C. verticillata					2	1½	1°				Fine ferny foliage
C. verticillata 'Grandiflora'					2	1½	1°				Fine ferny foliage; dark yellow flowers
C. verticillata 'Moonbeam'					1½	1½	1°				Fine ferny foliage; lemon-yellow flowers

☀ *sunny*   ☼ *semi-shady*   ☀ *shady*

Cortaderia

Pampas grass

These hardy perennials are among the largest of the ornamental grasses, forming large clumps of evergreen, arching leaves with very sharp edges. Tall plumes of flowers are produced throughout the summer.

Cortaderia selloana

The traditional use of pampas grass is as a lone specimen in a lawn, but modern uses include mixed borders, combined with daisy-flowered perennials and shrubs noted for their fall leaf color, and gravel areas. In early spring, cut out all dead leaves and stems—wear pruning gloves to avoid cuts from the leaf edges. Propagate by division in spring. No pest or disease problems.

	SPRING			SUMMER			FALL			WINTER			height (ft)	spread (ft)	min temp (°F)	moisture	sun/shade	colors	
Cortaderia selloana 'Pumila'	planting	planting	planting			flower	flower	flower					5	4	1°	well drained	sun	white	Ideal for smaller gardens
C. selloana 'Sunningdale Silver'	planting	planting	planting			flower	flower	flower					10	8	1°	well drained	sun	white	Rain-resistant flowers

Corydalis

Dwarf hardy perennials of varied habit and needs. *C. flexuosa* is especially recommended for partially shady conditions such as a woodland garden or beneath large deciduous shrubs, while *C. lutea* is ideal for a sunny rock garden or bank, or the front of a mixed border.

Corydalis flexuosa 'China Blue'

The former becomes dormant in summer, while the latter is evergreen, and both have attractive ferny foliage. Propagate by division in the fall or from seed when ripe in a cold frame. *C. lutea* self-seeds prolifically. Slugs and snails are the main problems.

Corydalis solida

	SPRING			SUMMER			FALL			WINTER			height (in)	spread (in)	min temp (°F)	moisture	sun/shade	colors	
Corydalis flexuosa 'China Blue'			flower	flower			planting	planting	planting				12	8	1°	moist	partial shade	blue	Humus-rich soil
C. lutea			flower	flower	flower	flower	flower	planting	planting				15	12	1°	well drained	sun	yellow	Also takes partial shade
C. solida	flower	flower	flower				planting	planting	planting				10	8	1°	well drained	sun	multicolored	Also takes partial shade

planting | flower | well drained | moist | wet

Cosmos

Cosmos atrosanguineus

**There are both annual and perennial cosmos.
C. atrosanguineus is a tuberous, frost-hardy herbaceous
perennial while *C. bipinnatus* and *C. sulphureus* cultivars
are annuals, half-hardy, and tender respectively.**

All have ferny foliage and daisy-like flowers. Grow in
mixed borders with ornamental grasses and other daisy-
flowered plants. *C. atrosanguineus* is good in a patio tub.
Deadhead regularly. Winter tubers of *C. atrosanguineus*
under glass, as for dahlias, where weather is severe.
Propagate in spring; annuals from seed under glass,
C. atrosanguineus from basal cuttings. These plants are
prone to aphids, gray mold, slugs, and snails.

	SPRING	SUMMER	FALL	WINTER	height (in)	spread (in)	min temp (°F)	moisture	sun/shade	colors	
Cosmos atrosanguineus	🌱🌱🌱	● ● ●	● ● ●		30	18	25°	◐	☼	■	Chocolate-scented flowers
C. bipinnatus 'Sea Shells'	🌱🌱🌱	● ● ●			36	18	34°	◐	☼	▮	Rolled petals
C. bipinnatus Sonata Series	🌱🌱🌱	● ● ●			12	12	34°	◐	☼	▮	Good for windy gardens
C. sulphureus Ladybird Series	🌱🌱🌱	● ● ●			12	8	41°	◐	☼	■	Semi-double flowers
C. sulphureus 'Sunny Orange Red'	🌱🌱🌱	● ● ●			24	12	41°	◐	☼	▨	Semi-double flowers

Crocosmia
Montbretia

**These hardy herbaceous perennials grow from corms and are valued for their
brilliantly colored, somewhat funnel-shaped flowers. They produce clumps
of erect, sword-shaped or grassy leaves.**

Grow montbretias in mixed borders with other
late-flowering perennials. Good in subtropical
plantings, especially *C.* 'Lucifer'. They also
look good planted among ornamental grasses.
Flowers can be cut and arranged indoors.

Provide a permanent organic mulch in
hard-winter areas. Some will need twiggy
sticks to support the foliage, which can flop
during wet weather, smothering nearby
plants. Propagate by division in spring.
Generally trouble-free.

Crocosmia 'Lucifer'

	SPRING	SUMMER	FALL	WINTER	height (in)	spread (in)	min temp (°F)	moisture	sun/shade	colors	
Crocosmia x crocosmiiflora	🌱🌱🌱	●			24	3	1°	◐	☼	▨	Can be invasive
C. x crocosmiiflora 'Emily McKenzie'	🌱🌱🌱	●			24	3	1°	◐	☼	■	Wide petals
C. 'Emberglow'	🌱🌱🌱	● ● ●			24	3	25°	◐	☼	■	Branching stems
C. 'Lucifer'	🌱🌱🌱	●			48	4	25°	◐	☼	■	Arching spikes
C. masoniorum	🌱🌱🌱	●			48	4	1°	◐	☼	▨	Arching spikes

☼ *sunny* ☀ *semi-shady* ● *shady*

Crocus

Crocuses grow from corms and all are dwarf in habit, most being hardy. Flowers are very similar, irrespective of species, being somewhat wine glass-shaped and opening best in full sun. The leaves, often appearing with or after the flowers, are somewhat grassy. Some crocuses flower in the fall, others in winter or spring.

All are most effective when planted in bold, informal drifts. They can be grown at the front of mixed borders and around the base of deciduous trees, especially the large-flowered Dutch crocuses like *C.* 'Jeanne d'Arc' and *C.* 'Pickwick'. Small-flowered kinds, such as the *C. chrysanthus* hybrids, including 'Blue Pearl' and 'E. A. Bowles', are good for rock gardens. Some are suitable for naturalizing in short grass, particularly *C. speciosus* and *C. tommasinianus*. Propagate by removing and replanting cormlets while parent corms are dormant. Some species self-seed prolifically, including *C. speciosus* and *C. tommasinianus*. Birds can peck at yellow flowers and cause damage—tightly stretch strands of thick black thread over them for protection. Mice and squirrels may eat the corms. Corm rot is another problem while corms are in store.

Crocus 'Jeanne d'Arc'

Crocus tommasinianus

Crocus 'Cream Beauty'

	SPRING	SUMMER	FALL	WINTER	height (in)	spread (in)	min temp (°F)	moisture	sun/shade	colors	
Crocus 'Blue Pearl' (Chrysanthus hybrid)	flower		planting		3	2	1°	moist	sun		Early flowering
C. 'Cream Beauty' (Chrysanthus hybrid)	flower		planting		3	2	1°	moist	sun		Early flowering
C. 'E. A. Bowles' (Chrysanthus hybrid)	flower		planting		3	2	1°	moist	sun		Early flowering
C. 'Jeanne d'Arc' (Dutch)	flower		planting		4	3	1°	moist	sun		Vigorous and showy
C. 'Ladykiller' (Chrysanthus hybrid)	flower		planting		3	2	1°	moist	sun		Early flowering
C. x *luteus* 'Golden Yellow' (Dutch)	flower		planting		4	3	1°	moist	sun		Can be grown in grass
C. 'Pickwick' (Dutch)	flower		planting		4	3	1°	moist	sun		Vigorous and showy
C. 'Remembrance' (Dutch)	flower		planting		4	3	1°	moist	sun		Vigorous and showy
C. 'Snow Bunting' (Chrysanthus hybrid)	flower		planting		3	2	1°	moist	sun		Early flowering
C. speciosus		planting	flower		6	2	1°	moist	sun		Brilliant orange styles
C. tommasinianus	flower		planting	flower	4	1	1°	moist	sun		Several cultivars available
C. 'Zwanenburg Bronze' (Chrysanthus hybrid)	flower		planting		3	2	1°	moist	sun		Early flowering

planting   flower | well drained   moist   wet

Cuphea

These tender subshrubs are usually grown as annuals. They are neat, bushy plants, producing masses of brilliantly colored tubular flowers throughout the summer.

Cuphea llavea 'Tiny Mice'

Used in summer bedding schemes, including subtropical displays, and in containers such as patio tubs and window boxes, they provide a pleasing display over many months. Cupheas mix effectively with purple verbenas, as well as with many other summer bedding plants. Raise plants from seed sown under glass in early spring. Plants can also be propagated from cuttings of young shoots in spring. Cupheas may be attacked by aphids.

	SPRING	SUMMER	FALL	WINTER	height (in)	spread (in)	min temp (°F)	moisture	sun/shade	colors	
Cuphea ignea	🌱🌱🌱	●●●	●●		30	36	41°	💧💧	☀	▮▯	Very free-flowering
C. llavea 'Tiny Mice'	🌱🌱🌱	●●●	●●		15	9	34°	💧💧	☀	▮▮	Neat, low bushes

Cyclamen

Cyclamen are tuberous perennials, the species described being hardy. The flowers of these miniature plants have swept-back petals and the rounded or heart-shaped leaves, often patterned with silver, make attractive carpets.

These are ideal plants for rock gardens, woodland gardens, and for planting in the partial shade of deciduous shrubs. Plant them in generous drifts for best effect. Cyclamen can be permanently mulched with leaf mold, applied when dormant. Propagate from seed sown as soon as ripe and germinated in a cold frame. *C. hederifolium* self-seeds prolifically. Problems are mice, squirrels, and vine weevil larvae.

Cyclamen coum

	SPRING	SUMMER	FALL	WINTER	height (in)	spread (in)	min temp (°F)	moisture	sun/shade	colors	
Cyclamen coum	●		🌱🌱🌱	●	3	4	1°	💧💧	◐	▮▯	Leaves may be patterned with silver
C. hederifolium		🌱🌱🌱	●●●		4	6	1°	💧💧	◐	▯	Flowers before the leaves

☀ *sunny*   ◐ *semi-shady*   ● *shady*

Dahlia

Dahlias are half-hardy herbaceous perennials with tuberous roots, grown for their long and prolific display of flowers in summer and fall. **D**ahlias can be grouped into border or bedding cultivars that are propagated vegetatively, and those that are grown as annuals from seed.

The border dahlias are tall and ideally suited to mixed borders, while the bedding cultivars are shorter and used for summer bedding or planting in patio tubs.

Their flowers are classified according to form: for example, Anemone-flowered, with crested blooms; Ball, with large ball-shaped flowers; Cactus, with double, spiky flowers; Collarette, with an inner collar or ring of shorter petals; Decorative, with wide-petaled, double flowers; Pompon, with small ball-shaped flowers; Semi-cactus, whose double flowers have pointed petals; Single, with one or two circles of petals; and Waterlily, with flattish flowers. The Miscellaneous group contains dahlias that do not fit into any of the other groups. Dwarf dahlias grown as annuals from seed are ideal for summer bedding or patio containers. All dahlias combine effectively with cannas,

Dahlia 'Snowstorm'

Dahlia 'Dahlietta'

🖐 *planting*　　⊙ *flower*　　💧 *well drained*　　💧 *moist*　　💧 *wet* chrysanthemums, gladioli, petunias, salvias, and verbenas. The flowers are excellent for cutting. Pinch out tips of young plants to encourage branching. Support tall cultivars with canes or wooden stakes. When flowering starts, liquid feed weekly with high-potash fertilizer. Keep well watered in dry weather. Deadhead all dahlias.

In the fall, when blackened by frost, lift border and bedding dahlias, cut down stems to 6in (15cm), dry off tubers, and store in trays of almost dry coir in a cool, frost-free place for the winter. Start into growth in early spring and propagate from basal stem cuttings. Alternatively, plant out dormant tubers in mid-spring—large clumps can be divided (each division must have at least one tuber and stem base). Raise annual types from seed under glass in early spring. Dahlias are prone to aphids, caterpillars, earwigs, powdery mildew, red spider mite, slugs, snails, tuber rot, and viruses.

Dahlia 'Bishop of Llandaff'

Dahlia 'Stolze von Berlin'

Dahlia 'Yellow Happiness'

	SPRING	SUMMER	FALL	WINTER	height (ft)	spread (ft)	min temp (°F)	moisture	sun/shade	colors	
D. 'Bishop of Llandaff' (Miscellaneous)					3	1½	34°				Deep red foliage
D. 'Claire de Lune' (Colerette)					3	2	34°				Rich yellow center
D. Coltness Hybrids					1½	1½	34°				Grown as annual; single flowers
D. 'Dahlietta'					2	2	34°				Dwarf bedding dahlia
D. 'David Howard' (Decorative)					2½	2	34°				Small flowers, coppery foliage
D. 'Figaro'					1½	1½	34°				Grown as annual; double flowers
D. 'Gerrie Hoek' (Waterlily)					4	2	34°				Blooms prolifically
D. 'Glorie van Heemstede' (Waterlily)					4	2	34°				Blooms prolifically
D. 'Jeanette Carter' (Decorative)					3½	2	34°				Miniature flowers
D. 'Jescot Julie' (Miscellaneous)					3	1½	34°				Orchid-flowered cultivar
D. 'Moonfire' (Miscellaneous)					2	1½	34°				Purple foliage
D. 'Moor Place' (Pompon)					3½	2	34°				Miniature flowers
D. 'My Love' (Semi-cactus)					3	2	34°				Small flowers
D. 'Redskin'					2	2	34°				Grown as annual; good for bedding
D. 'Rigoletto'					1½	1	34°				Grown as annual; good for bedding
D. 'Snowstorm' (Decorative)					3	2	34°				Excellent for cutting
D. 'Stolze von Berlin' (Ball)					3	2	34°				Miniature-flowered
D. 'Yellow Happiness' (Semi-cactus)					3	2	34°				Good for cutting

 sunny ☀ semi-shady ● shady

Delphinium

Delphiniums are mainly hardy herbaceous perennials but some are grown as hardy annuals. Characterized by their spikes of flowers, delphiniums are split into several groups. The Elatum Group (which includes 'Blue Nile', 'Bruce', Magic Fountains Group, and 'Mighty Atom') has fat spikes of flowers and is the most popular.

The Belladonna Group (such as 'Casablanca') has loose, branching spikes. The Pacific Hybrids (including the Summer Skies Group) are rather like Elatum delphiniums but are grown as annuals. *D. grandiflorum* is also usually grown as an annual and has open heads of flowers. Leaves of all kinds are usually lobed. Delphiniums are ideal for mixed borders, including cottage-garden borders, and combine effectively with many other plants including roses (particularly shrub roses), and plants with flat heads of flowers such

Delphinium 'Casablanca'

Delphinium 'Sunkissed'

Delphinium 'Blue Nile'

as achilleas. The flowers are excellent for cutting. Tall delphiniums need canes for support, one cane per stem. Shorter cultivars can be supported with twiggy sticks. Liquid feed fortnightly during the growing season and water well in dry weather. Cut back dead flower spikes to lower side shoots, and cut down all stems in the fall. Raise annuals from seed under glass in early spring. Propagate Belladonna and Elatum cultivars from basal stem cuttings in spring. Problems include leaf spot, powdery mildew, slugs, snails, and mosaic virus.

	SPRING	SUMMER	FALL	WINTER	height (ft)	spread (ft)	min temp (°F)	moisture	sun/shade	colors	
Delphinium 'Blue Nile' (Elatum Group)	🌱🌱🌱	●			5	2	1°	💧	☀	▨	Semi-double flowers
D. 'Bruce' (Elatum Group)	🌱🌱🌱	●			6	2	1°	💧	☀	▪	Semi-double flowers
D. 'Casablanca' (Belladonna Group)	🌱🌱🌱	●			4	1½	1°	💧	☀	☐	Loose, branching spikes
D. grandiflorum 'Blue Butterfly'	🌱🌱🌱	●			1½	1	1°	💧	☀	▦	Branching spikes
D. Magic Fountains Group (Elatum Group)	🌱🌱🌱	●			3	2	1°	💧	☀	▥	Good-quality spikes
D. Summer Skies Group (Pacific Hybrid)	🌱🌱🌱	●			5	2½	1°	💧	☀	▢	Semi-double flowers
D. 'Sunkissed' (Elatum Group)	🌱🌱🌱	●			5	2	1°	💧	☀	▥	Good-quality spikes

🌱 planting   ● flower   💧 well drained   💧 moist   💧 wet

Dianthus
Carnation *or* Pink

A large group of perennials, annuals, and biennials providing plants for various parts of the garden. The following are all completely hardy. Sweet williams (*Dianthus barbatus*) are favorite biennials, much used in cottage-garden borders.

Dianthus chinesis 'Strawberry Parfait'

Carnations grown as annuals, *D. caryophyllus* and *D. chinensis* (Indian pink), make a good display in mixed borders or containers. With regard to perennial dianthus, all of which are evergreen (often with grayish foliage), some are alpines and suitable for rock gardens, including *D. alpinus* and 'La Bourboule'. Old-fashioned pinks, including 'Dad's Favourite' and 'Mrs Sinkins', are great for cottage-garden borders. Modern pinks including 'Doris', 'Haytor White', 'Joy', and 'Laced Monarch', and border carnations such as 'Lavender Clove', are better for modern mixed borders.

All dianthus are suitable for borders, and combine well with roses—particularly shrub roses—and with gray- or silver-leafed shrubs and perennials such as santolinas and artemisias respectively. They are also effective with white-flowered gypsophila.

Flowers are excellent for cutting and many are highly fragrant. All dianthus are good for alkaline soils. Tall kinds may need the support of twiggy sticks. Deadhead dianthus regularly. Raise annuals from seed in early spring under glass; sweet williams from seed in an outdoor seed bed in late spring to early summer. Propagate perennials from cuttings in summer. Troubles for these plants include aphids, leaf spot, slugs, and snails.

	SPRING	SUMMER	FALL	WINTER	height (in)	spread (in)	min temp (°F)	moisture	sun/shade	colors
Dianthus alpinus (Alpine pink)		● ● ●			3	4	1°			Short-lived, deep pink or red
D. barbatus 'Giant Auricula-eyed' (biennial)		●			24	12	1°			Bicolored, pink, and red
D. caryophyllus Luminette Series (annual)		● ● ●			10	6	1°			Fragrant, also in pink and red
D. chinensis 'Fire Carpet' (annual)		● ● ●			8	6	1°			Single flowers
D. chinensis 'Strawberry Parfait' (annual)		● ● ●			6	6	1°			Large single flowers
D. 'Dad's Favourite' (Old-fashioned pink)		●			12	12	1°			Semi-double, fragrant, white, and red
D. 'Doris' (Modern pink)		● ● ●			12	12	1°			Double, fragrant flowers
D. 'La Bourboule' (Alpine pink)		● ● ●			3	8	1°			Single, fragrant flowers
D. 'Laced Monarch' (Modern pink)		●			18	12	1°			Double flowers, also pink and red
D. 'Mrs Sinkins' (Old-fashioned pink)		●			12	12	1°			Double, fringed, fragrant flowers

☼ *sunny*   ☼ *semi-shady*   ● *shady*

Diascia

Frost-hardy herbaceous perennials with a rather spreading habit and producing masses of lobed, tubular flowers on upright stems over a very long period.

Diascia 'Lilac Belle'

Excellent for the front of mixed borders, banks, and patio tubs or window boxes. Diascias combine well with alchemillas, cerinthes, eryngiums, lavenders, and small bush or ground cover roses. Remove dead flower heads regularly to ensure continuous flowering. Propagate by division in spring or from semi-ripe cuttings in summer. In cold areas, young plants need cool greenhouse protection during their first winter. Main problems are slugs and snails.

	SPRING	SUMMER	FALL	WINTER	height (in)	spread (in)	min temp (°F)	moisture	sun/shade	colors	
Diascia barberae 'Ruby Field'	🌱 🌱 🌱	● ● ●	● ●		10	24	25°	💧	☀		Very free-flowering
D. 'Coral Belle'	🌱 🌱 🌱	● ● ●	● ●		18	16	25°	💧	☀		Very free-flowering
D. 'Lilac Belle'	🌱 🌱 🌱	● ● ●	● ●		18	16	25°	💧	☀		Very free-flowering
D. rigescens	🌱 🌱 🌱	● ● ●			12	18	25°	💧	☀		Dense spikes of flowers

Dicentra

These are hardy herbaceous perennials with attractive, divided, ferny foliage and dangling, heart-shaped flowers. Dicentras are among the best plants for the dappled shade of woodland gardens, but can also be planted in similar conditions around deciduous shrubs in a mixed border.

Dicentra spectabilis 'Alba'

Dicentras associate well with spring or early summmer flowering shrubs, as well as with woodland and shade-loving perennials such as ajugas, corydalis, epimediums, and hostas. Keep mulched to ensure soil retains moisture. Propagate by division, ideally as soon as plants become dormant in the fall. Slugs and snails are the main problems.

Dicentra spectabilis

	SPRING	SUMMER	FALL	WINTER	height (ft)	spread (ft)	min temp (°F)	moisture	sun/shade	colors	
Dicentra 'Bountiful'	●	●	🌱 🌱 🌱		1	1½	1°	💧💧	◑		Pinnate foliage
D. formosa	●	●	🌱 🌱 🌱		1½	2	1°	💧💧	◑		Self-seeds prolifically
D. spectabilis	●	●	🌱 🌱 🌱		3	1½	1°	💧	◑		Flower stems arch over
D. spectabilis 'Alba'	●	● ●	🌱 🌱 🌱		3	1½	1°	💧	◑		Vigorous habit

🌱 *planting*   ● *flower*   💧 *well drained*   💧 *moist*   💧 *wet*

Digitalis
Foxglove

These plants are treated as hardy biennials, although some may live for a bit longer. Foxgloves are distinctive plants with spikes of longish, bell-like flowers. Being woodland plants, they look at home in the dappled shade of woodland gardens.

Alternatively, foxgloves can be grown in similar conditions in a shrub or mixed border, among large deciduous shrubs, where they will make a striking effect. Remove dead flower heads if you want to prevent self-seeding. Propagate from seed sown in pots in a cold frame during late spring. Plants may be attacked by leaf spot and powdery mildew.

Digitalis purpurea Excelsior Hybrid

	SPRING	SUMMER	FALL	WINTER	height (ft)	spread (ft)	min temp (°F)	moisture	sun/shade	colors	
Digitalis grandiflora		●			3	1½	1°				Shiny leaves
D. lutea		●			2	1	1°				Shiny, deep green leaves
D. x mertonensis		●			3	1	1°				Shiny, deep green leaves
D. purpurea		●			5	2	1°				Self-seeds freely
D. purpurea Excelsior Hybrids		●			5	2	1°				Flowers face outward
D. purpurea Foxy Hybrids		●			3	2	1°				Flowers conspicuously spotted

Dimorphotheca
African daisy

These half-hardy annuals are low-growing bushy plants producing daisy-like flowers, which need direct sun to remain open.

These plants have a long flowering period and are ideal for patio tubs, window boxes, and for summer bedding schemes, combining well with other daisy-flowered plants including argyranthemums, brachyscome, gazanias, and osteospermums, and with cerinthes and scaevolas. Remove dead flowers regularly. Raise plants from seed in early spring under glass. Can also be sown in flowering positions in mid- to late spring. Watch out for gray mold on the flowers.

Dimorphotheca sinuata

	SPRING	SUMMER	FALL	WINTER	height (in)	spread (in)	min temp (°F)	moisture	sun/shade	colors	
D. pluvialis 'Glistening White'		● ● ●			15	12	34°				Deep green aromatic foliage
D. sinuata (syn. *D. aurantiaca*)		● ● ●			12	12	34°				Medium green aromatic foliage

☀ *sunny*　 ☀ *semi-shady*　 ● *shady*

Doronicum
Leopard's bane

Doronicum orientale 'Magnificum'

Hardy herbaceous perennials valued for their early color, doronicums have cheerful yellow daisy-like flowers carried above heart-shaped leaves.

Essentially mixed-border plants, doronicums also look at home in the dappled shade of a woodland garden and combine beautifully with blue-flowered perennials such as lungworts (pulmonaria) and corydalis, and with biennial forget-me-nots (myosotis). Other good companions are dicentras, as well as spring-flowering shrubs such as yellow kerrias and various white-flowered spiraeas. Propagate by division in the fall, preferably early in the season. Problems include leaf spot and powdery mildew. Overly wet soils encourage the roots of this plant to rot.

	SPRING	SUMMER	FALL	WINTER	height (ft)	spread (ft)	min temp (°F)	moisture	sun/shade	colors	
Doronicum x *excelsum* 'Harpur Crewe'	●●●		🌱🌱🌱		2	2	1°	💧💧	☼	▨	Single flowers
D. 'Frühlingspracht' (syn. 'Spring Beauty')	●●●		🌱🌱🌱		1½	2	1°	💧💧	☼	▢	Double flowers
D. 'Miss Mason'	●●●		🌱🌱🌱		1½	2	1°	💧💧	☼	▢	Single flowers
D. orientale 'Magnificum'	●●●		🌱🌱🌱		1½	2	1°	💧💧	☼	▢	Large single flowers

Dorotheanthus
Livingstone daisy

Carpeting half-hardy annuals with succulent leaves and stems, and covered in brilliant daisy-like flowers, Livingstone daisies are easily grown.

Dorotheanthus bellidiformis 'Lunette'

The only disappointment is that the flowers of this plant open fully only in direct sun and remain closed in dull conditions. Use at the front of mixed borders, plant in cracks in paving, grow them on a sunny bank, or create displays in patio containers such as shallow bowls. Livingstone daisies are ideal for poor soils. Pick off the dead flower heads regularly. Raise plants from seed sown under cover in spring. Watch out for aphids, foot rot, slugs, and snails.

	SPRING	SUMMER	FALL	WINTER	height (in)	spread (in)	min temp (°F)	moisture	sun/shade	colors	
D. bellidiformis 'Lunette' (syn. 'Yellow Ice')	🌱🌱🌱	●●●			4	12	34°	💧💧	☼	▢	Flowers freely
D. bellidiformis 'Magic Carpet'	🌱🌱🌱	●●●			4	12	34°	💧💧	☼	▦	Flowers freely

🌱 planting   ● flower   💧 well drained   💧💧 moist   💧💧💧 wet

Echinacea
Coneflower

A tall, upright, hardy herbaceous perennial, echinacea has large daisy-like flowers, each with a conspicuous, brownish, cone-shaped center, carried on reddish stems.

An ideal plant for modern prairie-style borders. Mix it with ornamental grasses, asters, late heleniums, helianthus, monardas, rudbeckias, and golden rods (solidago). Also good with shrubs noted for fall leaf color such as rhus (sumachs). When flowers are over, cut back the stems to encourage more blooms. Propagate by division in spring or by root cuttings in winter. Not troubled by pests or diseases.

Echinacea purpurea 'White Swan'

	SPRING	SUMMER	FALL	WINTER	height (ft)	spread (ft)	min temp (°F)	moisture	sun/shade	colors	
Echinacea purpurea	🖐🖐🖐	●●●●			5	2	1°	💧	☀	■	Rough hairy foliage
E. purpurea 'Magnus'	🖐🖐🖐	●●●●			5	2	1°	💧	☀	■	Large flowers
E. purpurea 'White Swan'	🖐🖐🖐	●●●●			2	2	1°	💧	☀	□	Large flowers

Echinops
Globe thistle

Echinops ritro

Hardy herbaceous perennials, echinops are valued for their distinctive globe-shaped flower heads. The gray-green spiny foliage is often deeply cut and is a further attraction.

Excellent subjects for mixed borders, they combine well with shrubs of all kinds, perennials such as flat-headed achilleas, and with ornamental grasses, including Miscanthus. Globe thistles are also suited to more natural parts of the garden and will grow in infertile soils. The flowers can be dried for winter arrangements. Remove dead flower heads. Propagate by division in spring or from root cuttings during winter. The main pests are aphids.

	SPRING	SUMMER	FALL	WINTER	height (ft)	spread (ft)	min temp (°F)	moisture	sun/shade	colors	
Echinops bannaticus 'Blue Globe'	🖐🖐🖐	●●●			3	2	1°	💧	☀	■	Large flower heads
E. bannaticus 'Taplow Blue'	🖐🖐🖐	●●●			5	2	1°	💧	☀	■	One of the tallest varieties
E. ritro	🖐🖐🖐	●			2	2	1°	💧	☀	■	Young flower heads of steel blue
E. ritro 'Veitch's Blue'	🖐🖐🖐	●			3	2	1°	💧	☀	■	Repeat flowering

☀ sunny   ☀ semi-shady   ● shady

Echium
Viper's bugloss

This species is a hardy biennial of branching habit, carrying spikes of bowl-shaped flowers, each surrounded with a conspicuous green calyx. Blue is probably the most popular color, but there are cultivars available in other colors.

Echium vulgare 'Blue Bedder'

Viper's bugloss is suitable for filling gaps in mixed borders where it associates with many annual or perennial flowers, including poppies (papaver). It can also be used in patio tubs and window boxes. Raise plants from seed sown under cover in early summer, winter young plants in a frost-free greenhouse, and plant out in spring. Slugs and snails are the main pests.

	SPRING	SUMMER	FALL	WINTER	height (ft)	spread (ft)	min temp (°F)	moisture	sun/shade	colors	
Echium vulgare 'Blue Bedder'	🌱 🌱 🌱	🌱 ●			1½	1	1°	💧	☀	⬜	Bristly leaves
E. vulgare Dwarf Hybrids	🌱 🌱 🌱	🌱 ●			1½	1	1°	💧	☀	◨	Bristly leaves

Epimedium
Barrenwort

Hardy herbaceous or evergreen perennials of dwarf habit, spreading vigorously by rhizomes. Heart-shaped leaves may take on fall tints in some species, while spring foliage is often flushed with bronze.

Epimedium x versicolor

Clusters of small bowl- or cup-shaped flowers appear through the leaves and come in various colors. Epimediums are excellent for ground cover in woodland gardens, under deciduous trees, or around large deciduous shrubs in a mixed border. A permanent organic mulch in hard-winter areas is beneficial. Cut down the old leaves of herbaceous species in late winter. Propagate by separating the mats of rhizomes in the fall, or take rhizome cuttings in winter. Watch out for powdery mildew.

Epimedium grandiflorum 'Snow Queen'

	SPRING	SUMMER	FALL	WINTER	height (ft)	spread (ft)	min temp (°F)	moisture	sun/shade	colors	
Epimedium grandiflorum	● ● ●		🌱 🌱 🌱		1	1	1°	💧	◑	▨	Herbaceous
E. grandiflorum 'Snow Queen'	● ● ●		🌱 🌱 🌱		1	1	1°	💧	◑	⬜	Herbaceous
E. x *rubrum*	● ● ●		🌱 🌱 🌱		1	1	1°	💧	◑	⬛	Herbaceous
E. x *versicolor* 'Sulphureum'	● ● ●		🌱 🌱 🌱		1	3	1°	💧	◑	▨	Evergreen
E. x *youngianum* 'Niveum'	● ● ●		🌱 🌱 🌱		1	1	1°	💧	◑	⬜	Herbaceous

🌱 planting ● flower 💧 well drained 💧 moist 💧 wet

Eranthis
Winter aconite

A hardy dwarf herbaceous perennial growing from tubers, winter aconite is valued for its early yellow flowers.

Eranthis hyemalis is a good example. Plant in generous groups or drifts under or around deciduous shrubs and trees with winter and spring bulbs such as snowdrops (galanthus). Can be naturalized in grass. Good for alkaline soil. Propagate by separating clumps in spring. This plant is prone to slug damage.

Eranthis hyemalis

Erigeron
Fleabane

Erigeron karvinskianus

Hardy herbaceous perennials with showy, daisy-like flowers in various colors, fleabanes are ideal for the front of mixed borders. The flowers are good for cutting. Remove dead flower heads regularly.

Propagate by division in spring. Division every two years keeps plants young and vigorous. Alternatively, propagate from basal stem cuttings in spring. Watch out for powdery mildew, slugs, and snails.

	SPRING	SUMMER	FALL	WINTER	height (ft)	spread (ft)	min temp (°F)	moisture	sun/shade	colors	
Erigeron 'Charity'	🌱🌱🌱	●●●			2	1½	1°	💧	☀	■	Avoid soil drying out
E. 'Dignity'	🌱🌱🌱	●●●			1½	1½	1°	💧	☀	■	Avoid soil drying out
E. 'Dunkelste Aller' (syn. 'Darkest of All')	🌱🌱🌱	●●●			2	1½	1°	💧	☀	■	Avoid soil drying out
E. karvinskianus	🌱🌱🌱	●●●			1	3	1°	💧	☀	□	Good for cracks in paving

Eryngium
Eryngo *or* Sea holly

Hardy herbaceous or evergreen perennials of distinctive habit. The variously shaped but spiny foliage is very attractive, as are the branching heads of thistle-like flowers.

Grow in a mixed border or gravel area with ornamental grasses and achilleas. Flowers may be cut and dried. Propagate from root cuttings in winter. Watch out for black root rot, powdery mildew, slugs, and snails.

Eryngium protiflorum

	SPRING	SUMMER	FALL	WINTER	height (ft)	spread (ft)	min temp (°F)	moisture	sun/shade	colors	
Eryngium alpinum	🌱🌱🌱	●●●	●		2½	1½	1°	💧	☀	■	Conspicuous spiny flower bracts
E. giganteum	🌱🌱🌱	●●●			3	1	1°	💧	☀	■	Gray, spiny flower bracts
E. planum	🌱🌱🌱	●●●			3	1½	1°	💧	☀	□	Bluish, spiny flower bracts
E. tripartitum	🌱🌱🌱	●●●	●		3	1½	1°	💧	☀	■	Bluish flower bracts

☀ *sunny*   ☀ *semi-shady*   ● *shady*

Erysimum
Wallflower

The cultivars of *E.* x *allionii* (Siberian wallflower) and *E. cheiri* are hardy dwarf evergreen perennials grown as biennials. They flower very freely and come in many bright and pastel colors. Wallflowers are traditionally used in spring bedding schemes in combination with tulips and forget-me-nots (myosotis).

These plants are also useful gap fillers for mixed borders and are essential "ingredients" of cottage-garden borders. The dwarf compact kinds are suitable for patio containers and window boxes.

Erysimum cheiri Fair Lady Series

Erysimum 'Apricot Twist'

E. cheiri 'Harlequin'

Erysimums are ideal for alkaline soil, but avoid very wet conditions during winter, which can lead to the roots rotting off. Raise plants from seed sown in an outdoor seed bed in late spring or early summer. Transplant seedlings to a nursery bed. Plant young plants in flowering positions in the fall. Watch out for leaf spot, powdery mildew, slugs, snails, and mosaic virus. Wallflowers are also prone to a root disease of the cabbage family known as clubroot, which causes roots to swell up and growth to become stunted. Discard affected plants. It is most likely to occur on acid soils.

	SPRING	SUMMER	FALL	WINTER	height (in)	spread (in)	min temp (°F)	moisture	sun/shade	colors	
Erysimum x *allionii*	flower flower flower	planting	planting planting planting		24	12	1°	well drained	sun	▨	Fragrant flowers
E. 'Apricot Twist'	flower flower flower flower flower flower	planting	planting planting planting		24	24	1°	well drained	sun	▨	Short-lived perennial
E. cheiri Bedder Series	flower flower flower	planting	planting planting planting		12	12	1°	well drained	sun	▥	Fragrant flowers
E. cheiri 'Blood Red'	flower flower flower	planting	planting planting planting		18	18	1°	well drained	sun	▨	Fragrant flowers
E. cheiri 'Cloth of Gold'	flower flower flower	planting	planting planting planting		18	18	1°	well drained	sun	▢	Fragrant flowers
E. cheiri Fair Lady Series	flower flower flower	planting	planting planting planting		18	18	1°	well drained	sun	▥	Fragrant flowers
E. cheiri 'Harlequin'	flower flower flower	planting	planting planting planting		12	12	1°	well drained	sun	▨	Fragrant flowers
E. cheiri 'Persian Carpet'	flower flower flower	planting	planting planting planting		10	10	1°	well drained	sun	▨	Fragrant flowers
E. cheiri Prince Series	flower flower flower	planting	planting planting planting		8	8	1°	well drained	sun	▤	Very free-flowering

planting   ● flower   ◊ well drained   ◊◊ moist   ◊◊◊ wet

Erythronium
Dog's-tooth violet
or Trout lily

The erythroniums are hardy dwarf bulbs producing nodding, somewhat lily-like flowers with swept-back petals. The long, wide leaves are also attractive, and some species have dramatic bronze-marbled foliage.

As these bulbs like broken shade, grow them in a woodland garden, or below large deciduous shrubs or trees in a mixed border. *E. dens-canis* (European dog's-tooth violet) is suitable for naturalizing in grass, provided that it does not grow too long and dense. Propagate by division of clumps in summer or fall while dormant. Few problems—watch out for slugs and snails.

Erythronium californicum 'White Beauty'

	SPRING	SUMMER	FALL	WINTER	height (in)	spread (in)	min temp (°F)	moisture	sun/shade	colors	
Erythronium dens-canis	●●●		🌱🌱🌱		6	4	1°	●●	◐	▓	Leaves have purple markings
E. californicum 'White Beauty'	●●●		🌱🌱🌱		12	4	1°	●●	◐	□	Creamy flowers with orange-brown marks

Eschscholzia
California poppy

Eschscholzia californica hybrids

These hardy annuals have brilliantly colored bowl-shaped flowers and attractive pale or gray-green ferny foliage. The flowers need direct sun to open fully. These slim, dwarf plants can be used to fill gaps in a mixed border and for growing in gravel areas and on rock gardens.

These flowers combine well with small ornamental grasses, brachyscome, cerinthes, and felicias. Particularly good for infertile, dry soils. Propagate from seed sown in flowering positions in spring or early fall. Make successive sowings several weeks apart for a long display. Watch out for slugs and snails.

	SPRING	SUMMER	FALL	WINTER	height (in)	spread (in)	min temp (°F)	moisture	sun/shade	colors	
Eschscholzia caespitosa 'Sundew'	🌱🌱🌱	●●●	🌱🌱🌱		6	6	1°	●	☼	□	Fine, ferny foliage
E. californica	🌱🌱🌱	●●●	🌱🌱🌱		12	6	1°	●	☼	▨	Ferny foliage
E. californica 'Monarch Art Shades'	🌱🌱🌱	●●●	🌱🌱🌱		12	6	1°	●	☼	▦	Double flowers
E. californica Thai Silk Series	🌱🌱🌱	●●●	🌱🌱🌱		8	6	1°	●	☼	▓	Single or semi-double flowers

☼ *sunny*　　◐ *semi-shady*　　● *shady*

Euphorbia
Spurge

These are mainly hardy herbaceous or evergreen perennials, although *E. characias* and *E. mellifera* are hardy evergreen shrubby plants. All euphorbias are great character plants, the larger kinds making a definite statement in gardens and suitable for use as single specimens.

Spurges produce large flower heads, but it is the colored bracts surrounding the inconspicuous flowers that provide the color. Most spurges can be used effectively in mixed borders. For example, *E. amygdaloides* looks good with grassy carex or sedges. *E. dulcis* can be combined with alliums, geraniums, and late tulips. *E.* x *martinii* looks great with gray-leafed shrubs and dwarf glaucous grasses. The hardy annual *E. marginata* could be included in a cool, green and white color scheme. *E. characias* is excellent as a specimen plant

Euphorbia amygdaloides var. robbiae

Euphorbia x martinii

Euphorbia mellifera

Euphorbia characias

and could be grown in patio tubs. *E. polychroma* combines well with early flowering perennials, such as doronicums and pulmonarias. The prostrate *E. myrsinites* is suitable for a rock garden, grouped with aubrieta and aurinia. Propagate perennials in spring, by division or from basal stem cuttings. Propagate shrubby types from stem-tip cuttings in spring or summer. Raise annuals from seed sown in flowering positions during spring. Watch out for aphids, gray mold and, on some species, rust.

	SPRING	SUMMER	FALL	WINTER	height (in)	spread (in)	min temp (°F)	moisture	sun/shade	colors	
Euphorbia amygdaloides var. robbiae					30	12	1°				Spreads vigorously, evergreen
E. characias					48	48	25°				Evergreen, biennial stems
E. characias subsp. *wulfenii*					48	48	25°				Evergreen, biennial stems
E. dulcis 'Chameleon'					12	12	1°				Purple foliage, herbaceous
E. marginata (annual)					36	12	1°				White-variegated leaves
E. x *martinii*					36	36	1°				Evergreen, young leaves flushed purple
E. mellifera					72	96	25°				Fragrant flowers, evergreen
E. myrsinites					4	12	1°				Evergreen gray foliage
E. polychroma					15	24	1°				Herbaceous

🛠 *planting* ● *flower* 🌢 *well drained* 🌢 *moist* 🌢 *wet*

Felicia
Blue daisy

Felicia amelloides 'Santa Anita'

These half-hardy annuals and the tender subshrub grown as an annual, *F. amelloides*, are mat-forming and bushy plants respectively. They produce masses of daisy flowers in blue and other colors.

These plants are popular for summer bedding and containers in combination with other daisy-flowered bedding plants such as gazanias. Propagate annuals from seed in spring under cover, subshrubs from semi-ripe cuttings in late summer. Problem-free.

	SPRING			SUMMER			FALL			WINTER		height (in)	spread (in)	min temp (°F)	moisture	sun/shade	colors	
Felicia amelloides	🌱	🌱	🌱	●	●	●	●	●					12	12	41°	💧💧	☀	▦	Tolerates poor soil
F. amelloides 'Santa Anita'	🌱	🌱	🌱	●	●	●	●	●					12	12	41°	💧💧	☀	▦	Extra-large flowers
F. amelloides variegated	🌱	🌱	🌱	●	●	●	●	●					12	12	41°	💧💧	☀	▦	White-variegated foliage
F. bergeriana	🌱	🌱	🌱	●	●	●							12	12	34°	💧💧	☀	▦	Tolerates poor soil
F. heterophylla 'Blue and Rose Mixed'	🌱	🌱	🌱	●	●	●							10	10	34°	💧💧	☀	▦	Tolerates poor soil

Freesia

Normally thought of as half-hardy greenhouse pot plants in frost-prone climates, freesias can be obtained as heat-treated corms (to stimulate bloom production) for outdoor flowering in the summer.

Named cultivars with fragrant flowers in a range of colors are available and their flowers are good for cutting. Plant in a sheltered position in border or patio tubs and window boxes. Discard corms after flowering. Watch out for aphids.

Freesia 'Striped Jewel'

Fritillaria
Fritillary

Fritillaria imperialis 'Maxima Lutea'

Fritillarias are hardy bulbs with nodding, bell-shaped flowers. *F. imperialis* (crown imperial) is suitable for a mixed border (but smells of foxes!) while *F. meleagris* (snake's-head fritillary) can be naturalized in grass.

The crown imperial combines well with shrubs, including rhododendrons, and must have exceedingly good drainage. Propagate from offsets or bulbils when dormant. Prone to slugs and snails.

	SPRING			SUMMER			FALL			WINTER		height (in)	spread (in)	min temp (°F)	moisture	sun/shade	colors	
Fritillaria imperialis				●			🌱	🌱	🌱				48	12	1°	💧💧	☀	▦	Easily grown. Powerful odor
F. imperialis 'Maxima Lutea'				●			🌱	🌱	🌱				48	12	1°	💧💧	☀	▢	Easily grown
F. meleagris	●	●	●				🌱	🌱	🌱				12	3	1°	💧	☀	▦	Snake's-head fritillary. Easily grown

☀ *sunny*   ◐ *semi-shady*   ● *shady*

Fuchsia

Fuchsias are frost-tender to frost-hardy deciduous or evergreen shrubs, but the ones considered here are grown as summer bedding plants. They make bushy or, in some cultivars, trailing plants, and they flower profusely, producing a succession of dangling, usually bell-shaped single or double flowers, often with swept-back petals, and mainly in combinations of blue, red, pink, and white.

Fuchsias bloom over a very long period. They make superb container plants, the trailing cultivars being especially suitable for hanging baskets. But the bush forms can also be grown in baskets as centerpieces. Bush fuchsias also make good dot plants in summer bedding schemes and combine well with a wide

Fuchsia 'Red Spider'

Fuchsia 'Eva Boerg'

range of summer bedding plants, including begonias and impatiens. They can also be used as fillers in a mixed border. Propagate plants from semi-ripe cuttings in late summer, and winter the young plants in a cool, frost-free greenhouse. Discard the old parent plants at the end of the season. Pinch out tips of young plants to encourage bushy growth, and also pinch out the resulting side shoots. Fuchsias may be attacked by aphids, gray mold, red spider mites, rust, and vine weevil grubs.

	SPRING	SUMMER	FALL	WINTER	height (in)	spread (in)	min temp (°F)	moisture	sun/shade	colors	
Fuchsia 'Annabel'	planting	flower	flower		24	24	34°	well drained	sun		Double flowers
F. 'Ballet Girl'	planting	flower	flower		18	24	34°	well drained	sun		Double flowers
F. 'Cascade' (trailing)	planting	flower	flower		6	18	34°	well drained	sun		Single flowers
F. 'Checkerboard'	planting	flower	flower		36	30	34°	well drained	sun		Single flowers
F. 'Dollar Princess'	planting	flower	flower		18	18	34°	moist	sun		Double flowers
F. 'Eva Boerg' (trailing)	planting	flower	flower		6	18	34°	moist	sun		Semi-double flowers
F. 'Golden Marinka' (trailing)	planting	flower	flower		6	18	34°	well drained	sun		Gold and green variegated foliage
F. 'Leonora'	planting	flower	flower		30	24	34°	well drained	sun		Single flowers
F. 'Red Spider' (trailing)	planting	flower	flower		6	24	34°	moist	sun		Single flowers
F. 'Thalia'	planting	flower	flower		36	36	34°	moist	sun		Long tubular flowers
F. 'Voodoo'	planting	flower	flower		18	18	34°	well drained	sun		Giant double flowers
F. 'Winston Churchill'	planting	flower	flower		24	24	34°	well drained	sun		Double flowers

planting   flower | well drained   moist   wet

Gaillardia
Blanket flower

Gaillardia pulchella is a hardy annual with a well-branched habit. The others are hardy herbaceous perennials but are generally short-lived.

Grown for their bright daisy flowers, gaillardias are good for prairie-style borders combined with ornamental grasses. Asters are other good companions. Flowers are suitable for cutting. Propagate all from seed in spring under cover. Perennials can also be divided in spring. Watch out for slugs and snails. Remove dead blooms.

Gaillardia 'Kobold'

	SPRING	SUMMER	FALL	WINTER	height (ft)	spread (ft)	min temp (°F)	moisture	sun/shade	colors	
Gaillardia 'Burgunder'					2	1½	1°				Good for poor soil
G. 'Dazzler'					2	1½	1°				Good for poor soil
G. 'Kobold' (syn. 'Goblin')					1	1	1°				Good for poor soil
G. pulchella Plume Series					1	1	1°				Double flowers. Annual

Galanthus
Snowdrop

Galanthus nivalis

Hardy dwarf bulbs valued for their early flowers, usually as winter is merging into spring. Grow around shrubs in a mixed border, under deciduous trees, or in a woodland garden.

The dangling bell-shaped blooms are white, marked with green. Propagate by splitting clumps and replanting as soon as flowering is over. This is also the best planting time for these flowers. Watch out for gray mold and Narcissus bulb fly.

	SPRING	SUMMER	FALL	WINTER	height (in)	spread (in)	min temp (°F)	moisture	sun/shade	colors	
Galanthus 'Atkinsii'					8	3	1°				Strong grower
G. nivalis					4	4	1°				Fragrant flowers
G. nivalis 'Flore Pleno'					4	4	1°				Double flowers

Gaura

Gaura lindheimeri

A hardy herbaceous perennial of bushy habit, G. lindheimeri produces airy sprays of star-shaped flowers over an incredibly long period.

It is ideal for a prairie-style border in combination with ornamental grasses such as *Stipa gigantea*. Propagate in spring by division or basal stem cuttings. No problems from pests or diseases.

	SPRING	SUMMER	FALL	WINTER	height (ft)	spread (ft)	min temp (°F)	moisture	sun/shade	colors	
Gaura lindheimeri					4	3	1°				Flowers age to pink
G. lindheimeri 'Siskiyou Pink'					4	3	1°				Tolerates drought

☀ *sunny*   ◑ *semi-shady*   ● *shady*

Gazania

Half-hardy evergreen perennials grown as annuals, gazanias are dwarf spreading plants generally with deep green leaves with white undersides, but they may also be gray in color.

Large daisy-like flowers mainly open only in direct sun, although cultivars are being bred to perform better in cloudy weather. Grow in summer bedding schemes or patio tubs and window boxes with other daisy-flowered bedding plants such as blue felicias. Good for seaside gardens. Regularly remove dead flowers. Raise from seed in spring under cover. Take semi-ripe cuttings in late summer and winter young plants in a cool, frost-free greenhouse. Watch out for gray mold.

Gazania 'Daybreak Red Stripe'

Flowers

G

	SPRING	SUMMER	FALL	WINTER	height (in)	spread (in)	min temp (°F)	moisture	sun/shade	colors	
Gazania Chansonette Series	planting planting planting	flower flower flower			8	8	34°	well drained	sun		Flowers are zoned
G. Daybreak Series	planting planting planting	flower flower flower			8	8	34°	well drained	sun		Flowers are zoned
G. Mini-star Series	planting planting planting	flower flower flower			8	8	34°	well drained	sun		Some flowers zoned
G. Sundance Series	planting planting planting	flower flower flower			10	10	34°	well drained	sun		Very free-flowering

Gentiana
Gentian

Gentiana 'Multiflora'

A variable genus of hardy perennials generally valued for their brilliant blue flowers, the blooms being mainly trumpet-shaped.

There are low mat-forming plants for the rock or scree garden, including evergreen *G. acaulis* (trumpet gentian), semi-evergreen *G. sino-ornata*, which needs acid soil, and evergreen *G. verna* (spring gentian) which may be short-lived. Taller species for the mixed border or woodland garden include herbaceous *G. asclepiadea* (willow gentian). Gentians need shade from the hottest sun. Propagate by division in spring. Watch out for slugs and snails.

	SPRING	SUMMER	FALL	WINTER	height (in)	spread (in)	min temp (°F)	moisture	sun/shade	colors	
Gentiana acaulis	planting planting flower	flower			3	10	1°	moist	part sun		Forms mats of growth
G. 'Multiflora'	planting planting planting		flower flower		3	12	1°	moist	part sun		Needs acid soil
G. sino-ornata	planting planting planting		flower flower flower		3	12	1°	moist	part sun		Needs acid to neutral soil
C. verna	planting planting flower	flower			2	4	1°	moist	part sun		May be short-lived

planting *planting*   flower *flower*   well drained *well drained*   moist *moist*   wet *wet*

Geranium
Cranesbill

A large genus of hardy herbaceous and evergreen perennials. They are mainly low-growing, bushy plants notable for their long display of bowl- or saucer-shaped flowers in shades of blue, magenta, and pink, plus white. The leaves are generally lobed, often hand-shaped.

The leaves of some geraniums are aromatic and may have brown or bronze markings, while some species take on autumnal leaf tints. Smaller geraniums, including *G. cinereum*, are excellent for rock or scree gardens. The others are ideal for mixed borders, where they associate well with many other plants, including old and modern shrub roses, ground-cover roses, flowering and foliage shrubs, perennials such as

Geranium 'Johnson's Blue'

delphiniums, alchemilla, and hostas, and dwarf ornamental grasses. Geraniums are especially at home in cottage-garden borders combined with old-fashioned annuals and perennials. Some, including *G. macrorrhizum* and cultivars, are suitable for woodland gardens. Cranesbills need little attention apart from regular removal of flower stems when blooms have finished, and old foliage. Propagate by division or basal cuttings in spring. Problems include caterpillars, powdery mildew, slugs, snails, vine weevil grubs, and viruses.

Geranium x oxonianum 'Wargrave Pink'

	SPRING	SUMMER	FALL	WINTER	height (in)	spread (in)	min temp (F)	moisture	sun/shade	colors	
Geranium cinereum 'Ballerina'					6	12	1°				Gray-green foliage
G. endressii					18	24	1°				Takes partial shade
G. 'Johnson's Blue'					18	24	1°				Takes partial shade. Bright blue flowers
G. macrorrhizum					18	24	1°				Takes partial shade. Pink flowers
G. macrorrhizum 'Album'					18	24	1°				Takes partial shade
G. x oxonianum 'A.T. Johnson'					12	24	1°				Takes partial shade
G. x oxonianum 'Wargrave Pink'					24	30	1°				Takes partial shade
G. psilostemon					48	24	1°				Takes partial shade. Unusual flowers

☼ *sunny*   ☼ *semi-shady*   ☀ *shady*

Geum
Avens

Geums are hardy herbaceous perennials with large pinnate leaves and bowl- or saucer-shaped, often brilliantly colored flowers on thin wiry stems produced over a long period.

Geum 'Lady Stratheden'

These are ideal plants for frontal positions in a mixed border and really look at home in cottage-garden borders. Avens combine well with other hardy perennials including achilleas, aquilegias, and geraniums, and with old or modern shrub roses. Avoid wet soils as they can cause roots to rot. Propagate by division in spring. Caterpillars may find the leaves appetizing, so watch out and protect the plants accordingly.

	SPRING	SUMMER	FALL	WINTER	height (ft)	spread (ft)	min temp (°F)	moisture	sun/shade	colors	
Geum 'Borisii'	🌱🌱●	●●●			1½	1	1°	💧	☀	◼	Pinnate, hairy leaves
G. 'Fire Opal'	🌱🌱🌱	●●●			2½	2	1°	💧	☀	◼	Semi-double flowers
G. 'Lady Stratheden'	🌱🌱🌱	●●●			2	2	1°	💧	☀	◻	Semi-double flowers
G. 'Mrs J. Bradshaw'	🌱🌱🌱	●●●			2	2	1°	💧	☀	◼	Semi-double flowers
G. rivale 'Leonard's Variety'	🌱🌱	●●●			1½	2	1°	💧	☀	◻	Flowers profusely

Gladiolus

These half-hardy plants grow from corms and produce widely flaring, funnel-shaped flowers in spikes in a wide color range. The leaves are sword-like. Various groups include the popular Grandiflorus or large-flowered gladioli noted for substantial spikes, one per corm, flower size ranging from giant to miniature.

Gladiolus 'Early Yellow'

Butterfly gladioli have closely packed, flaring flowers, sometimes with ruffled petals, blotched in the throat. As the flowers are good for cutting, grow gladioli in rows on the vegetable plot. Alternatively, plant them in groups in a mixed border. Combine them with modern shrub roses, other corms such as crocosmias, or cannas and dahlias. Feed fortnightly with a high-potash liquid fertilizer from the time the flower spikes are developing. Continue for a few weeks after flowering. Where frosts occur lift the corms in the

Gladiolus 'May Bride'

🌱 *planting*   ● *flower*   💧 *well drained*   💧 *moist*   💧 *wet*

fall when the foliage is yellowing and snap the corms off the stems. Dry off and then separate out the new corms (discarding the old) for storing in a dry, frost-proof place for the winter. Propagate from cormlets removed when dormant and "sow" them like seeds in spring outdoors. Watch out for aphids, corm rot, and slugs.

	SPRING	SUMMER	FALL	WINTER	height (in)	spread (in)	min temp (°F)	moisture	sun/shade	colors	
Gladiolus Butterfly Hybrids		●●●			30	6	34°	◐◑	☀	▨	Flowers have blotched throats
G. 'Early Yellow' (Grandiflorus)		●●●			36	6	34°	◐◑	☀	☐	Ruffled flowers
G. 'Green Woodpecker' (Grandiflorus)		●●●			60	6	34°	◐◑	☀	☐	Ruffled flowers
G. 'Jester' (Grandiflorus)		●●●			36	6	34°	◐	☀	■	Trumpet-like flowers
G. 'May Bride' (Grandiflorus)		●●●			36	6	34°	◐◑	☀	☐	Trumpet-like flowers
G. 'Violetta' (Grandiflorus)		●●●			36	6	34°	◐◑	☀	■	Trumpet-like flowers

Gypsophila

Gypsophila elegans **is a hardy annual with clouds of tiny flowers.** *G. paniculata* **(baby's breath) cultivars are hardy herbaceous perennials with similar blooms.** *G. repens*, **a partially evergreen perennial, forms mats of growth that become smothered with starry flowers.**

The latter is good for a rock or scree garden, but the others are ideal for mixed borders, combined with such plants as dianthus (pinks and carnations) and roses. Flowers of larger species are good for cutting. Raise annuals from seed in spring in flowering positions. Propagate perennials in spring; cultivars from basal stem cuttings, species from seed under cover. Generally trouble-free.

	SPRING	SUMMER	FALL	WINTER	height (ft)	spread (ft)	min temp (°F)	moisture	sun/shade	colors	
Gypsophila elegans 'Covent Garden'		●●●			2	1	1°	◐	☀	☐	Alkaline soil preferred. Annual
G. paniculata 'Bristol Fairy'		●●●			3	3	1°	◐◑	☀	☐	Double flowers
G. paniculata 'Flamingo'		●●●			3	3	1°	◐◑	☀	☐	Double flowers

☀ sunny   ◑ semi-shady   ● shady

Gypsophila paniculata 'Flamingo'

Helenium
Sneezeweed

Helenium 'Moerheim Beauty'

These hardy herbaceous perennials have daisy-like flowers with conspicuous dome-like brown or yellow centers. The blooms are produced over a long period.

Heleniums are suitable for mixed borders in combination with perennials such as rudbeckias, helianthus, dahlias, asters, and ornamental grasses including miscanthus and stipa. The flowers are good for cutting. Tall cultivars need supports such as twiggy sticks. Remove dead flower heads regularly. Propagate in spring, by division every two years or from basal cuttings. Plants may be troubled by leaf spot.

	SPRING	SUMMER	FALL	WINTER	height (ft)	spread (ft)	min temp (°F)	moisture	sun/shade	colors	
Helenium 'Bruno'	planting	flower			4	2	1°	well drained	sun	▦	Brown center
H. 'Butterpat'	planting	flower			3	2	1°	well drained	sun	▢	Brown-yellow center
H. 'Moerheim Beauty'	planting	flower			3	2	1°	well drained	sun	▨	Brown center; copper-red florets
H. 'Wyndley'	planting	flower			2½	2	1°	well drained	sun	▩	Brown center; yellow ray-florets

Helianthemum
Rock rose *or* Sun rose

Hardy evergreen shrubs of prostrate, ground-covering habit, rock roses are spangled over a long period with brilliantly colored flowers resembling small single roses. In some cultivars, the foliage is grayish.

Generally grown on rock gardens or screes in combination with other rock plants such as *Iberis sempervirens*, sedums, saxifrages, and *Euphorbia myrsinites*. Also good for covering a bank. They thrive in chalky soils. When flowering is over, cut back all shoots to within 1in (2.5cm) of the old wood. Propagate from softwood cuttings in spring or early summer. Not troubled by pests or diseases.

Helianthemum 'Wisley Primrose'

	SPRING	SUMMER	FALL	WINTER	height (ft)	spread (ft)	min temp (°F)	moisture	sun/shade	colors	
Helianthemum 'Fire Dragon'	planting	flower			1	1	1°	well drained	sun	▨	Grayish foliage
H. 'Jubilee'	planting	flower			1	1	1°	well drained	sun	▢	Double flowers
H. 'Rhodanthe Carneum'	planting	flower			1	1½	1°	well drained	sun	▢	Gray foliage
H. 'Wisley Primrose'	planting	flower			1	1½	1°	well drained	sun	▢	Gray-green foliage

planting · flower · well drained · moist · wet

Helianthus
Sunflower

Helianthus annuus, **along with its cultivars, is the popular hardy annual that can grow to great heights and produce gigantic flowers. The others described here are hardy herbaceous perennials. All produce large daisy-like flowers with conspicuous, generally darker centers.**

The main color is yellow but other colors are now making an appearance. Sunflowers are suitable for mixed or prairie-style borders, especially in combination with tall ornamental grasses such as miscanthus, and other daisy-flowered perennials including asters, *Echinacea purpurea*, and rudbeckias. Solidago or golden rod is another effective

companion. Fall-coloring shrubs such as rhus and cotinus make good backgrounds. Dwarf annual cultivars can be grown in patio tubs. The flowers are suitable for cutting. These plants are good for chalky and dry soils. Tall sunflowers will need supports.

Perennials appreciate a permanent mulch of bulky organic matter such as garden compost to prevent rapid drying out of the soil. Propagate in spring, perennials by division every two years or from basal cuttings, and annuals from seed sown under cover or in flowering positions. With regard to pests and diseases, watch out for powdery mildew, slugs, and snails.

Helianthus annuus 'Double Shine'

Helianthus 'Lemon Queen'

	SPRING	SUMMER	FALL	WINTER	height (ft)	spread (ft)	min temp (°F)	moisture	sun/shade	colors	
Helianthus annuus 'Double Shine'	🖐🖐🖐	● ● ●			4	1½	1°	💧🌢	☼	▨	Double flowers
H. annuus 'Giant Yellow'	🖐🖐🖐	● ● ●			16	2	1°	💧🌢	☼	▨	Large, yellow single flowers
H. annuus 'Ruby Sunset'	🖐🖐🖐	● ● ●			5	2	1°	💧🌢	☼	■	Medium-size single flowers
H. annuus 'Russian Giant'	🖐🖐🖐	● ● ●			10	2	1°	💧🌢	☼	☐	Large single flowers
H. annuus 'Teddy Bear'	🖐🖐🖐	● ● ●			3	1½	1°	💧🌢	☼	▨	Double flowers
H. 'Capenoch Star'	🖐🖐🖐		● ● ●		5	3	1°	🌢💧	☼	☐	Single flowers
H. 'Lemon Queen'	🖐🖐🖐		● ● ●		5	4	1°	💧🌢	☼	☐	Single flowers
H. 'Loddon Gold'	🖐🖐🖐		● ● ●		5	3	1°	🌢💧	☼	▨	Double flowers

☼ *sunny*   ☀ *semi-shady*   ● *shady*

Heliotropium
Heliotrope

This half-hardy deciduous shrub is generally grown as an annual summer bedding plant in frost-prone climates. Cultivars have fragrant, purple, violet-blue, or white flowers and bloom continuously over a long period.

Include heliotrope as dot plants in summer bedding schemes—also in patio tubs and window boxes, where they combine well with many other summer bedding plants including pelargoniums, begonias, impatiens, petunias, tagetes (marigolds), and *Salvia splendens* (scarlet sage). Propagate from semi-ripe cuttings in late summer, and winter young plants in a cool, frost-free greenhouse. Discard old plants at the end of the season. Generally trouble-free.

Heliotropium 'Nagano'

	SPRING	SUMMER	FALL	WINTER	height (ft)	spread (ft)	min temp (°F)	moisture	sun/shade	colors	
Heliotropium 'Marine'	planting	flower			1½	1½	34°	well drained	sun	■	Large flower heads
H. 'Nagano'	planting	flower			2	2	34°	well drained	sun	■	Good for bedding

Helleborus
Hellebore

Helleborus niger

Hardy evergreen or herbaceous perennials with lobed or divided leaves and heads of bowl-shaped flowers. The dwarf *H. niger* or Christmas rose is the earliest to flower.

The others, such as *H.* x *hybridus* cultivars, are taller plants. In a mixed border plant around winter- or spring-flowering shrubs, with bergenias and dwarf bulbs such as snowdrops (galanthus) and early-flowering narcissus. Provide a permanent mulch of bulky organic matter. Propagate by division in spring after flowering, *H. argutifolius* and *H. foetidus* from seed when ripe in a garden frame. Watch out for aphids, black root rot, leaf spot, slugs, and snails.

Helleborus x *hybridus*

	SPRING	SUMMER	FALL	WINTER	height (ft)	spread (ft)	min temp (°F)	moisture	sun/shade	colors	
Helleborus argutifolius	flower/planting		planting	flower	4	3	1°	wet	sun/shade	□	Neutral or alkaline soil
H. foetidus	flower/planting		planting	flower	2½	1½	1°	wet	sun/shade	■	Neutral or alkaline soil
H. x *hybridus* cultivars	flower/planting		planting	flower	1½	1½	1°	wet	sun/shade	▦	Neutral or alkaline soil
H. niger	flower/planting		planting	flower	1	1½	1°	wet	sun	□	Common name is "Christmas Rose"
H. niger 'Potter's Wheel'	flower/planting		planting	flower	1	1½	1°	wet	sun/shade	□	Neutral or alkaline soil
H. x *sternii*	flower/planting		planting	flower	1	1	1°	wet	sun/shade	□	Neutral or alkaline soil, also takes full sun

planting　　flower　　well drained　　moist　　wet

Hemerocallis
Daylily

Hardy herbaceous or evergreen perennials with large, lily-like flowers, hemerocallis come in a wide range of colors and have broad, arching, grassy foliage. Each flower lasts for only one day but blooms are produced in succession over a long period.

Daylilies are essential plants for a mixed border, in combination with agapanthus, crocosmias, kniphofias, old or modern shrub roses, and ornamental grasses. Provide a permanent mulch of bulky organic matter. Liquid feed fortnightly during the flowering period. Divide plants every two years in spring. Problems include aphids, rust, slugs, and snails.

Hemerocallis 'Golden Chimes'

	SPRING	SUMMER	FALL	WINTER	height (ft)	spread (ft)	min temp (F)	moisture	sun/shade	colors	
H. 'Catherine Woodbery'	plant	shady			2½	2	1°	●●	sunny	▨	Evergreen; star-shaped flowers
H. 'Golden Chimes'	plant	shady			3	1½	1°	●●	sunny	▨	Evergreen; star-shaped flowers
H. 'Hyperion'	plant	shady			3	2½	1°	●●	sunny	☐	Evergreen; night-flowering; fragrant
H. 'Pink Damask'	plant	shady			3	2	1°	●●	sunny	▨	Star-shaped flowers
H. 'Stafford'	plant	shady			2½	2	1°	●●	sunny	▰	Evergreen; star-shaped flowers
H. 'Stella de Oro'	plant	shady			1	1½	1°	●●	sunny	☐	Evergreen; circular flowers

Heuchera
Coral flower

Heuchera 'Palace Purple'

Hardy evergreen or partially evergreen perennials, heucheras produce low mounds of fairly large, lobed leaves, and heads of tiny flowers on upright, wiry stems. In recent years many cultivars with colorful foliage have become available.

Heucheras, especially those with attractive leaves, make superb ground cover around shrubs in mixed borders or woodland gardens. The flowers are suitable for cutting. Provide a permanent mulch of bulky organic matter, topping up annually. Plants are best divided every few years in early fall. Vine weevil grubs may attack the roots.

	SPRING	SUMMER	FALL	WINTER	height (ft)	spread (ft)	min temp (F)	moisture	sun/shade	colors	
H. micrantha var. diversifolia 'Palace Purple'		shady	plant		2	2	1°	●●	sunny	☐	Bronze-red foliage; takes partial shade
H. 'Pewter Moon'		shady	plant		1½	1	1°	●●	sunny	▨	Leaves marbled gray; takes partial shade
H. 'Red Spangles'		shady	plant		1½	1	1°	●●	sunny	▰	Large, showy flowers; takes partial shade

☀ *sunny*   ◑ *semi-shady*   ● *shady*

Hosta
Plantain lily

These hardy herbaceous perennials are grown mainly for their large leaves and, although most flower reasonably well, several produce particularly good displays of blooms as well as having attractive foliage.

The flowers are bell-shaped or tubular. Hostas are used mainly as ground cover among shrubs, in woodland gardens and around pools. They also grow quite well in patio tubs. Ensure that the soil remains moist, as dry conditions are seldom tolerated. Mulch permanently with organic matter such as leaf mold, garden compost, or peat substitute. Propagate by division in spring. Very prone to slugs and snails; also vine weevil grubs.

Hosta 'Ground Master'

	SPRING	SUMMER	FALL	WINTER	height (ft)	spread (ft)	min temp (°F)	moisture	sun/shade	colors	
Hosta 'Ground Master'	🖐🖐🖐	☀			1½	2	1°	💧	☀	▦	Cream-edged leaves
H. 'Honeybells'	🖐🖐🖐	☀			3	3	1°	💧	☀	☐	Fragrant; light green foliage
H. lancifolia	🖐🖐🖐	☀			2	2½	1°	💧	☀	■	Deep green foliage
H. 'Royal Standard'	🖐🖐🖐	☀			3	3	1°	💧	☀	☐	Fragrant; light green foliage
H. ventricosa	🖐🖐🖐	☀			3	3	1°	💧	☀	■	Deep green foliage

Hyacinthoides
Bluebell

Bluebells are hardy bulbs with spikes of bell-shaped flowers, mainly in blue shades, and clumps of broad, strap-like leaves. *H. non-scripta* is the English bluebell, *H. hispanica* the more robust Spanish bluebell.

Bluebells look good in bold drifts around shrubs, in woodland gardens, and in long grass where they can be allowed to naturalize. Bluebells spread rapidly from self-sown seed, so cut off seed heads if you want to prevent this. Propagate by removing and replanting offsets when dormant in summer or fall. Bluebells are not troubled by pests or diseases, but rabbits sometimes eat the leaves.

Hyacinthoides non-scripta growing in woodland.

	SPRING	SUMMER	FALL	WINTER	height (in)	spread (in)	min temp (°F)	moisture	sun/shade	colors	
Hyacinthoides hispanica	☀		🖐🖐🖐		15	4	1°	💧	☀	▦	Vigorous grower
H. non-scripta	☀		🖐🖐🖐		12	4	1°	💧	☀	■	Spreads rapidly from seed

🖐 *planting*   ☀ *flower*   💧 *well drained*   💧 *moist*   💧 *wet*

Hyacinthus orientalis 'Pink Pearl'

Iberis amara

Hyacinthus
Hyacinth

Cultivars of *H. orientalis* are hardy bulbs with short, thick, heavy spikes of fragrant flowers, which are generally planted for spring bedding in combination with *Bellis perennis* (double daisies), violas or pansies, and tulips.

Hyacinths are also good for patio tubs and window boxes, but in these the bulbs may be damaged by severe frosts. When the display is over, lift the bulbs to make way for summer bedding and replant in a mixed border. After flowering, feed with a liquid fertilizer weekly until the leaves die down. Propagate by removing offsets when dormant. Not troubled by pests or diseases.

	SPRING	SUMMER	FALL	WINTER	height (in)	spread (in)	min temp (°F)	moisture	sun/shade	colors	
Hyacinthus orientalis 'City of Haarlem'	●		✿✿✿		8	3	1°	◐	☼	☐	Takes partial shade
H. orientalis 'Delft Blue'	●		✿✿✿		8	3	1°	◐	☼	☐	Takes partial shade
H. orientalis 'L'Innocence'	●		✿✿✿		8	3	1°	◐	☼	☐	Takes partial shade
H. orientalis 'Ostara'	●		✿✿✿		8	3	1°	◐	☼	■	Takes partial shade
H. orientalis 'Pink Pearl'	●		✿✿✿		8	3	1°	◐	☼	■	Takes partial shade

Iberis
Candytuft

***Iberis amara* and *I. umbellata* (globe candytuft) are hardy annuals with domed or flat heads of flowers. They can be grown at the front of mixed borders, among roses or in patio containers. *I. sempervirens* is a hardy, dwarf, evergreen shrubby plant for the rock or scree garden, combined with such plants as helianthemums and saxifrages.**

After flowering, lightly trim *I. sempervirens* to ensure a compact habit. Raise annuals from seed in spring or fall, sowing in flowering positions.

Propagate *I. sempervirens* from semi-ripe cuttings in summer. Root them in a cold frame or with gentle bottom heat in a greenhouse. Watch out for caterpillars, slugs, and snails.

	SPRING	SUMMER	FALL	WINTER	height (in)	spread (in)	min temp (°F)	moisture	sun/shade	colors	
Iberis amara 'Giant Hyacinth Flowered'	✿✿✿	●●●	✿✿✿		12	6	1°	◐	☼	☐	Good for alkaline soil
I. sempervirens	✿✿●	●			12	12	1°	◐	☼	☐	Good for alkaline soil
I. umbellata Fairy Series	✿●●	●●●	✿✿✿		6	6	1°	◐	☼	▦	Multicolored flowers

☼ *sunny*   ☀ *semi-shady*   ● *shady*

H
I

Flowers

Impatiens
Busy Lizzie

Impatiens walleriana cultivars (busy Lizzie) and the **New Guinea Group** are frost-tender perennials generally grown as annuals. **Busy Lizzies** are dwarf, bushy plants, producing flat, spurred flowers in a wide range of brilliant and pastel colors over a long period. The **New Guinea Group** generally make larger, yet well-branched plants, with similar, usually strongly colored, flowers and more attractive foliage, which may be bronze or variegated.

Impatiens walleriana Super Elfin Series

Impatiens are rated as major summer bedding plants, combining well with many other bedding subjects such as fuchsias, begonias, ageratum, lobelia, heliotrope, cannas, celosias, nicotiana, pelargoniums, petunias, scaevola, and verbena. They are widely planted in patio containers and window boxes, and can also be used as centerpieces for hanging baskets.

Alternatively, baskets can be completely filled with busy Lizzies to create a hanging ball of color. Impatiens also look attractive surrounding shrubs in a mixed border. They are particularly good for growing in partial

Impatiens New Guinea Group

 planting   flower   well drained   moist   wet

I. walleriana 'Mosaic Rose'

shade, but will thrive in sun provided that it is not excessively strong and the soil remains moist. Protect plants from wind. Keep well watered and liquid feed every three to four weeks. Raise plants from seed in spring under glass. Impatiens can also be propagated from softwood cuttings in spring or summer. The buds and flowers may be affected by gray mold in damp summers. Watch out for damping off among seedlings.

	SPRING	SUMMER	FALL	WINTER	height (in)	spread (in)	min temp (°F)	moisture	sun/shade	colors	
Impatiens New Guinea Group 'Tango'					12	12	41°				Bronze-flushed foliage
I. walleriana Accent Series					8	8	41°				Compact habit
I. walleriana Carousel Series					12	12	41°				Double flowers
I. walleriana Confection Series					12	12	41°				Double flowers
I. walleriana Expo Series					8	8	41°				Includes bicolors
I. walleriana 'Mega Orange Star'					10	10	41°				Very large flowers
I. walleriana 'Mosaic Lilac'					8	8	41°				Very early flowering
I. walleriana 'Mosaic Rose'					8	8	41°				Unusual effect
I. walleriana 'Stardust Mixed'					10	10	41°				Flowers dusted with white
I. walleriana Super Elfin Series					6	6	41°				Very compact

Ipomoea
Morning glory

These fast-growing, frost-tender twining climbers are grown as annuals. The large, flaring or trumpet-shaped flowers are produced against a background of large, often lobed or heart-shaped leaves.

Grow ipomoeas up a pergola, wall, or fence or, in a mixed border, through large shrubs. They look good combined with *Tropaeolum peregrinum* (canary creeper). These climbers need a sheltered position, as they dislike cold drying winds. Raise plants in spring under glass, first soaking the seeds for a day in tepid water to soften the hard seed coats. Watch out for powdery mildew. Also prone to virus.

Ipomoea tricolor 'Heavenly Blue'

	SPRING	SUMMER	FALL	WINTER	height (ft)	spread (ft)	min temp (°F)	moisture	sun/shade	colors	
Ipomoea nil 'Scarlett O'Hara'					16	3	45°				Vigorous habit
I. tricolor 'Flying Saucers'					12	2	45°				Vigorous habit
I. tricolor 'Heavenly Blue'					12	2	45°				Vigorous habit

☼ *sunny*   ☀ *semi-shady*   ● *shady*

Iris

This is a large and diverse group of plants whose flowers consist of three upright inner petals (the standards) and three outer reflexed or horizontal petals (the falls). Most popular are the hardy rhizomatous perennials that grow from thick rhizomes or horizontal stems. Bearded irises—herbaceous kinds with surface rhizomes and fans of erect, sword-shaped leaves—are included in this group.

The flowers of bearded irises come in a very wide range of colors and have a "beard" of hairs on the falls. Cultivars are classified according to height, and range from miniature dwarf bearded to tall bearded. Beardless rhizomatous irises, with underground rhizomes, include the herbaceous *I. sibirica* cultivars with grassy

Iris confusa

Iris reticulata 'Harmony'

Iris danfordiae

foliage and the grassy leafed, evergreen, winter-flowering *I. unguicularis*.

There is a big group of irises that grow from bulbs. These range from miniature bulbs, such as *I. danfordiae* and *I. reticulata*, to tall Dutch irises whose flowers are particularly good for

🖑 planting   ⦿ flower   ◧ well drained   ◖ moist   ◆ wet

Iris reticulata

Iris 'Jane Phillips'

plot specially for cutting. When planting, the upper half of the rhizomes of bearded irises should be above soil level, but the rhizomes of beardless irises are covered with soil. Lift and divide rhizomatous irises every three years in early summer after flowering. Mulch only beardless irises. Propagate bulbous irises by dividing congested clumps of bulbs in the fall. Irises are prone to gray mold, leaf spot, rhizome rot, slugs, and snails.

cutting. The rhizomatous irises are indispensable plants for mixed borders and are among the main ingredients of cottage-garden borders. They associate well with other early flowering hardy herbaceous plants including peonies, oriental poppies (*Papaver orientale*), and lupines. They also look good with early flowering roses, especially shrub roses. Miniature bulbs are generally grown on rock or scree gardens, while Dutch irises can be grown in mixed borders or in rows on the vegetable

	SPRING	SUMMER	FALL	WINTER	height (in)	spread (in)	min temp (°F)	moisture	sun/shade	colors	
Iris 'Arctic Fancy'	●	🌱🌱🌱			20	18	1°	💧💧	☼	▨	Bearded. Blue beard
I. confusa	●	🌱🌱🌱			36	12	25°	💧💧	☼	☐	Flowers have yellow crests
I. danfordiae	●		🌱🌱🌱	●●●	6	3	1°	💧💧	☼	☐	Bulb. One of the earliest
I. Dutch, 'Golden Harvest'	●●● ●●	🌱🌱🌱			30	4	1°	💧💧	☼	☐	Bulb. Good for cutting
I. Dutch, 'Wedgewood'	●●● ●●	🌱🌱			30	4	1°	💧💧	☼	▨	Bulb. Good for cutting
I. 'Frost and Flame'	●	🌱🌱🌱			30	24	1°	💧💧	☼	☐	Bearded. Orange beard
I. 'Gingerbread Man'	●	🌱🌱🌱			14	12	1°	💧💧	☼	▨	Bearded. Blue beard
I. 'Jane Phillips'	●	🌱🌱🌱			30	24	1°	💧💧	☼	☐	Bearded. An old variety, but attractive
I. 'Pigmy Gold'	●	🌱🌱🌱			16	24	1°	💧	☼	☐	Bearded. Good for front of border
I. reticulata	●		🌱🌱🌱	●	6	3	1°	💧💧	☼	▨	Bulb. Good for rock garden
I. reticulata 'Cantab'	●		🌱🌱🌱	●	6	3	1°	💧💧	☼	▨	Bulb. Yellow crest on falls
I. reticulata 'Harmony'	●		🌱🌱🌱	●	6	3	1°	💧	☼	▨	Bulb. Yellow blotch on falls
I. sibirica 'Dreaming Yellow'	●	🌱🌱🌱			30	24	1°	💧💧	☼	☐	Beardless. Ruffled falls
I. sibirica 'Perry's Blue'	●	🌱🌱🌱			30	24	1°	💧💧	☼	☐	Beardless. An old variety, but attractive
I. 'Staten Island'	●	🌱🌱🌱			30	24	1°	💧💧	☼	▨	Bearded. Eye-catching flowers
I. unguicularis	● 🌱🌱			●	12	24	1°	💧💧	☼	▨	Beardless. Fragrant; good for alkaline soil

☼ *sunny*   ◑ *semi-shady*   ● *shady*

Kniphofia

Red hot poker
or Torch Flower

The hardy herbaceous perennials described here are distinctive plants with clumps of grassy foliage and thick spikes of tubular flowers.

In a mixed border these plants combine well with ornamental grasses such as cortaderia, miscanthus, and stipa, and with hardy perennials including agapanthus, flat-headed achilleas, and crocosmias. They also look good in gravel areas and in association with architecture and paving. Young plants are best mulched with dry straw in winter to protect roots from hard frost.

Propagate by division in spring. However, bear in mind that kniphofias do not like to be disturbed, so lift plants only when it is necessary to divide clumps. Rarely troubled by pests or diseases.

Kniphofia 'Royal Standard'

	SPRING	SUMMER	FALL	WINTER	height (ft)	spread (ft)	min temp (°F)	moisture	sun/shade	colors	
Kniphofia 'Little Maid'	planting	flower	flower		2	1½	1°	well drained	sun	□	Slim flower spikes
K. 'Percy's Pride'	planting	flower	flower		4	2	1°	well drained	sun	□	Buds tinted green
K. 'Royal Standard'	planting	flower			3	2	1°	well drained	sun	□	Red buds
K. 'Samuel's Sensation'	planting	flower	flower		5	2½	1°	well drained	sun	■	Flowers tinted yellow with age

Lagurus

Hare's tail

Lagurus ovatus

This hardy annual grass has tufts of light green leaves and hairy, egg-shaped flower heads on thin stems.

This plant's flowers are good for cutting and drying but should be gathered while still young. *Lagurus ovatus* can be grown in a mixed border with daisy flowered annuals such as cornflowers (centaurea), English marigolds (calendulas), coreopsis and strawflowers (bracteantha), as well as other annuals like love-in-a-mist (nigella), limnanthes and cerinthe. Ideal for sandy soils and seaside gardens. Raise plants from seed in spring, sown in flowering position. Not troubled by pests or diseases.

planting	flower	well drained	moist	wet

Lamium
Deadnettle

Lamium maculatum 'Pink Pearls'

Lamiums are hardy carpeting perennials with attractive foliage and whorls of two-lipped flowers. They make good ground cover in shade, particularly around shrubs or in woodland gardens, and may also be used to cover shady banks.

The evergreen *L. galeobdolon* (yellow archangel) is very vigorous but the herbaceous *L. maculatum* cultivars are much more restrained. Make sure that *L. galeobdolon* does not smother other plants—it is easily dug up if it invades another plant's territory. Propagate by division in fall or spring. Watch out for slugs and snails, which can spoil the foliage.

	SPRING	SUMMER	FALL	WINTER	height (in)	spread (in)	min temp (°F)	moisture	sun/shade	colors	
Lamium galeobdolon 'Hermann's Pride'		● ● ●			24	72	1°	◖◗	◐		Leaves heavily splashed silver
L. maculatum 'Aureum'		● ● ●			8	24	1°	◖◗	◐		Yellow foliage
L. maculatum 'Beacon Silver'		● ● ●			8	24	1°	◖◗	◐		Silver foliage
L. maculatum 'Pink Pearls'		● ● ●			8	24	1°	◖◗	◐		Leaves marked silver

Lathyrus
Everlasting pea
or Sweet pea

The everlasting pea, *L. latifolius*, is a hardy herbaceous perennial while sweet peas, *L. odoratus* cultivars, are hardy annuals. They are mainly climbers, although dwarf bushy sweet peas have been bred. Many sweet pea cultivars are very fragrant.

The everlasting pea is a favorite cottage-garden plant and looks great scrambling through shrubs. Sweet peas can be grown up wigwams or obelisks in mixed borders. Dwarf sweet peas are ideal for patio containers. Flowers are excellent for cutting. Feed sweet peas fortnightly with liquid fertilizer and deadhead regularly. Sow sweet peas in the fall or early spring in a cold frame or in flowering positions in mid-spring. Propagate perennials by division in spring. Watch out for aphids, black root rot, foot rot, powdery mildew, slugs, snails, and viruses.

Lathyrus latifolius

	SPRING	SUMMER	FALL	WINTER	height (in)	spread (in)	min temp (°F)	moisture	sun/shade	colors	
Lathyrus latifolius		● ● ● ●			72	48	1°	◖◗	☼		Bluish-green foliage
L. odoratus 'Beaujolais'		● ● ●			72	6	1°	◖◗	☼		Large flowers
L. odoratus 'Noel Sutton'		● ● ●			72	6	1°	◖	☼		Long, firm stems
L. odoratus Old-fashioned Scented Mix		● ● ●			72	6	1°	◖◗	☼		Small but very fragrant flowers
L. odoratus 'Pink Cupid'		● ● ● ●			6	18	1°	◖◗	☼		Good for containers
L. odoratus 'Winston Churchill'		● ● ● ●			72	6	1°	◖◗	☼		Frilled flowers

☼ *sunny*   ◐ *semi-shady*   ● *shady*

Laurentia

Also known as Solenopsis, *Laurentia axillaris* is a small tender perennial with deeply cut leaves and star-shaped flowers that appear in profusion over a very long period.

Laurentia is used for summer bedding, especially in patio containers and window boxes. It is also a good subject for hanging baskets. Try combining it with *Bidens ferulifolia*, brachyscome, calceolarias, diascias, and gazanias. Remove dead flower heads regularly to ensure continuous flowering. Propagate from seeds in spring under glass or from softwood cuttings in summer. Winter young plants in a cool greenhouse. Watch out for aphids.

Laurentia axillaris

	SPRING	SUMMER	FALL	WINTER	height (in)	spread (in)	min temp (°F)	moisture	sun/shade	colors
Laurentia axillaris	planting	flower	flower		12	12	41°	well drained	sun	Very free-flowering
L. axillaris Charm Series	planting	flower	flower		12	12	41°	well drained	sun	Very free-flowering
L. axillaris 'Fantasy Blue'	planting	flower	flower		12	12	41°	well drained	sun	Very free-flowering

Lavatera
Mallow

Lavatera trimestris 'Silver Cup'

***Lavatera trimestris* cultivars are hardy annuals with lobed leaves and flaring, trumpet-shaped flowers in shades of pink or white.**

Excellent for a cottage garden or modern mixed border, particularly in association with shrub roses, mallows also mix well with other annuals such as clarkia and *Salvia viridis* (annual clary sage). These plants also look good with gray-leafed plants such as lavenders and artemisias. The blooms last well when cut for flower arrangements. Protect plants from wind. Raise plants from seed in spring, under glass or in flowering positions. Watch out for leaf spot, stem rot, and rust.

	SPRING	SUMMER	FALL	WINTER	height (ft)	spread (ft)	min temp (°F)	moisture	sun/shade	colors
Lavatera trimestris 'Loveliness'	planting	flower			3	1½	1°	well drained	sun	Old variety but still popular
L. trimestris 'Mont Blanc'	planting	flower			1½	1	1°	well drained	sun	Deep green leaves
L. trimestris 'Silver Cup'	planting	flower			2½	1½	1°	well drained	sun	Large flowers

planting   flower   well drained   moist   wet

Leucanthemum
Shasta daisy

Leucanthemum x superbum cultivars are hardy herbaceous perennials, invaluable for their long display of white, single or double daisy flowers.

Leucanthemum x superbum 'Snowcap'

Vigorous plants, forming substantial clumps, they combine well with many other hardy perennials, particularly those with strong colors such as *Lychnis chalcedonica* (Maltese cross) and oriental poppies (*Papaver orientale*). The flowers are suitable for cutting. Provide supports for tall cultivars. Propagate by division in spring or fall. To keep plants young and vigorous, divide them every two to three years. Plants may be troubled by aphids, earwigs, leaf spot, slugs, and snails.

	SPRING	SUMMER	FALL	WINTER	height (ft)	spread (ft)	min temp (°F)	moisture	sun/shade	colors
Leucanthemum x superbum 'Esther Read'	🌱🌱🌱	●●●●	●🌱🌱		2	2	1°	💧	☀	Double flowers
L. x superbum 'Snowcap'	🌱🌱🌱	●●●●	●🌱🌱		1½	1½	1°	💧	☀	Single flowers
L. x superbum 'Wirral Supreme'	🌱🌱🌱	●●●●	●🌱🌱		3	2½	1°	💧	☀	Double flowers

Leucojum
Snowflake

These hardy bulbs, which are rather similar to snowdrops (Galanthus), have bell-shaped flowers, mainly in white, and strap-shaped or grassy foliage.

Snowflakes vary in size, the larger *L. aestivum* and *L. vernum* being suited to mixed borders, where they look good drifted informally among shrubs, or naturalized in grass, while the tiny *L. autumnale* is suitable for a rock garden. Propagate by division of clumps, either in spring immediately after flowering, or in fall, *L. autumnale* while dormant in summer. Leucojums may be attacked by narcissus bulb fly, slugs, and snails.

Leucojum aestivum 'Gravetye Giant'

	SPRING	SUMMER	FALL	WINTER	height (in)	spread (in)	min temp (°F)	moisture	sun/shade	colors
Leucojum aestivum	●●🌱		🌱🌱🌱		24	3	1°	💧	☀	Deep green foliage
L. aestivum 'Gravetye Giant'	●●🌱		🌱🌱🌱		36	4	1°	💧	☀	Vigorous
L. autumnale		🌱🌱🌱	●		4	2	1°	💧	☀	Grassy foliage
L. vernum	●🌱🌱		🌱🌱🌱		8	3	1°	💧	☀	Deep green foliage

☀ sunny   ☀ semi-shady   ● shady

Liatris
Gayfeather

The hardy herbaceous perennial *L. spicata* is valued for substantial spikes of pink or white flowers produced late in the season among clumps of grassy foliage. Liatris grows from swollen stems that look like corms.

The blooms of these plants, which attract bees, are suitable for cutting. Grow in mixed borders with ornamental grasses, especially *Stipa gigantea*, and with late-flowering perennials such as golden rod (solidago), asters, echinaceas, and rudbeckias. Gayfeather dislikes wet soil in winter. Propagate by dividing clumps in spring. Watch out for slugs and snails, which are partial to young foliage.

Liatris spicata

	SPRING	SUMMER	FALL	WINTER	height (ft)	spread (ft)	min temp (°F)	moisture	sun/shade	colors	
Liatris spicata	🗑🗑🗑	✹ ✹	✹		4	1½	1°	💧	☀	▨	Flowers open from top of spike
L. spicata 'Kobold'	🗑🗑🗑	✹ ✹	✹		1½	1	1°	💧	☀	■	Deep purple flower heads

Ligularia

Ligularia przewalskii

Hardy herbaceous perennials, ligularias are vigorous plants with large, rounded or lobed leaves and spikes of yellow or orange daisy-like flowers. They are excellent for moist spots in the garden, including the edge of woodland gardens, and are especially at home planted around pools or on stream banks.

Grow with shrubs in a mixed border, provided the soil is moist enough. Other good companions include rodgersias, hemerocallis, carex or sedges, waterside irises, and ferns. Ensure protection from wind. Propagate by division in spring. Slugs and snails are partial to the young foliage.

	SPRING	SUMMER	FALL	WINTER	height (ft)	spread (ft)	min temp (°F)	moisture	sun/shade	colors	
Ligularia dentata 'Desdemona'	🗑🗑🗑	✹ ✹	✹		3	3	1°	💧	☀	▨	Brown-flushed foliage, purple beneath
L. 'Gregynog Gold'	🗑🗑🗑	✹	✹		6	3	1°	💧	☀	▨	Large rounded leaves
L. przewalskii	🗑🗑🗑	✹			6	3	1°	💧	☀	□	Deeply cut hand-shaped leaves

🗑 *planting*   ✹ *flower*   💧 *well drained*   💧 *moist*   💧 *wet*

Lilium
Lily

A large group of hardy bulbs of diverse habit, the flowers may be shaped like a Turkscap (with reflexed petals), or they may be trumpet-, funnel-, bowl-, or star-shaped. Many lilies have fragrant blooms. Lilies are classified into nine divisions.

Many species and hybrids are easy to grow (including all those described here), while others are more challenging. Lilies are superb in woodland gardens or shrub borders, in combination with rhododendrons, pieris, Japanese maples, magnolias, and other shrubs. They prefer their roots shaded by low-growing shrubs and woodland perennials but like their heads in the sun. Lilies are also good for patio tubs, again with their root area shaded. The flowers are suitable for cutting. Lilies like humus-rich, acid to neutral soil, although some thrive in alkaline soils. If any are known to be stem rooting (producing roots at the base of the stems), plant these deeper than normal, at least three times the height of the bulb. Propagate from offsets or bulblets when dormant. Pests and diseases include aphids, bulb aphids, bulb rot, gray mold, slugs, snails, and viruses.

Lilium 'Star Gazer'

Flowers

L

Lilium 'Enchantment' *Lilium* 'Magic Pink' *Lilium* 'Red Night'

	SPRING	SUMMER	FALL	WINTER	height (in)	spread (in)	min temp (°F)	moisture	sun/shade	colors	
Lilium candidum (Species)		●	✿ ✿ ✿		72	12	1°	💧💧	☼	☐	Trumpet-shaped flowers.
L. 'Casa Blanca' (Oriental hybrid)		●	✿ ✿ ✿		48	6	1°	💧💧	☼	☐	Bowl-shaped, fragrant flowers
L. 'Connecticut King' (Asiatic hybrid)	●		✿ ✿ ✿		36	6	1°	💧💧	☼	▨	Star-shaped flowers
L. 'Enchantment' (Asiatic hybrid)	✸		✿ ✿ ✿		24	6	1°	💧	☼	▨	Star-shaped flowers
L. lancifolium (Species)		● ✸	✿ ✿		60	6	1°	💧	☼	▨	Stem rooting; turkscap flowers
L. 'Magic Pink' (Oriental hybrid)		●	✿ ✿ ✿		48	4	1°	💧💧	☼	☐	Bowl-shaped, slightly fragrant flowers
L. 'Red Night' (Asiatic hybrid)		● ●	✿ ✿ ✿		36	12	1°	💧💧	☼	▨	Unscented, cup-shaped flowers
L. speciosum (Species)		● ✸	✿ ✿		60	12	1°	💧💧	☼	▯	Stem rooting; turkscap flowers; very fragrant
L. 'Star Gazer' (Oriental hybrid)		✸	✿ ✿ ✿		48	6	1°	💧💧	☼	▰	Star-shaped flowers

☼ *sunny* ☼ *semi-shady* ● *shady*

Limnanthes
Poached egg plant

A hardy annual, *Limnanthes douglasii*, the best species, has flowers reminiscent of a poached egg (hence the common name), which attract bees.

Limnanthes douglasii is a very attractive and cheerful plant for mixed borders, and makes a fine companion for nigella (love-in-a-mist), echiums (viper's bugloss), signet marigolds (tagetes), and dwarf grasses such as *Festuca glauca* (blue fescue). This is also a good annual for sowing in rock or scree gardens. Propagate from seed sown in flowering positions during spring or fall. Put cloches over fall sowings in winter. Limnanthes also self-sows prolifically. It is not troubled by pests or diseases.

Limnanthes douglasii

Limonium
Statice

Limonium sinuatum cultivar

***Limonium sinuatum* cultivars are frost-hardy perennials that are usually grown as annuals. The heads of brightly colored flowers, which are produced on winged stems, are suitable for cutting and drying.**

Grow in a mixed border with eryngiums (sea holly), echinops (globe thistles), *Gypsophila paniculata* cultivars, osteospermums, gazanias, and argyranthemums, or in rows on the vegetable plot especially for cutting. Statice is particularly recommended for seaside gardens and it thrives in sandy soils. Propagate from seed sown in early spring under glass. Plants may become infected with powdery mildew.

	SPRING	SUMMER	FALL	WINTER	height (ft)	spread (ft)	min temp (°F)	moisture	sun/shade	colors	
Limonium sinuatum Forever Series	🌱🌱🌱	●●●●	●		1½	1	25°	💧	☀	▨	Dense flower spikes
L. sinuatum Fortress Series	🌱🌱🌱	●●●●	●		2	1	25°	💧	☀	▥	Branching habit
L. sinuatum Sunburst Series	🌱🌱🌱	●●●●	●		2½	1	25°	💧	☀	▧	Creates a "warm" effect

🌱 planting   ● flower   💧 well drained   💧 moist   💧 wet

Linaria
Toadflax

Linaria maroccana cultivars are dainty, hardy annuals with masses of small, two-lipped flowers in a wide range of bright colors. Grow toadflax at the front of mixed borders or in gravel areas.

Also try this plant in gaps in paving. It is a good choice for cottage gardens and can look charming in window boxes and patio tubs. Suitable companions include border pinks and carnations (dianthus), and silver- or gray-foliage plants such as artemisias, catmints (nepeta), and lavenders. Especially suitable for sandy soils. Propagate from seed in spring, sowing in flowering positions. Toadflax also self-sows prolifically. Watch out for aphids and powdery mildew.

	SPRING	SUMMER	FALL	WINTER	height (in)	spread (in)	min temp (°F)	moisture	sun/shade	colors	
Linaria maroccana 'Fairy Bouquet'	🌱🌱🌱	●●●			8	6	1°	💧💧	☀		Very free-flowering
L. maroccana 'Fairy Lights'	🌱🌱🌱	●●●			12	6	1°	💧💧	☀		Contrasting white centers
L. marocanna 'Northern Lights'	🌱🌱🌱	●●●			15	6	1°	💧💧	☀		Includes bicolors

Liriope
Lilyturf

A hardy evergreen perennial, lilyturf grows from tuberous roots. Spikes of pale violet or white flowers appear from clumps of grassy foliage late in the year.

An excellent plant for shady places in a woodland garden or shrub border, planted in a large mass it makes fine ground cover. Good companions include other ground cover plants such as ivies (hedera), *Pachysandra terminalis*, and periwinkles (vinca). Winter and spring bulbs such as snowdrops (galanthus) and dwarf narcissus also look good growing through the foliage. Lilyturf prefers acid or lime-free soil. Propagate by division in spring. Slugs and snails are partial to young foliage.

Liriope muscari 'John Burch'

	SPRING	SUMMER	FALL	WINTER	height (ft)	spread (ft)	min temp (°F)	moisture	sun/shade	colors	
Liriope muscari	🌱🌱🌱		●●●		1	1½	1°	💧💧	●		Deep green foliage
L. muscari 'John Burch'	🌱🌱🌱		●●●		1	1½	1°	💧💧	●		Gold-variegated leaves

☀ sunny   ☀ semi-shady   ● shady

Lobelia

The most popular lobelias are _L. erinus_ cultivars, grown as half-hardy annuals. Low bushy or trailing plants, they are used for summer bedding, often for edging beds, and are also good for containers—the trailing kinds are especially suitable for hanging baskets.

These plants produce masses of tiny two-lipped flowers over a very long period and combine well with many other summer bedding plants including begonias, pelargoniums, marigolds (tagetes), and scarlet salvias. The traditional color is blue, but various other colors are available. Very different in habit are the hardy herbaceous perennials, ideal for planting at the edge of a pool, or in a mixed border if the soil is sufficiently moist, where they look best in

Lobelia erinus 'Mrs Clibran'

Lobelia erinus 'Crystal Palace'

Lobelia erinus 'Cascade Mixed'

combination with shrubs and hostas. These include _L. cardinalis_ (cardinal flower) and _L._ 'Queen Victoria', neither very long-lived; _L. x speciosa_ cultivars, often grown as annuals; and _L. siphilitica_ (blue cardinal flower), which looks good in a woodland garden or shrub border. Feed annuals fortnightly with low-nitrogen liquid fertilizer when well established. Raise annuals from seed under glass in late winter. Propagate perennials by division in spring, or from stem cuttings in summer. Watch out for slugs and snails.

Flowers

L

	SPRING	SUMMER	FALL	WINTER	height (in)	spread (in)	min temp (°F)	moisture	sun/shade	colors	
Lobelia cardinalis	planting	flower	flower		36	12	1°	moist	sun		Bronze-flushed foliage
L. erinus 'Cambridge Blue'	planting	flower	flower	planting	6	6	34°	moist	sun/shade		Compact bushy habit
L. erinus Cascade Series	planting	flower	flower	planting	6	12	34°	moist	sun/shade		Trailing
L. erinus 'Crystal Palace'	planting	flower	flower	planting	6	6	34°	moist	sun/shade		Compact bushy habit
L. erinus Fountain Series	planting	flower	flower	planting	6	12	34°	moist	sun/shade		Trailing
L. erinus 'Mrs Clibran'	planting	flower	flower	planting	6	6	34°	moist	sun/shade		Compact bushy habit
L. erinus Riviera Series	planting	flower	flower	planting	6	6	34°	moist	sun/shade		Compact bushy habit
L. 'Queen Victoria'	planting	flower	flower		36	12	1°	moist	sun/shade		Beetroot-colored foliage
L. siphilitica	planting	flower	flower		36	12	1°	moist	sun/shade		Pale green foliage
L. x speciosa Fan Series	planting	flower	flower	planting	24	8	1°	moist	sun/shade		Bronze-flushed or deep green foliage

planting   flower   well drained   moist   wet

Lobularia
Sweet alyssum

Cultivars of _L. maritima_ are low, carpeting hardy annuals covered with heads of small, four-petaled, fragrant flowers. Mainly white, other colors are available.

These plants are used for summer bedding, often for edging beds, and are good in containers, including hanging baskets. Traditionally combined with bedding lobelia, sweet alyssum associates well with many other summer bedding plants, and is especially useful as a foil for strong or "hot" colors. Good for seaside gardens. Regularly trim off dead flowers with shears. Propagate from seed in spring, under glass or in flowering positions. Watch out for slugs and snails.

Lobularia maritima cultivar

	SPRING	SUMMER	FALL	WINTER	height (in)	spread (in)	min temp (°F)	moisture	sun/shade	colors	
Lobularia maritima 'Carpet of Snow'					4	12	1°				Good ground cover
L. maritima Easter Bonnet Series					4	8	1°				Early into flower
L. maritima 'Oriental Night'					4	8	1°				Compact habit
L. maritima 'Rosie O'Day'					4	8	1°				Compact habit
L. maritima 'Snow Crystals'					8)(	12	1°				Dome-shaped habit

Lunaria
Honesty

Lunaria annua is grown as a hardy biennial while _L. rediviva_ is a hardy herbaceous perennial. Both produce heads of four-petaled flowers above somewhat heart-shaped, saw-edged leaves.

Lunaria rediviva

The translucent silvery or buff seed pods that follow the flowers are suitable for drying. Both species are ideal for a wild or woodland garden but also look at home in a mixed border planted around shrubs, and among perennials such as hostas and astilbes. Lunaria is also a good choice for cottage gardens. Raise plants from seed in late spring in a nursery bed and divide perennials in spring. Both self-sow. Prone to virus. Plants showing symptoms of virus should be pulled up and discarded as there is no cure.

Lunaria annua 'Variegata'

	SPRING	SUMMER	FALL	WINTER	height (ft)	spread (ft)	min temp (°F)	moisture	sun/shade	colors	
Lunaria annua 'Variegata'					3	1	1°				White-variegated leaves
L. rediviva					3	1	1°				Scented flowers

☼ sunny   ☀ semi-shady   ● shady

Lupinus
Lupine

These hybrid lupines are hardy herbaceous perennials producing fat spikes of flowers above clumps of hand-shaped leaves.

These are virtually "essential" plants for the mixed border, invaluable for combining with other early flowering perennials such as oriental poppies (*Papaver orientale*), peonies, bearded irises, and delphiniums. Ornamental onions (allium) are also good companions, as are old and modern shrub roses. Lupines prefer acid, sandy soil. The perennial hybrid lupines are best propagated from basal cuttings in spring. Problems include leaf spot, powdery mildew, slugs, snails, and viruses.

Lupinus 'The Page'

Lupinus 'Polar Princess'

	SPRING	SUMMER	FALL	WINTER	height (ft)	spread (ft)	min temp (°F)	moisture	sun/shade	colors	
Lupinus 'Chandelier'	planting	flower			3	2½	1°	well drained	sun		Long flowering period
L. 'Noble Maiden'	planting	flower			3	2½	1°	well drained	sun		Long flowering period
L. 'Polar Princess'	planting	flower			3	2½	1°	well drained	sun		Long flowering period
L. 'The Governor'	planting	flower			3	2½	1°	well drained	sun		Long flowering period
L. 'The Page'	planting	flower			3	2½	1°	well drained	sun		Long flowering period

Lychnis

Lychnis coronaria

A diverse genus of hardy plants, lychnis often have brilliant or strongly colored, star-shaped or flat, lobed flowers.

L. chalcedonica (Jerusalem or Maltese cross) is a popular herbaceous perennial and can be used to create dazzling combinations, particularly with flat-headed achilleas or day lilies (hemerocallis). *L. coronaria* (rose campion) is a short-lived perennial raised regularly from seed. It looks good with other silver-leafed perennials such as artemisias, and with shrub roses. *L. flos-cuculi* (ragged robin) is a herbaceous perennial for the woodland or wild garden. Propagate in spring, from seed under cover, by division or from basal cuttings. Watch out for slugs and snails.

	SPRING	SUMMER	FALL	WINTER	height (ft)	spread (ft)	min temp (°F)	moisture	sun/shade	colors	
Lychnis chalcedonica	planting	flower flower flower			3	1	1°	moist	sun		Provide supports
L. coronaria	planting	flower			2¾	1	1°	well drained	sun		Silver-gray foliage
L. flos-cuculi	planting flower	flower			2½	2	1°	moist	part sun		Deeply cut petals

🌱 *planting* ● *flower* 🖤 *well drained* 🖤 *moist* 🖤 *wet*

Lysimachia

Lysimachias are hardy herbaceous perennials, except for *L. nummularia* (creeping Jenny) which is evergreen.

The latter is a prostrate groundcover plant that can become invasive, but the others are border plants with spikes of starry or cup-shaped flowers. Grow creeping Jenny among shrubs in a woodland garden or mixed border—it looks good combined with ajugas. The taller perennials are suitable for mixed borders, poolside planting, or wild gardens, in combination with hemerocallis (daylilies), ligularias, and rodgersias. Propagate by division in spring. Watch out for slugs and snails.

Lysimachia nummularia

Lysimachia punctata

L

M

Flowers

	SPRING	SUMMER	FALL	WINTER	height (in)	spread (in)	min temp (°F)	moisture	sun/shade	colors	
Lysimachia ciliata 'Firecracker'	🖐🖐🖐	☀			30	24	1°	💧💧	☀	☐	Reddish-brown foliage
L. clethroides	🖐🖐🖐	☀			36	24	1°	💧💧	☀	☐	Curved flower spikes
L. nummularia	🖐🖐🖐	●●●			2	36	1°	💧💧	◐	☐	Very vigorous habit
L. punctata	🖐🖐🖐	☀			36	24	1°	💧💧	☀	☐	Vigorous habit

Malcolmia
Virginian stock

Malcolmia maritima

A hardy annual, Virginian stock bears a long succession of scented, four-petaled flowers. Grow at the front of mixed borders, in cottage gardens, in cracks in paving, or in a gravel area.

This annual thrives in coastal gardens. Grow with other hardy annuals, or with annual ornamental grasses. Propagate from seed in spring, sowing in flowering positions. Sow every five or six weeks to ensure a long period of flowering. Plants also self-seed. Generally no problems from pests or diseases, but this annual dislikes very warm, humid weather.

☀ *sunny*　◐ *semi-shady*　● *shady*

Matthiola
Stock

The hardy *M. incana* cultivars, grown as annuals or biennials for bedding or containers, are valued for their spikes of fragrant flowers that are good for cutting. Ideal for mixed borders, these plants are also at home in cottage gardens.

Brompton stocks and the Legacy Series are grown as biennials; the Cinderella Series and Ten Week stocks are treated as annuals. *M. longipetala* subsp. *bicornis* (night-scented stock) is a hardy annual, useful for filling gaps in borders. All prefer alkaline soil. Sow annuals in early spring under glass. Biennials are sown in mid-summer in a cold frame or seed bed, planted out in the fall and protected with cloches, or wintered in a cold frame and planted out in spring.

Sow night-scented stock in flowering positions in spring. Watch out for aphids, club root (see Erysimum, page 76), gray mold, and virus.

Matthiola incana Brompton Mixed

	SPRING	SUMMER	FALL	WINTER	height (in)	spread (in)	min temp (°F)	moisture	sun/shade	colors
Matthiola incana Brompton Mixed	planting · flower	planting · flower · flower	flower · planting · planting		18	12	1°	well drained	sun	Double or single fragrant flowers
M. incana Cinderella Series	planting planting planting	flower flower flower			10	8	1°	well drained	sun	Double flowers
M. incana Legacy Series	planting planting planting	planting flower flower	planting planting planting		18	12	1°	well drained	sun	Double flowers
M. incana Ten Week Mixed	planting planting planting	flower flower flower			12	8	1°	well drained	sun	Fragrant double flowers
M. longipetala subsp. *bicornis*	planting planting planting	flower flower flower			12	8	1°	well drained	sun	Night-scented

planting · flower · well drained · moist · wet

108

Mimulus
Monkey flower

Various hardy hybrids are generally grown as annuals for summer bedding or display in containers. They have brilliantly colored, tubular, flaring flowers, often spotted with a contrasting color.

These plants also look good planted in the moist soil beside a pool, say with hostas and astilbes. *M. cardinalis* (scarlet monkey flower) is a hardy herbaceous perennial for the poolside or bog garden. All these plants like soil with a high humus content. Water well in dry weather. When growing in containers such as patio tubs and window boxes, make sure that the potting mix does not dry out, as this will curtail growth and flowering. Raise annuals from seed in spring under glass. Propagate perennials in spring, by division or from softwood cuttings. Watch out for powdery mildew, slugs, and snails.

Mimulus 'Puck'

	SPRING	SUMMER	FALL	WINTER	height (in)	spread (in)	min temp (°F)	moisture	sun/shade	colors	
Mimulus 'Calypso'					8	12	1°				Flowers often spotted and bicolored
M. cardinalis					36	24	1°				Pale green foliage
M. Magic Series					8	12	1°				Small flowers, often bicolored
M. 'Puck'					8	12	1°				Apricot blush

Miscanthus

These hardy herbaceous perennial grasses are valued as much for their foliage as for their airy panicles of flowers produced late in the season.

The dead foliage and flowers remain attractive through winter. Miscanthus are great for combining with a wide range of hardy perennials in mixed borders, including late-flowering kinds, and with shrubs, especially those with autumnal leaf tints or berries. They also look good in gravel areas and beside pools. Propagate by division in spring. Not troubled by pests or diseases.

Miscanthus sinensis 'Silberfeder'

	SPRING	SUMMER	FALL	WINTER	height (ft)	spread (ft)	min temp (°F)	moisture	sun/shade	colors	
Miscanthus sinensis 'Rotsilber'					4	3	1°				Leaves have central white stripe
M. sinensis 'Silberfeder'					8	4	1°				Flowers freely

☼ sunny   ☼ semi-shady   ● shady

Molucella

Bells of Ireland

Molucella laevis

A half-hardy annual, *M. laevis* has somewhat inconspicuous flowers, each surrounded by a large, light green calyx. When the seeds form, these calyces become papery and at this stage the seed heads are good for drying.

Molucella is suitable for a sunny mixed border and looks good combined with dwarf ornamental grasses or with shrub roses. Also combines well with nigella (love-in-a-mist) and *Nemophila menziesii* (baby blue-eyes).

Raise plants from seed in spring under glass, or in flowering positions toward the end of spring. This plant is not troubled by pests or diseases.

Monarda

Bergamot

Hardy herbaceous perennials, monardas have aromatic foliage and whorled heads of tubular flowers, attractive to bees, on stiff, upright stems.

These plants are particularly suited to prairie-style borders mixed with ornamental grasses such as miscanthus, and with later-flowering perennials including *Aster* x *frikartii* 'Mönch', rudbeckias, echinacea, helianthus, and golden rods (solidago).

Monarda 'Beauty of Cobham'

Monarda 'Violet Queen'

Bergamot does not like very wet soil in winter or summer drought. Propagate in spring, by division or from basal cuttings. Powdery mildew, slugs, and snails are the main problems, although mildew-resistant cultivars are becoming available.

	SPRING	SUMMER	FALL	WINTER	height (ft)	spread (ft)	min temp (°F)	moisture	sun/shade	colors	
Monarda 'Beauty of Cobham'	planting planting planting	flower flower flower	flower		3	2	1°	moist	sun		Leaves flushed purple
M. 'Cambridge Scarlet'	planting planting planting	flower flower flower	flower		3	2	1°	moist	sun		Old, but still a good cultivar
M. 'Croftway Pink'	planting planting planting	flower flower flower	flower		3	2	1°	moist	sun		Old, but still a good cultivar
M. 'Violet Queen'	planting planting planting	flower flower flower	flower		3	2	1°	moist	sun		Good modern cultivar

planting | flower | well drained | moist | wet

Muscari
Grape hyacinth

Grape hyacinths are hardy dwarf bulbs. *M. armeniacum* has grassy foliage and short, stumpy spikes of tubular flowers. It is a particularly robust bulb and spreads quickly, hence its selection here.

As muscari will take partial shade, plant it around shrubs in mixed borders, in bold groups or drifts, with other small spring bulbs such as miniature narcissus and erythroniums. This grape hyacinth is also suitable for a woodland garden, for naturalizing in grass, and for planting on rock gardens. Propagate by splitting up and replanting established clumps when dormant in summer or fall. Apart from possible virus, it is free from problems.

Muscari armeniacum

Myosotis
Forget-me-not

Myosotis sylvatica cultivars are hardy dwarf biennials producing a haze of tiny flowers, principally in shades of blue, in spring. They are used mainly in spring bedding schemes, particularly as a carpet for bedding tulips, and also combine well with wallflowers (Erysimum) and double daisies (Bellis).

Similar combinations could be used in patio containers and window boxes. Forget-me-nots are delightful when planted in informal drifts around spring-flowering deciduous shrubs, such as Forsythia or Spiraea, or in woodland gardens. Raise plants from seed sown in an outdoor seed bed in early summer and plant out in the fall. Will also self-sow freely. Watch out for powdery mildew, slugs, and snails.

Myosotis 'Royal Blue'

Myosotis sylvatica 'Blue Ball'

	SPRING	SUMMER	FALL	WINTER	height (in)	spread (in)	min temp (°F)	moisture	sun/shade	colors	
Myosotis sylvatica 'Blue Ball'	● ● ●	●			6	6	1°	◆◆	☀	▨	Very compact habit
M. sylvatica 'Royal Blue'	● ● ●	●			12	8	1°	◆◆	☀	▨	Taller than most
M. sylvatica 'Spring Symphony Mixed'	● ● ●	●			8	8	1°	◆◆	☀	▥	Very compact habit

☼ sunny   ☀ semi-shady   ● shady

M

Flowers

111

Narcissus
Daffodil

One of the classic heralds of spring is swathes of golden daffodils, growing anywhere from coastal meadows to the foothills of mountains. There are now more than 50 species of narcissus and thousands of cultivars have been developed.

Daffodils are among the most popular of hardy bulbs. Variable in habit, they range from miniature species and hybrids to tall cultivars with large flowers. Leaves may be strap-shaped or, in miniature species, somewhat grassy. Basically, the flowers consist of a trumpet- or cup-shaped corona surrounded by flat or reflexed petals (perianth segments).

Daffodils are classified into 12 divisions (indicated in brackets in the table opposite). Gardeners are not too concerned with divisions, but it is interesting to note that the most popular are: the Trumpet daffodils with a large, trumpet-shaped corona; Large-cupped, with a large, cup-shaped corona; Double, with double flowers; Cyclamineus, with reflexed petals and long corona; Triandrus, Jonquilla, and Tazetta with clusters of small flowers; and Split Corona, with a flat corona that is deeply split (often likened to a fried egg).

Narcissus 'Dove Wings'

Narcissus 'Geranium'

Narcissus Tête-à-Tête'

Daffodils have many uses, but they generally look best when they are grown informally, rather than in formal bedding schemes. For example, plant generous groups or drifts among shrubs in a mixed border or woodland garden. Plant them in a lawn under deciduous trees. Grow taller kinds in long grass. Miniature daffodils are suitable for rock gardens, for grouping around small shrubs, or even for naturalizing in short grass.

🖉 planting　　☀ flower　　💧 well drained　　💧 moist　　💧 wet

For the most delightful effects with these flowers, grow daffodils with spring-flowering trees and shrubs where possible, such as flowering cherries and forsythia. Daffodils are also suitable for containers such as patio tubs and window boxes. They make particularly good cut flowers. If the soil is light or you are planting in grass, set the bulbs slightly more deeply. Acid soil is best for Cyclamineus and Triandrus daffodils, and slightly alkaline for Jonquilla and Tazetta cultivars.

After flowering remove dead heads and feed weekly with a high-potash liquid fertilizer until the foliage starts yellowing. Never remove foliage until it is completely dead. Lift and divide congested clumps when dormant. Propagate by removing offsets when dormant. Daffodils are prone to bulb rot, narcissus bulb fly, slugs, snails, and viruses. Contact with the sap of daffodils may irritate skin.

Narcissus 'February Gold'

Narcissus 'Beryl' *Narcissus* 'Minnow' *Narcissus* 'Actaea'

	SPRING	SUMMER	FALL	WINTER	height (in)	spread (in)	min temp (°F)	moisture	sun/shade	colors	
Narcissus 'Actaea' (Poeticus)	●		🌱🌱🌱		18	6	1°	💧💧	☀		Very fragrant
N. 'Belcanto' (Split corona)	●		🌱🌱🌱		18	6	1°	💧💧	☀		Large flowers
N. 'Beryl' (Cyclamineus)	●		🌱🌱🌱		8	3	1°	💧💧	☀		Prefers cool conditions
N. 'Bobbysoxer' (Jonquilla)	●		🌱🌱🌱		6	3	1°	💧💧	☀		Two flowers to each stem
N. 'Dove Wings' (Cyclamineus)	●		🌱🌱🌱		12	3	1°	💧	☀		Prefers cool conditions
N. 'February Gold' (Cyclamineus)	●		🌱🌱🌱		12	3	1°	💧💧	☀		Prefers cool conditions
N. 'Geranium' (Tazetta)	●		🌱🌱🌱		15	3	1°	💧💧	☀		Fragrant flowers
N. 'Golden Ducat' (Double)	●		🌱🌱🌱		15	6	1°	💧💧	☀		Large flowers
N. 'Ice Follies' (Large-cupped)	●		🌱🌱🌱		15	6	1°	💧💧	☀		Robust grower
N. 'Minnow' (Tazetta)	●		🌱🌱🌱		6	3	1°	💧💧	☀		Robust habit
N. 'Tête à Tête' (Miscellaneous)	●		🌱🌱🌱		6	3	1°	💧💧	☀		Several flowers per stem

☼ sunny   ☀ semi-shady   ● shady

Nemesia

Nemesia strumosa cultivars are half-hardy annuals with heads of small, two-lipped flowers in a wide range of bright colors, often bicolored. Used for summer bedding, patio containers, and window boxes, they should be mass planted for best effect.

Nemesias do not need other plants associated with them as they make a fine show on their own, but if desired, try them with *Salvia farinacea* cultivars, *Nemophila menziesii* (baby blue-eyes), and *Scaevola*

aemula. Best in slightly acid soil, nemesias dislike hot dry conditions, so keep them cool and water as necessary. Raise plants from seed in spring under glass. Black root rot and foot rot may be troublesome.

Nemesia strumosa cultivar

Nemesia strumosa 'Sundrops Mixed'

	SPRING	SUMMER	FALL	WINTER	height (in)	spread (in)	min temp (°F)	moisture	sun/shade	colors	
Nemesia strumosa Carnival Series	🌱🌱🌱	●●●			8	6	34°	💧	☀		Compact habit of growth
N. strumosa 'KLM'	🌱🌱🌱	●●●			10	6	34°	💧	☀		Flowers have yellow throat
N. strumosa 'Sundrops Mixed'	🌱🌱🌱	●●●			10	6	34°	💧	☀		Early flowering

Nemophila
Baby blue-eyes

Nemophila menziesii, the best species, is a small hardy annual with pinnate grayish-green leaves and shallow bowl-shaped flowers in summer. Suitable for mixed borders, patio containers, and window boxes, nemophila is ideal for combining with more strongly colored annuals, such as nemesias.

Other effective companions are *Argyranthemum* 'Jamaica Primrose' and *Limnanthes douglasii* (poached egg plant). Seeds can be sown in spring or fall in flowering positions. Once introduced to a garden, plants will increase by self-sowing. Apart from aphids, there are no problems from pests or diseases.

Nemophila menziesii 'Snowstorm'

🌱 *planting*   ● *flower*   💧 *well drained*   💧 *moist*   💧 *wet*

Nepeta
Catmint

Nepeta x faassenii

Nepeta 'Six Hills Giant'

Hardy herbaceous perennials, the catmints have aromatic foliage and spikes of two-lipped flowers, mainly in blue and purple shades, over a long period. The blooms attract bees. Grow nepeta in a mixed border, including cottage-garden borders.

Catmints combine particularly well with roses of all kinds (old and modern), and with geraniums, peonies, and lupines. After flowering, trim plants lightly with shears to encourage more blooms to follow and compact growth. Propagate by division in spring or fall. Watch out for powdery mildew, slugs, and snails.

	SPRING	SUMMER	FALL	WINTER	height (ft)	spread (ft)	min temp (°F)	moisture	sun/shade	colors
Nepeta x faassenii					1½	1½	1°		sunny	Aromatic grayish leaves
N. nervosa					2	1	1°		sunny	Aromatic grayish leaves
N. sibirica 'Souvenir d'André Chaudron'					1½	1½	1°		sunny	Aromatic grayish leaves
N. 'Six Hills Giant'					3	2	1°		sunny	Aromatic grayish leaves

Nerine

A hardy bulb valued for its late flowering, *Nerine bowdenii* produces heads of lily-like blooms with reflexed petals, the wide strap-like leaves appearing after the flowers.

The blooms are good for cutting. The best place to grow nerine is at the foot of a wall that receives plenty of sun, in combination with schizostylis and fall-flowering sedums. Plant shallowly, with tips just below the surface. In areas prone to hard frosts keep the root area covered with dry leaves or straw for the winter. Apply a general-purpose fertilizer in spring. Propagate by dividing clumps when dormant in summer. Watch out for slugs and snails.

Nerine bowdenii

☀ *sunny*   ◐ *semi-shady*   ● *shady*

Nicotiana
Tobacco plant

Nicotianas are grown as half-hardy annuals and produce a long display of tubular or widely flaring flowers, which open mainly in the evening. However, some, including the _N. x sanderae_ cultivars and 'Lime Green', open in the daytime.

These are ideal for mass planting in summer bedding schemes where they combine well with many other bedders including verbenas, petunias, _Cosmos bipinnatus_, _Salvia farinacea_, and pelargoniums. The larger _N. alata_ and _N. sylvestris_ are effective in subtropical bedding schemes, with foliage plants such as cannas. Provide supports for tall plants. Raise plants from seed under cover in spring. Watch out for aphids, gray mold, and viruses.

	SPRING	SUMMER	FALL	WINTER	height (ft)	spread (ft)	min temp (°F)	moisture	sun/shade	colors	
Nicotiana alata (syn. _N. affinis_)	planting	flower			5	1½	34°	well drained	sun/part		Night-scented
_N._ 'Lime Green'	planting	flower			2	1	34°	well drained	sun/part		Unusual color
_N._ x _sanderae_ Domino Series	planting	flower			1½	1	34°	well drained	sun/part		Flowers face upward
_N._ x _sanderae_ Havana Series	planting	flower			1	1	34°	well drained	sun/part		Compact habit of growth
_N._ x _sanderae_ Merlin Series	planting	flower			1	1	34°	well drained	sun/part		Ideal for containers
_N._ x _sanderae_ Nicki Series	planting	flower			1½	1	34°	well drained	sun/part		Fragrant flowers
_N._ x _sanderae_ 'Sensation Mixed'	planting	flower			2½	1	34°	well drained	sun/part		Fragrant flowers
N. sylvestris	planting	flower			5	2	34°	well drained	sun/part		Fragrant; flowers do not open in full sun

Nigella
Love-in-a-mist

Nigella damascena is a hardy annual with feathery bright green foliage and flattish flowers, mainly in blue shades but also in other colors, with a ruff of foliage. Grow love-in-a-mist in a mixed border with other annuals such as calendulas (English marigolds) and poppies (papaver), together with annual grasses.

Nigella damascena 'Persian Jewels'

The flowers are good for cutting and the balloon-like seed pods can be dried for winter arrangements. Raise plants from seed sown in their flowering positions. Sown in the fall, they will flower earlier in the following year, but cover the young plants with cloches over the winter. Alternatively, sow in spring for later flowering. Love-in-a-mist is not troubled by pests or diseases.

	SPRING	SUMMER	FALL	WINTER	height (in)	spread (in)	min temp (°F)	moisture	sun/shade	colors	
Nigella damascena 'Miss Jekyll'	planting	flower	planting		18	8	1°	well drained	sun		Good old cultivar
N. damascena 'Persian Jewels'	planting	flower	planting		15	8	1°	well drained	sun		Good range of modern colors

planting · flower | well drained · moist · wet

Flowers

Nymphaea
Waterlily

Waterlilies are the most popular flowering aquatics for garden pools. Those described here are hardy herbaceous perennials. Waterlilies have rounded leaves that float on the water, and they produce somewhat star-shaped or bowl-shaped flowers just above the surface.

Some waterlilies are vigorous and spreading, suited only to large pools and lakes, but the ones described are more restrained and suitable for medium to small

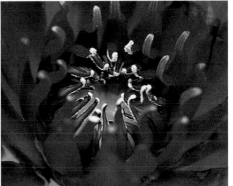

Nymphaea 'Escarboucle'

Nymphaea 'James Brydon'

Nymphaea tetragora syn.pygmaea

pools. *N.* 'Pygmaea Helvola' is ideal for minipools. Waterlilies are planted in plastic aquatic baskets, using heavy loam or commercial aquatic mix, the surface covered with a layer of pea gravel. Stand the basket on bricks so that the crown of the plant is just under the water, and

gradually lower the basket as the plant grows by removing bricks until the crown is covered with 6–24in (15–60cm) or more of water according to plant size (the larger the plant, the deeper the water). Propagate by division in spring. Waterlilies are prone to leaf spot and root rot.

	SPRING	SUMMER	FALL	WINTER	height (in)	spread (in)	min temp (°F)	moisture	sun/shade	colors	
Nymphaea 'Escarboucle'	🌱 🌱 🌱	◉ ◉ ◉			24	60	1°		☼	■	Good for medium to large pool
N. 'James Brydon'	🌱 🌱 🌱	◉ ◉ ◉			18	48	1°		☼	▨	Good for medium to large pool
N. 'Pygmaea Helvola'	🌱 🌱 🌱	◉ ◉ ◉			6	15	25°		☼	□	Good for mini- to small pool

☼ *sunny*   ☼ *semi-shady*   ● *shady*

Oenothera
Sundrops

Hardy herbaceous perennials, these sundrops have large, showy, bowl-shaped, yellow flowers over a long period. Individual flowers last about one day.

O. fruticosa is suitable for a mixed border, combined with shrubs such as cistus, lavenders and rosemary (rosmarinus), and ornamental grasses including *Stipa gigantea*.

Cultivars of *O. speciosa* also combine well with ornamental grasses in a border. Sundrops are especially suited to poor soils and are intolerant of very wet soil in winter. Propagate in spring, by division or from softwood cuttings. Watch out for black root rot, leaf spot, powdery mildew, and attention from slugs and snails.

Oenothera speciosa 'Siskiyou'

	SPRING	SUMMER	FALL	WINTER	height (ft)	spread (ft)	min temp (°F)	moisture	sun/shade	colors	
Oenothera fruticosa 'Fyrverkeri' ('Fireworks')	🌱 🌱	● ● ● ●			1½	1	1°	💧	☀	☐	Foliage flushed with brown
O. speciosa 'Siskiyou'	🌱 🌱	● ● ●	●		1	1	1°	💧	☀	⬛	Neat bushy habit

Osteospermum

Mainly evergreen half-hardy to hardy subshrubs and perennials generally grown as annuals, osteospermums are dwarf bushy plants producing masses of daisy-like flowers over a very long period.

The flowers come in a range of colors. Osteospermums are now firmly established as major summer bedding plants and they are excellent in patio containers and window boxes. Bold groups at the front of mixed borders are also effective. Attractive combinations can be created with many other summer bedding plants, including argyranthemums in contrasting colors, brachyscome, diascias, dimorphotheca,

Osteopernum 'Pink whirls'

Osteospermum 'Sunny Alex'

Flowers

O

🌱 *planting*　　● *flower*　　💧 *well drained*　　💧 *moist*　　💧 *wet*

felicia, gazanias, nemophila, pelargoniums, tagetes (marigolds), verbenas, and foliage plants that are used for bedding such as *Aeonium* 'Zwartkop' and *Plectranthus argentatus*. Deadhead plants on a regular basis to ensure continuous flowering.

Propagate from semi-ripe cuttings in late summer, winter young plants under glass and plant out in the following spring when frosts are over. Sow seeds under glass in spring. Watch out for aphids, otherwise free from problems.

	SPRING	SUMMER	FALL	WINTER	height (ft)	spread (ft)	min temp (F)	moisture	sun/shade	colors
Osteospermum 'Buttermilk'					2	2	34°		☀	Deep blue center
O. jucundum					1	2	25°		☀	Purplish center
O. 'Silver Sparkler'					2	2	34°		☀	Purple center; variegated leaves
O. 'Sunny Alex'					1½	2	34°		☀	Good modern cultivar
O. 'Weetwood'					2	2	25°		☀	Yellow center
O. 'Whirligig'					2	2	34°		☀	Blue center

Paeonia
Peony

Paeonia lactiflora cultivars are hardy herbaceous perennials producing large bowl- or cup-shaped flowers. Especially recommended for cottage gardens, peonies also look at home in modern mixed borders.

Paeonia lactiflora 'Bowl of Beauty'

Effective companions include *Alchemilla mollis*, ornamental alliums (onions), aquilegias (columbines), delphiniums, tall bearded irises, lupines, and oriental poppies (*Papaver orientale*). Peonies are superb with shrub roses, particularly old cultivars or the New English roses, and with silver- or gray-leafed shrubs such as lavenders and santolinas (cotton lavenders). Peonies like a rich soil containing plenty of humus. Supports such as bamboo canes may be needed for the flower stems to prevent rain from flattening them. Peonies have a very long life but once planted do not like to be disturbed, so lift them only if you want to propagate the plants by division in spring. Watch out for peony wilt (stems wilt and turn brown at the base and should be cut out), and viruses.

	SPRING	SUMMER	FALL	WINTER	height (ft)	spread (ft)	min temp (F)	moisture	sun/shade	colors
Paeonia lactiflora 'Bowl of Beauty'					3	3	1°		☀	Anemone-form flowers
P. lactiflora 'Duchess de Nemours'					2½	2½	1°		☀	Scented, double flowers
P. lactiflora 'Félix Crousse'					2½	2½	1°		☀	Scented, double flowers
P. lactiflora 'Sarah Bernhardt'					3	3	1°		☀	Scented, double flowers

☀ *sunny*   ◑ *semi-shady*   ● *shady*

Papaver
Poppy

Poppies form a large group of perennials, annuals, and biennials with showy bowl-shaped flowers, often in brilliant colors, followed by attractive seed heads, which can be dried for winter flower arrangements. Hardy annuals include *P. commutatum*, *P. rhoeas* Shirley Series, and *P. somniferum* (opium poppy).

Papaver orientale 'Perry's White'

The best-known hardy biennial is *P. croceum* (Iceland poppy). Hardy perennials include the flamboyant cultivars of *P. orientale* (oriental poppy). Poppies combine beautifully with many plants and should be in every garden. The annuals and biennials are especially lovely with ornamental annual grasses such as *Lagurus ovatus* (hare's tail), and with other ephemerals such as cornflowers (centaurea) and love-in-a-mist (nigella). The perennial oriental poppies combine superbly with tall bearded irises, lupines, delphiniums, and aquilegias (columbines). Dwarf perennials should be planted in front of oriental poppies to hide the foliage, which becomes rather shabby after flowering. Raise annuals and biennials from seed in spring, sowing in flowering

Papaver orientale 'Allegro'

positions as they dislike disturbance. Propagate perennials from root cuttings in fall or winter, rooting them in a cold frame and planting out in spring. Aphids are the main problems with poppies.

Papaver orientale 'Lenchfener'

Papaver orientale 'John Metcalf'

Papaver orientale 'Cedric Morris'

	SPRING	SUMMER	FALL	WINTER	height (in)	spread (in)	min temp (°F)	moisture	sun/shade	colors	
Papaver commutatum 'Lady Bird'	🌱 🌱 🌱	● ● ●		▯	18	6	1°	💧	☼	◼	Ferny foliage
P. croceum Garden Gnome Group	🌱 🌱 🌱	● ● ●			8	6	1°	💧	☼	▨	Low, compact habit
P. 'Lenchfener'	🌱 🌱 ●	● ● ●			30	24	1°	💧	☼	▢	Good modern cultivar
P. orientale 'Allegro'	🌱 🌱 ●	● ●			30	24	1°	💧	☼	◕	A really brilliant color
P. orientale 'Cedric Morris'	🌱 🌱	● ●			30	24	1°	💧	☼	●	Gray, hairy leaves
P. orientale 'John Metcalf'	🌱 🌱 ●	● ●			30	24	1°	💧	☼	▣	Good modern cultivar
P. orientale 'Perry's White'	🌱 🌱	● ● ●			30	24	1°	💧	☼	●	Sturdy flower stems
P. rhoeas Shirley Series	🌱 🌱 🌱	● ● ●			36	12	1°	💧	☼	▦	Single to double flowers
P. somniferum 'Peony Flowered'	🌱 🌱 🌱	● ● ●			36	12	1°	💧	☼	▦	Frilled, double flowers

🌱 planting   ● flower   💧 well drained   💧 moist   💧 wet

Papaver orientale 'Allegro' (side label)

P

Flowers

Pelargonium

The seed-raised zonal pelargoniums listed here are tender, bushy, evergreen perennials grown as annuals. They produce large rounded heads of mainly single flowers over a very long period.

Ivy-leafed pelargoniums are tender, trailing, evergreen perennials, also grown as annuals, with ivy-shaped leaves and rounded heads of single or double flowers. They include seed-raised strains and cultivars propagated from cuttings. The zonal pelargoniums are major summer bedding plants and suitable for mass planting in formal beds. They combine well with many other bedders including petunias, *Lobelia erinus* cultivars, ageratum, verbenas,

Pelargonium 'Vista Deep Rose'

and *Lobularia maritima* cultivars. Good dot plants for these pelargoniums include cannas, *Cordyline australis*, and silver-leafed *Senecio cineraria* cultivars. Zonals can also be used in patio containers and window boxes with the same companions. Ivy-leafed pelargoniums are usually grown in containers for summer display, particularly hanging baskets and window boxes. Effective companions include trailing lobelias, ageratum, verbenas, and petunias. Regularly deadhead plants. Sow seeds in late winter under glass. Propagate from semi-ripe cuttings in late summer, and winter young plants under glass. Prone to aphids, caterpillars, foot rot, gray mold, rust, and vine weevil grubs.

Pelargonium 'Sensation Scarlet'

	SPRING	SUMMER	FALL	WINTER	height (in)	spread (in)	min temp (°F)	moisture	sun/shade	colors	
Pelargonium 'Amethyst' (Ivy-leafed)	🌱🌱🌱	●●●●			12	18	34°	💧💧	☀		Semi-double flowers
P. 'Luna' (Ivy-leafed)	🌱🌱🌱	●●●●			12	18	34°	💧💧	☀		Shiny green foliage
P. Multibloom Series (Zonal, seed-raised)	🌱🌱🌱	●●●●		🌱	12	12	34°	💧💧	☀		Single flowers produced in clusters
P. Sensation Series (Zonal, seed-raised)	🌱🌱🌱	●●●●		🌱	12	12	34°	💧💧	☀		Single, rain-tolerant flowers
P. 'Speckles' (Zonal, seed-raised)	🌱🌱🌱	●●●●		🌱	12	12	34°	💧	☀		Flowers speckled and splashed
P. 'Summer Showers' (Ivy-leafed, seed-raised)	🌱🌱🌱	●●●●		🌱	6	24	34°	💧💧	☀		Very free-flowering
P. Vista Series (Zonal, seed-raised)	🌱🌱🌱	●●●●		🌱	15	12	34°	💧💧	☀		Uniform growth, free-flowering
P. 'Wico' (Ivy-leafed)	🌱🌱🌱	●●●●			12	18	34°	💧	☀		Glossy green foliage

☀ *sunny*   ☀ *semi-shady*   ● *shady*

Penstemon

Frost-hardy to fully hardy herbaceous, partially evergreen, or evergreen perennials. Penstemons also bear masses of tubular flowers, with two lobed lips, over a long period. Most have narrow spear-shaped leaves.

Penstemon 'Apple Blossom'

Grow in mixed borders, especially in cottage gardens. Suitable companions include silver- or gray-leafed plants such as artemisias, catmints (nepeta), lavenders, and *Stachys byzantina*. Effective, too, with shrub roses, especially old roses, and with alstroemerias, dianthus (border carnations and pinks), and ornamental grasses such as miscanthus. Nicotianas and verbenas are good annual companions. Where frosts are hard protect plants with a thick mulch of dry straw, bracken, or leaves over winter. Deadhead regularly. Propagate from semi-ripe cuttings in summer or by division in spring. Watch out for powdery mildew, slugs, and snails.

	SPRING	SUMMER	FALL	WINTER	height (ft)	spread (ft)	min temp (°F)	moisture	sun/shade	colors	
Penstemon 'Alice Hindley'	planting	flower	flower		3	1½	25°	well drained	sun	■	Produces large leaves
P. 'Andenken an Friedrich Hahn'	planting	flower	flower		2½	2	25°	well drained	sun	■	Narrow leaves, vigorous, and well branched
P. 'Apple Blossom'	planting	flower	flower		2	2	25°	well drained	sun	□	Narrow leaves, small flowers
P. 'Evelyn'	planting	flower	flower		2	1	1°	well drained	sun	■	Narrow leaves, small flowers
P. 'Pennington Gem'	planting	flower	flower		2½	1½	25°	well drained	sun	□	Narrow leaves, large flowers
P. 'Stapleford Gem'	planting	flower	flower		2	1½	1°	well drained	sun	▨	Large leaves and flowers

Perovskia

A hardy subshrub, *P.* 'Blue Spire' is grown for its spikes of blue flowers and ferny, gray foliage and stems. A good choice for dry parts of the garden, including gravel gardens and areas, it even grows well in poor or chalky soils.

It is an excellent plant for seaside gardens where it looks good with other maritime plants including tamarisk (tamarix), *Eryngium maritimum* (sea holly), *Limonium latifolium* (sea lavender), and *Crambe maritima* (sea kale). In other gardens suitable companions include shrub roses and late-flowering perennials such as rudbeckias. In spring cut back all last year's stems to a permanent, low, woody framework. Propagate from semi-ripe cuttings in summer. Perovskia is not troubled by pests or diseases.

Perovskia 'Blue Spire'

planting	● flower	♦ well drained	♦ moist	♦ wet

Petunia

Although correctly perennials, petunias are often grown as half-hardy annuals. They produce masses of flattish, five-lobed flowers over a very long period.

Petunias grow well in poor to moderately fertile soils and are good for coastal gardens where they combine well with gazanias, portulaca, and succulents including *Dorotheanthus bellidiformis* (Livingstone daisy), lampranthus, and *Carpobrotus edulis* (Hottentot fig). Petunias are mainly used in summer bedding schemes and containers, where they combine effectively with many other summer bedders including pelargoniums, scarlet salvias, verbenas, bedding dahlias, osteospermums, tagetes (marigolds), fuchsias, and impatiens. Deadhead regularly. Raise plants from seed in spring under glass. Petunias are prone to aphids, foot rot, slugs, snails, and viruses.

Petunia Surfinia Series 'Blue Vein'

Petunia Million Bells Series 'Cherry'

	SPRING	SUMMER	FALL	WINTER	height (in)	spread (in)	min temp (°F)	moisture	sun/shade	colors	
P. Carpet Series (Multiflora Group)	🌱🌱🌱	●●●●	●●●		10	36	34°	💧	☀	⬛	Small flowers, good for bedding schemes
P. 'Fantasy Mixed' (Milliflora Group)	🌱🌱🌱	●●●●	●●●		12	18	34°	💧	☀	⬜	Good for containers, mixed colors
P. Million Bells Series (Milliflora Group)	🌱🌱🌱	●●●●	●●●		6	48	34°	💧	☀	▥	Trailing habit, ideal for containers
P. Picotee Series (Grandiflora Group)	🌱🌱🌱	●●●●	●●●		12	36	34°	💧	☀	▦	Large, white-edged flowers
P. Surfinia Series (Grandiflora Group)	🌱🌱🌱	●●●●	●●●		12	48	34°	💧	☀	▦	Good for containers; buy as plugs

Phacelia
California bluebell

A hardy annual, *P. campanularia* is valued for its blue, bell-shaped flowers, which are attractive to bees. Grow it in a sunny position in mixed borders and, as it thrives in dry soils, in gravel gardens.

For an attractive blue theme, combine phacelia with other blue-flowered annuals such as *Centaurea cyanus* (cornflower) and *Nemophila menziesii* (baby blue-eyes). Raise plants from seed in spring or early fall, sowing in flowering positions. Spring sowings quickly come into flower. Where winters are very wet or very cold, protect young plants with cloches over winter. Generally trouble-free.

Phacelia campanularia 'Ocean Waves'

☀ *sunny*　　🌤 *semi-shady*　　🌑 *shady*

Phlox

Phlox grow both as annuals and perennials. The *P.* x *drummondii* cultivars are frost-hardy annuals with flattish, lobed flowers. They are usually bedded out for summer display and can also be planted at the front of mixed borders. The annual phlox look especially at home in cottage gardens. They are also suitable for containers.

Effective companions for annual phlox include *Salvia farinacea* cultivars, heliotrope, and gray-foliage plants such as the half-hardy bedding shrub *Helichrysum petiolare*. Regular deadheading, although fiddly and time-consuming, adds several weeks or even months to the display. *P. paniculata* cultivars are hardy herbaceous perennials with heads of flattish, scented flowers on tall, erect stems. They are ideal for mixed borders (including cottage-garden borders) in combination with old and modern shrub

Phlox paniculata 'Spitfire'

roses, tall campanulas, *Echinacea purpurea*, rudbeckias, solidago (golden rod), and tall achilleas. *P. subulata* (moss phlox) cultivars are hardy, evergreen, mat-forming perennials for the rock or scree garden, with masses of flattish flowers early in the season. They combine well with *Aurinia saxatilis*, aubrieta, and helianthemum cultivars. Raise annuals from seed in early spring under glass. Propagate *P. paniculata* cultivars by division in spring or fall, from root cuttings in winter, or from basal cuttings in spring. Propagate *P. subulata* cultivars from softwood cuttings in spring. Phlox are prone to leaf spot and powdery mildew.

Phlox paniculata 'Starfire'

	SPRING	SUMMER	FALL	WINTER	height (in)	spread (in)	min temp (°F)	moisture	sun/shade	colors	
Phlox x *drummondii* 'African Sunset'	planting	flower			4	8	25°	well drained	sun		Bushy habit
P. x *drummondii* 'Tapestry'	planting	flower			18	12	25°	well drained	sun		Very fragrant flowers
P. x *drummondii* 'Twinkling Stars'	planting	flower			6	6	25°	well drained	sun		Starry flowers
P. paniculata 'Brigadier'	planting	flower	flower		36	18	1°	moist	sun		Strong-growing cultivar
P. paniculata 'Bright Eyes'	planting	flower	flower		48	24	1°	moist	sun		Distinctive cultivar
P. paniculata 'Fujiyama'	planting	flower	flower		30	18	1°	moist	sun		Large conical flower heads
P. paniculata 'Spitfire'	planting	flower	flower		36	10	1°	moist	sun		Dense flower heads
P. paniculata 'Starfire'	planting	flower	flower		36	18	1°	moist	sun		Deep green foliage
P. subulata 'Lilacina' (syn. 'G.F. Wilson')	planting flower				3	18	1°	well drained	sun		Vigorous habit
P. subulata 'Temiskaming'	planting flower				3	12	1°	well drained	sun		A slow grower

planting   flower   well drained   moist   wet

Flowers

Phygelius

Frost-hardy evergreen shrubs, phygelius have a suckering habit and look more like perennials. Tubular flowers on upright stems are produced over a long period.

Grow in a mixed border with agapanthus and kniphofias. Give them sufficient space as they have a spreading habit and do not look good when hemmed in by other plants. Remove dead flower heads regularly. In frosty areas phygelius can be grown like herbaceous perennials by cutting down stems in spring. They can also be grown in a sheltered spot and mulched in winter with dry material such as straw. Propagate from softwood cuttings in spring. Generally trouble-free.

Phygelius rectus 'Moonraker'

	SPRING	SUMMER	FALL	WINTER	height (ft)	spread (ft)	min temp (°F)	moisture	sun/shade	colors	
Phygelius aequalis 'Yellow Trumpet'	🌱🌱🌱	●●●			3	3	25°	💧	☼	▢	Very free-flowering
P. capensis	🌱🌱🌱	●●●			4	4	16°	💧	☼	▨	Deep green foliage
P. rectus 'African Queen'	🌱🌱🌱	●●●			3	3	25°	💧	☼	▨	Long swags of flowers
P. rectus 'Moonraker'	🌱🌱🌱	●●●			5	4	25°	💧	☼	▢	Slightly curved flowers

Physostegia
Obedient plant

Physostegia virginiana

***Physostegia virginiana* is a hardy perennial with branching spikes of tubular flowers over a long period. The common name refers to the fact that when the flowers are moved they stay in that position.**

Grow in a mixed border with *Echinacea purpurea*, solidago (golden rod), *Rudbeckia fulgida*, and ornamental grasses such as *Stipa gigantea*. The flowers are suitable for cutting. Propagate by division in the fall or early spring. Watch out for slugs and snails.

Polemonium
Jacob's ladder

A hardy herbaceous perennial, *Polemonium caeruleum* has branching heads of bell-shaped flowers and attractive pinnate foliage.

Grow Jacob's ladder in a mixed border, or in a more natural part of the garden, including long-grass areas. Good companions in a border include *Achillea* 'Moonshine', *Allium cristophii*, *Euphorbia characias* subsp. *wulfenii*, and lupines. Remove dead flowers regularly. Propagate by division in spring. Watch out for powdery mildew.

Polemonium caeruleum

☼ *sunny*   ☼ *semi-shady*   ● *shady*

Polygonatum
Solomon's seal

Polygonatum x _hybridum_ is a hardy herbaceous perennial with slightly arching stems bearing clusters of dangling, tubular flowers followed by black berries.

The leaves, carried horizontally, are broadly spear-shaped. Ideal for a shady border in combination with shrubs. A woodland garden also makes a good home, combined with plants such as hostas and primulas. Propagate by division in spring. Slugs and snails cause damage, as do the caterpillars of Solomon's seal sawfly (pick off or spray with rotenone or pyrethrum).

Polygonatum x hybridum

Potentilla
Cinquefoil

Potentilla 'William Rollison'

The hardy herbaceous potentillas have flowers like small roses over a very long period and clumps of hand-shaped foliage. They are ideal for a mixed border, especially in cottage gardens.

Mix them with other perennials such as artemisias, especially *A. ludoviciana* 'Silver Queen' with silver foliage, and plant them around shrub roses and with lavenders. Suitable for poor soils. Propagate by division in spring. This plant does not have any problems with pests or diseases.

	SPRING	SUMMER	FALL	WINTER	height (ft)	spread (ft)	min temp (°F)	moisture	sun/shade	colors	
Potentilla 'Gibson's Scarlet'	🌱🌱🌱	● ● ●			1½	1½	1°	💧	☀	⬛	Single flowers
P. 'William Rollison'	🌱🌱🌱	● ● ●			1½	1½	1°	💧	☀	⬜	Semi-double flowers

Primula

A diverse group of mainly hardy, herbaceous and evergreen perennials. _P. auricula_ (auricula) cultivars are dwarf evergreens forming rosettes of broad leaves and heads of flattish flowers in a wide range of colors, often zoned in a contrasting color.

Primula denticulata

Border auriculas are the most popular, ideal for frontal positions in mixed borders and delightful in cottage gardens. *P. denticulata* (drumstick primrose) is distinct with its ball-shaped flowers, ideal for a moist shady border or woodland garden mixed with hostas and other shade-loving perennials such as ferns. Candelabra primulas, such as *P. japonica*, with whorls of blooms carried in tiers, are grown in the same way and also look good beside a pool. The Primrose and Polyanthus Groups are dwarf rosette-forming evergreen or herbaceous plants

Primula vulgaris

🌱 *planting*　　● *flower*　　|　　💧 *well drained*　　💧 *moist*　　💧 *wet*

Primula veris

with flattish flowers on relatively short stems. The Primrose Group includes the common primrose, *P. vulgaris*, and *P.* 'Wanda', ideal for the front of shady borders or woodland gardens. Colored primroses such as 'Husky Mixed' are grown as biennials for spring bedding or containers. The Polyanthus Group includes perennials such as *P.* 'Guinevere', while some, such as the Crescendo Series, are grown as biennials for spring display in beds and containers. They have taller flower stems than primroses. *P. veris*, the cowslip, is ideal for growing in a wildflower meadow. Propagate perennials by division in the fall. Raise biennials and perennials from seed in a cold frame in spring, grow on in a shady nursery bed, and plant out in the fall. Primulas are prone to gray mold, slugs, snails, and vine weevil grubs.

Primula 'Wanda'

	SPRING	SUMMER	FALL	WINTER	height (in)	spread (in)	min temp (°F)	moisture	sun/shade	colors	
Primula auricula (border cultivars)					6	8	1°				Plants often white mealy and fragrant
P. Crescendo Series (Polyanthus Group)					12	12	1°				Thick, sturdy stems
P. denticulata					12	12	1°				Other colors available
P. 'Husky Mixed' (Primrose Group)					6	6	1°				Very clear, bright colors
P. japonica (Candelabra primula)					18	12	1°				Rosettes of leaves
P. veris					9	9	1°				Fragrant flowers
P. vulgaris					6	12	1°				Slightly fragrant flowers
P. 'Wanda' (Primrose Group)					4	12	1°				Purple-green foliage

Pulmonaria
Lungwort

These hardy evergreen ground-hugging perennials are valued for their clusters of small, flaring, tubular flowers produced early in the season and for their large, roughly hairy leaves, which are marked with silver in many species and cultivars.

Grow as ground-cover plants around shrubs in shady borders and woodland gardens, and combine them with spring-flowering bulbs. When flowering is over cut off all the old leaves to encourage fresh new foliage.

Plants are best lifted and divided every three years, in the fall or as soon as flowering has finished. Also propagate from root cuttings in winter. Watch out for powdery mildew, slugs, and snails.

Left: *Pulmonaria saccharata*

	SPRING	SUMMER	FALL	WINTER	height (in)	spread (in)	min temp (°F)	moisture	sun/shade	colors	
Pulmonaria officinalis					9	18	1°				Leaves spotted silver
P. rubra					15	30	1°				Fresh green foliage
P. saccharata					12	24	1°				Leaves spotted silver
P. 'Sissinghurst White'					12	18	1°				Leaves spotted silver

☼ *sunny*   ◑ *semi-shady*   ● *shady*

Pulsatilla
Pasque flower

The pasque flower, *P. vulgaris*, is a dwarf hardy herbaceous perennial with large, sumptuous, nodding, bell-shaped flowers covered in silky hairs held above attractive ferny foliage.

Ideal for a rock or scree garden, or for planting in gaps in paving, combine the pasque flower with other spring-flowering rock plants such as *Aurinia saxatilis*. It dislikes root disturbance so once planted leave alone, except when propagation by root cuttings is required in winter. The main pests are slugs and snails.

Pulsatilla vulgaris

Ranunculus
Buttercup

A variable genus including hardy herbaceous perennials such as *R. aconitifolius* 'Flore Pleno' (bachelor's buttons), tuberous-rooted *R. ficaria* (lesser celandine) cultivars, and *R. gramineus*.

Ranunculus asiaticus 'Accolade'

Flowers are generally saucer- or bowl-shaped but are fully double in some cultivars. These are good mixed-border plants, although *R. ficaria* cultivars are grown as ground cover in shady woodland gardens or shrub borders. *R. asiaticus* (Persian buttercup) cultivars are half-hardy tuberous perennials, planted in spring and wintered as dormant tubers in a frost-free place (store in dry peat substitute). Most prefer partial shade. Propagate hardy perennials by division in the fall or spring. Watch out for aphids, powdery mildew, slugs, and snails.

	SPRING	SUMMER	FALL	WINTER	height (in)	spread (in)	min temp (°F)	moisture	sun/shade	colors
Ranunculus aconitifolius 'Flore Pleno'					24	18	1°			Double flowers
R. asiaticus 'Accolade'					12	8	34°			Double flowers
R. asiaticus Turban Group					12	8	34°			Double flowers
R. ficaria 'Brazen Hussy'					2	12	1°			Dark brown foliage
R. gramineus					12	6	1°			Grassy foliage

Reseda
Mignonette

Reseda luteola

A hardy annual, *Reseda luteola* is valued for its cone-shaped heads of very fragrant flowers produced over a long period. A favorite cottage-garden plant, it can be grown at the front of mixed borders, especially around old shrub roses.

The flowers, which attract bees, are good for cutting. A suitable choice for a wildflower area and especially recommended for chalky soils. Remove dead flower heads regularly. Raise from seed sown in spring or fall in flowering positions, covering fall-sown seedlings with cloches over winter in hard-frost areas. Not troubled by pests or diseases.

planting   flower | well drained   moist   wet

Rodgersia

Rodgersia pinnata 'Superba'

This hardy herbaceous perennial produces large hand-shaped leaves and cone-shaped heads of flowers. Rodgersia should be grown at the edges of pools, in bog gardens, and in moist borders.

Effective companions include hostas, astilbes, moisture-loving irises, lobelias such as *L. cardinalis*, *L.* 'Queen Victoria', and *L.* x *speciosa* cultivars, *Mimulus cardinalis*, and ferns, including the royal fern, *Osmunda regalis*. It likes sheltered conditions and plenty of humus in the soil. Propagate by division in spring before growth starts. The main pests are slugs and snails.

Rudbeckia
Coneflower

Rudbeckias are mainly hardy herbaceous perennials producing large, showy, daisy-like flowers, each with a conspicuous central cone, over a long period. *R. hirta* (black-eyed Susan) cultivars are short-lived and usually grown as annuals. *R. fulgida* (also known as black-eyed Susan) cultivars are long-lived perennials.

Rudbeckia fulgida var. *deamii*

Rudbeckia fulgida var. *sullivantii* 'Goldsturm'

Coneflowers are essential plants for mixed borders and staples of prairie-style borders. Effective companions are asters, achilleas, sunflowers (helianthus), monardas, golden rod (solidago), *Echinacea purpurea*, and ornamental grasses such as miscanthus and stipa. The flowers are excellent for cutting. Rudbeckias are suitable for heavy soils if well drained. Raise annuals from seed in spring under glass. Propagate perennials by division in spring or fall. Rudbeckias are prone to slug and snail damage.

	SPRING	SUMMER	FALL	WINTER	height (in)	spread (in)	min temp (°F)	moisture	sun/shade	colors
Rudbeckia fulgida var. *deamii*					24	18	1°			Black cone
R. fulgida var. *sullivantii* 'Goldsturm'					24	18	1°			Large flowers, black cone
R. hirta 'Marmalade'					18	12	1°			Compact habit
R. hirta 'Rustic Dwarfs'					24	18	1°			Some flowers are bicolored
R. hirta 'Toto'					10	10	1°			Deep brown cone

sunny · semi-shady · shady

Salpiglossis

Salpiglossis sinuata hybrid

This half-hardy annual has widely flaring flowers in a range of dazzling colors and grows best outdoors in warm dry summers. Try it in mixed borders or patio containers.

Due to the strong, rich colors of this plant, companions are not really needed, except for those that have a "cooling" effect such as gypsophila and gray-leafed *Helichrysum petiolare*. The flowers are suitable for cutting. Salpiglossis needs a sheltered spot in the garden and supporting with twiggy sticks. Deadhead regularly. Raise plants from seed in spring under glass. The main problems are aphids, black root rot, foot rot, and gray mold.

	SPRING	SUMMER	FALL	WINTER	height (ft)	spread (ft)	min temp (°F)	moisture	sun/shade	colors	
Salpiglossis sinuata Bolero Hybrids	🌱🌱🌱	●●●●	●		2	1	34°	💧	☀	▦	May need supports
S. sinuata Casino Series	🌱🌱🌱	●●●●	●		2	1	34°	💧	☀	▦	Rain-tolerant

Salvia
Sage

The salvias described here range from hardy and half-hardy perennials to hardy annuals but all have spikes of tubular, two-lipped flowers, the upper lip being shaped like a hood. The stems of salvias are unusual in that they are square, as opposed to rounded as in most other plants. Cultivars of *S. farinacea* (mealycup sage) and *S. splendens* (scarlet sage) are perennials but are grown as half-hardy annuals for summer bedding schemes.

Salvia splendens 'Blaze of Fire'

S. farinacea looks good with many other summer bedding plants, such as argyranthemums, osteospermums, pelargoniums (zonal and ivy-leafed), bedding begonias, and petunias, while the hot and strong colors of *S. splendens* need cooling down with silver-foliage plants such as *Senecio cineraria* 'Silver Dust'. White-flowered bedding plants such as *Lobularia maritima* and some of the osteospermums or argyranthemums would also work well. Scarlet sage is also suitable for containers such as patio tubs and window boxes. *S. viridis* (annual clary) is a hardy annual with colorful flower bracts but inconspicuous flowers, good for cutting and drying or using fresh. The hardy perennials *S. nemorosa* and

🌱 planting ● flower 💧 well drained 💧 moist 💧 wet

S. x *sylvestris* are ideal for mixed borders, combined with flat-headed achilleas, rudbeckias, eryngiums, heleniums, and verbascums. Propagate salvias in spring, half-hardy annuals from seed under glass, hardy annuals in flowering positions, and

hardy perennials by division or from basal cuttings. Various pests and diseases attack salvias, including aphids, black root rot, foot rot, slugs, and snails.

	SPRING	SUMMER	FALL	WINTER	height (in)	spread (in)	min temp (°F)	moisture	sun/shade	colors	
Salvia farinacea 'Strata'	🌱🌱🌱	● ● ● ● ●			24	12	34°	💧💧	☀	▯	Narrow spikes of flowers
S. farinacea 'Victoria'	🌱🌱🌱	● ● ● ● ●			24	12	34°	💧💧	☀	▮	Narrow spikes of flowers
S. nemorosa 'Ostfriesland'	🌱🌱🌱	● ● ● ● ●			18	18	1°	💧💧	☀	▮	Bushy habit
S. splendens 'Blaze of Fire'	🌱🌱🌱	● ● ● ● ●			15	12	34°	💧💧	☀	▮	Light green foliage
S. splendens 'Firecracker'	🌱🌱🌱	● ● ● ● ●			10	10	34°	💧💧	☀	▮	Dark green foliage
S. splendens Phoenix Series	🌱🌱🌱	● ● ● ● ●			12	12	34°	💧💧	☀	▨	Dark green foliage
S. x *sylvestris* 'Rose Queen'	🌱🌱🌱	● ● ●			30	12	1°	💧💧	☀	▯	Gray-green leaves
S. viridis 'Bouquet'	🌱🌱🌱	● ● ● ●			18	8	1°	💧💧	☀	▯	Colored flower bracts
S. viridis 'Claryssa'	🌱🌱🌱	● ● ● ●			15	8	1°	💧💧	☀	▨	Colored flower bracts

☀ *sunny*   ☀ *semi-shady*   ● *shady*

Saxifraga
Saxifrage

Hardy, mainly evergreen perennials that grow as mats or low cushions and mounds, saxifrages have small bowl- or star-shaped flowers.

Saxifraga x urbium 'Variegata'

These plants are grown mainly in rock and scree gardens in combination with other alpines such as sempervivums (houseleeks) and sedums (stonecrops), and with miniature spring bulbs. *S. fortunei* is herbaceous or partially evergreen with rounded, lobed leaves and heads of starry flowers, an excellent choice for a woodland garden or shady shrub border. *S. x urbium* (London pride) with rosettes of spoon-shaped leaves produces sprays of minute starry flowers. A vigorous mat-former, it is used as ground cover in shady places. Propagate saxifrages in spring, by division or removing rosettes and treating them as cuttings. Watch out for aphids, slugs, snails, and the grubs of vine weevil.

	SPRING	SUMMER	FALL	WINTER	height (in)	spread (in)	min temp (°F)	moisture	sun/shade	colors	
Saxifraga fortunei	planting planting planting	flower flower			12	12	1°	moist	part		Leaves have purple undersides
S. 'Gregor Mendel'	flower planting planting				4	8	1°	moist	sun		Best in alkaline soil
S. 'Jenkinsiae'	flower planting planting				2	6	1°	well drained	part		Best in alkaline soil
S. x urbium	planting planting planting	flower flower flower			12	18	1°	moist	sun		Tolerates infertile soil

Scabiosa
Scabious

Mainly hardy herbaceous perennials, scabious are essential plants for cottage gardens and mixed borders. The flower heads have a domed-shaped center of tiny flowers surrounded by broad petal-like flowers.

Scabiosa 'Butterfly Blue'

The flowers, good for cutting, attract butterflies and bees. *S. atropurpurea* (sweet scabious) is a short-lived plant grown as a hardy annual. All are suitable for mixed borders, combined with shrub roses, artemisias, gypsophilas, and eryngiums. Scabious are good for chalky soils but dislike wet soil in winter. Remove dead flowers regularly. Support annuals with twiggy sticks. Divide perennials every three years in spring. Propagate from basal cuttings in spring. Raise annuals from seed in early spring under glass or mid-spring in flowering positions. No problems from pests or diseases.

	SPRING	SUMMER	FALL	WINTER	height (in)	spread (in)	min temp (°F)	moisture	sun/shade	colors	
Scabiosa atropurpurea 'Double Mixed'	planting planting	flower flower flower			36	8	1°	well drained	sun		Double flowers
S. 'Butterfly Blue'	planting planting planting	flower			15	15	1°	well drained	sun		Grayish-green foliage
S. caucasica 'Clive Greaves'	planting planting planting	flower			24	24	1°	well drained	sun		Grayish-green foliage
S. caucasica 'Miss Willmott'	planting planting planting	flower			36	24	1°	well drained	sun		Grayish-green foliage

planting *planting*   flower *flower*   well drained *well drained*   moist *moist*   wet *wet*

S

Flowers

Scaevola
Fairy fan flower

A tender evergreen perennial of trailing habit, _S. aemula_ 'Blue Wonder', the best of the scaevolas, has small blooms in the shape of a fan over a very long period.

It is generally grown as an annual in patio tubs, window boxes, and hanging baskets and combines effectively with diascias, _Lobelia erinus_ cultivars, osteospermums, ivy-leafed pelargoniums, petunias (especially the Million Bells Series), and the gray-foliage plant _Helichrysum petiolare_. Several other cultivars are available. Propagate from softwood cuttings in summer, and winter young plants in a cool greenhouse, planting out when frosts are over. Scaevola is not troubled by pests or diseases.

Scaevola aemula 'Blue Wonder'

Schizanthus
Poor man's orchid

Schizanthus pinnatus

A tender annual of bushy habit, _S. pinnatus_, the best schizanthus, has widely flared, two-lipped, multicolored flowers set against attractive ferny foliage.

Being tender, it is best grown in a very sheltered spot, either in a mixed border or in patio containers or window boxes. The flowers are good for cutting. Best effects are achieved by combining schizanthus with foliage plants, such as the gray-leafed _Helichrysum petiolare_. Pinch out tips of young plants to create bushy specimens. Raise plants from seed in spring under glass. No problems from pests or diseases.

☼ _sunny_   ◑ _semi-shady_   ● _shady_

Schizostylis
Kaffir lily

Schizostylis coccinea and its cultivars are moderately hardy perennials growing from fleshy rhizomes and with narrow, upright, sword-like leaves that remain virtually year-round. Star-shaped blooms are carried in spikes, reminiscent of small gladioli, and provide welcome color late in the year.

These flowers are suitable for cutting. Grow schizostylis in a sheltered position, in a mixed border or at the base of a warm wall that receives plenty of sun year-round. Combine them with other late-flowering plants, such as dwarf hardy chrysanthemums, colchicums, *Crocus speciosus*, *Nerine bowdenii*, and fall-flowering sedums. Dwarf ornamental grasses can be included in the planting scheme, such as the dainty *Stipa tenuissima*.

Schizostylis coccinea 'Sunrise'

Schizostylus coccinea 'Major'

Mulch the root area of schizostylis in winter with bulky organic matter such as well-rotted garden compost or leaf mold, to serve as frost protection. Although schizostylis need well-drained conditions, the soil should remain moist at all times as the fleshy rhizomes must not be allowed to dry out. If time permits, remove dead flowers regularly. Remove dead foliage as necessary. Propagate schizostylis in spring by dividing established clumps. In any case, plants are best divided every three years or so. There are few problems, although hard frost will damage the flowers. The dreaded slugs and snails may decide to make a meal of young shoots.

	SPRING	SUMMER	FALL	WINTER	height (ft)	spread (ft)	min temp (°F)	moisture	sun/shade	colors	
Schizostylis coccinea	planting		flower		2	1	16°	moist	sun		Robust grower
S. coccinea 'Jennifer'	planting		flower		2	1	16°	moist	sun		Large blooms
S. coccinea 'Major'	planting		flower		2	1	16°	moist	sun		Large blooms
S. coccinea 'Mrs Hegarty'	planting		flower		2	1	16°	moist	sun		Flowers later than most
S. coccinea 'Sunrise'	planting		flower		2	1	16°	moist	sun		Large blooms
S. coccinea 'Viscountess Bynge'	planting		flower		2	1	16°	moist	sun		Prone to frost damage

planting   flower   well drained   moist   wet

Scilla

Scillas are hardy dwarf bulbs valued for their early star- or bell-shaped flowers, mainly in shades of blue. Plant in bold informal drifts among shrubs or under deciduous trees, or in short grass.

Scilla siberica

Scillas are also suitable for planting in small groups on rock gardens. Combine them with other miniature bulbs, including narcissus (especially the early-flowering Cyclamineus cultivars) and crocuses. They appreciate soil that is well laced with humus. Propagate by detaching offsets when dormant in summer. Few pests and diseases affect scillas, but watch out for viruses.

	SPRING	SUMMER	FALL	WINTER	height (in)	spread (in)	min temp (°F)	moisture	sun/shade	colors	
Scilla bifolia	●		🌱🌱🌱		4	2	1°	💧	☀	▣	Starry flowers
S. siberica	●		🌱🌱🌱		8	2	1°	💧	☀	▢	Bell-shaped flowers
S. siberica 'Spring Beauty'	●		🌱🌱🌱		8	2	1°	💧	☀	▣	Vigorous habit

Sedum
Stonecrop

A variable group of succulent perennials, those described here being fully hardy and herbaceous in habit, with flattish heads of small star-shaped flowers.

Grow them at the front of a mixed border, combining the late-flowering kinds with such plants as *Anemone* x *hybrida* and *Anemone hupehensis* cultivars, schizostylis, hardy chrysanthemums, *Nerine bowdenii*, ornamental grasses, and fall-coloring shrubs such as berberis, rhus, and cotinus. Sedums are especially suitable for slightly chalky soils. Propagate in spring, by division or from basal stem cuttings. Regular division of clumps every three years improves performance. Watch out for black root rot, foot rot, slugs, and snails.

Sedum spectabile 'Brilliant'

	SPRING	SUMMER	FALL	WINTER	height (ft)	spread (ft)	min temp (°F)	moisture	sun/shade	colors	
Sedum aizoon 'Euphorbioides'	🌱🌱🌱	● ● ●			1½	1	1°	💧	☀	▢	Pale green foliage
S. 'Herbstfreude' (syn. 'Autumn Joy')	🌱🌱🌱		●		2	2	1°	💧	☀	▣	Glaucous foliage
S. 'Ruby Glow'	🌱🌱🌱	● ● ●	●		1	1½	1°	💧	☀	▣	Red stems, purple flushed leaves
S. spectabile 'Brilliant'	🌱🌱🌱	● ●			1½	1½	1°	💧	☀	▣	Gray-green foliage
S. spectabile 'Iceberg'	🌱🌱🌱	● ●			1½	1½	1°	💧	☀	▢	Light gray-green foliage

S

Flowers

☀ *sunny*   ☀ *semi-shady*   ● *shady*

Sidalcea
False mallow

Hardy herbaceous perennials, sidalceas have lobed leaves and spikes of widely flaring, five-petaled flowers in shades of pink. They look especially at home in cottage gardens, but are also suitable for modern mixed borders.

Best results in slightly acid, sandy soil containing plenty of humus. Very wet soil is anathema to sidalceas. A dry organic winter mulch (for example, straw) protects roots from severe frosts. When flowering is over, reducing stems by half to two-thirds encourages another flush of flowers. This plant's flowers are excellent for cutting. Propagate by division in spring. Watch out for rust, slugs, and snails.

Sidalcea 'Elsie Heugh'

	SPRING	SUMMER	FALL	WINTER	height (ft)	spread (ft)	min temp (°F)	moisture	sun/shade	colors	
Sidalcea 'Croftway Red'	planting	flower			3	1½	1°	well drained	sun	■	Comes into flower early
S. 'Elsie Heugh'	planting	flower			3	1½	1°	well drained	sun	■	Fringed petals
S. 'Rose Queen'	planting	flower			3	1½	1°	well drained	sun	■	Bushy habit
S. 'William Smith'	planting	flower			3	1½	1°	well drained	sun	■	Old but reliable cultivar

Silene
Campion, catchfly

Silenes have rounded, five-petaled, often notched flowers. Rock or scree garden species include the hardy, dwarf, evergreen perennials *S. acaulis* (moss campion) and *S. schafta*.

Among the hardy annuals, *S. coeli-rosa* (rose of heaven) makes a good gap filler for the mixed border (flowers are suitable for cutting) and *S. pendula* (nodding catchfly), with pendulous flowers, is suitable for a hanging basket. The hardy herbaceous perennial *S. dioica* looks most at home in a natural or wildflower area. Silenes are good for chalky soils. Raise hardy annuals from seed in spring or fall in flowering positions. Propagate perennials in spring, by division or from basal stem cuttings. Prone to powdery mildew, slugs, and snails.

Silene dioica

	SPRING	SUMMER	FALL	WINTER	height (in)	spread (in)	min temp (°F)	moisture	sun/shade	colors	
Silene acaulis	planting	flower			2	0	1°	well drained	sun	■	Mossy foliage
S. coeli-rosa Angel Series	planting	flower	planting		12	6	1°	well drained	sun	■	Good cut flower
S. dioica	planting	flower			30	24	1°	moist	part shade	■	Double-flowered cultivar available
S. pendula 'Peach Blossom'	planting	flower	planting		6	10	1°	well drained	sun	■	Double flowers

🌱 *planting*   ● *flower*   💧 *well drained*   💧 *moist*   💧 *wet*

Sisyrinchium

A hardy perennial with erect, evergreen, iris-like leaves, *S. striatum* produces spikes of small bowl-shaped flowers. The popular cultivar 'Aunt May' has cream and green striped leaves.

The flowers are produced over a fairly long period, from early to mid-summer. Height is up to 36in (90cm), although the cultivar is shorter, at only 18in (45cm) in height, and spread is about 8in (20cm). Grow in a mixed border or gravel garden with other early summer perennials such as oriental poppies (*Papaver orientale*) and *Kniphofia* 'Royal Standard'. Suitable for chalky and poor soils, but very wet soil in winter is anathema to sisyrinchiums. In very wet winters support a pane of glass over the plants, or use a cloche, to keep off the rain. Propagate by division in spring. Sisyrinchiums can also self-seed freely so seedlings may be a source of new plants. Prone to black root rot.

Solidago
Golden rod

Solidago 'Goldenmosa'

Hardy herbaceous perennials of vigorous habit, the golden rods are valued for their late color, provided by sprays of small, daisy-like, yellow flowers that are suitable for cutting.

Grow in a mixed or prairie-style border with asters, hardy chrysanthemums, rudbeckias, late-flowering heleniums, helianthus, monardas, *Echinacea purpurea*, and ornamental grasses such as *Miscanthus sinensis* cultivars. Solidago also looks good with shrubs noted for the color of their leaves in the fall, particularly rhus (sumachs). These perennials are suitable for poor and sandy soils. Propagate by division in spring or fall, or from basal stem cuttings in spring. Solidagos are prone to powdery mildew.

	SPRING	SUMMER	FALL	WINTER	height (ft)	spread (ft)	min temp (°F)	moisture	sun/shade	colors	
Solidago 'Crown of Rays'	🌱🌱🌱	● ●	● ●		2	1½	1°	◌◌	☼	⬜	Flat, spreading flower heads
S. 'Goldenmosa'	🌱🌱🌱	● ●	● ●		2½	1½	1°	◌◌	☼	⬜	Very bushy habit

☼ *sunny*   ◐ *semi-shady*   ● *shady*

x Solidaster

This hardy herbaceous perennial is a hybrid between a solidago and an aster and it looks like a yellow-flowered aster, with sprays of small daisy-like flowers. Like solidago, these flowers, which are produced in great abundance, are excellent for cutting for indoor floral arrangements.

x *Solidaster* is used in the same way as solidago and looks good with the same plant combinations. Cut down the dead flower heads as soon as flowering is over. Propagate this perennial in spring, either by division or from basal stem cuttings. It benefits from regular division every three years. Watch out for powdery mildew, which may flare up if the summer is hot and dry.

x Solidaster luteus 'Lemore'

	SPRING	SUMMER	FALL	WINTER	height (ft)	spread (ft)	min temp (°F)	moisture	sun/shade	colors	
x *Solidaster luteus*	🌱 🌱 🌱	● ● ●	●		3	1	1°	💧	☀	☐	Very free-flowering
x *S. luteus* 'Lemore'	🌱 🌱 🌱	● ● ●	●		2½	1	1°	💧	☀	☐	Very free-flowering

Stachys
Betony

Stachys macrantha 'Superba'

These hardy herbaceous perennials have spikes of tubular, often hooded flowers arising from rosettes of wrinkled leaves. All stachys have square as opposed to rounded stems. The flowers attract insects, including butterflies and bees.

Stachys is suitable for a mixed border, where it combines effectively with old shrub roses, lavenders, cistus, and rosemary (rosmarinus). Hardy perennials that make suitable companions include artemisias and salvias. These two species will tolerate a position in partial shade. Propagate by division in spring just as plants are starting into growth. Stachys is prone to attacks by slugs and snails.

	SPRING	SUMMER	FALL	WINTER	height (ft)	spread (ft)	min temp (°F)	moisture	sun/shade	colors	
Stachys macrantha 'Superba'	🌱 🌱 🌱	● ● ●	●		2	1½	1°	💧	☀	■	Deep green foliage
S. officinalis	🌱 🌱 🌱	● ● ●	●		2	1½	1°	💧	☀	■	Forms a carpet of foliage

🌱 planting ● flower 💧 well drained 💧 moist 💧 wet

Flowers

S

Stipa
Feather grass

This hardy perennial grass forms tufts of narrow, evergreen or partially evergreen leaves. However, it is mainly grown for its impressive heads of oat-like flowers. *S. gigantea*, the best species, is generally used as an effective contrast with many hardy perennials.

This plant looks particularly good with flat-headed achilleas, or with the bold spikes of kniphofias, or with the rounded heads of agapanthus, or with the brilliant flowers of crocosmias—one could go on indefinitely. It also contrasts well with many shrubs. Good, too, for a gravel garden. Propagate by division in spring. Not troubled by pests or diseases.

Stipa gigantea

Sutera

A tender perennial with masses of small, five-petaled flowers over a long period, sutera has a wide spreading, partially trailing habit. It is ideal for hanging baskets with other summer bedders such as impatiens, lobelia, begonias, and petunias.

Sutera cordata 'Snowflake'

Sutera is best grown as an annual. Seeds are not available, but young plants can be bought from garden centers in spring. Propagate from softwood cuttings in summer, and winter the young plants in a frost-free greenhouse for planting out the following year. Cuttings may also be taken in spring from older plants wintered under glass. There are few problems from pests and diseases but aphids may congregate on shoot tips in summer.

	SPRING	SUMMER	FALL	WINTER	height (in)	spread (in)	min temp (°F)	moisture	sun/shade	colors	
Sutera cordata 'Pink Domino'	🌱🌱🌱	✹✹✹	✹✹		6	18	37°	💧💧	☼	▨	Very free-flowering
S. cordata 'Snowflake'	🌱🌱🌱	✹✹✹	✹✹		6	18	37°	💧💧	☼	☐	Very free-flowering

☼ *sunny*   ◑ *semi-shady*   ● *shady*

Symphytum
Comfrey

Hardy herbaceous perennials of dwarf habit, symphytum species and cultivars have large, elliptic, rough hairy leaves and clusters of pendulous, tubular flowers. They are used as ground cover in shrub borders, woodland gardens, and other moist places with partial shade.

Grow with other plants that like similar conditions such as bluebells (hyacinthoides), forget-me-nots (myosotis), lily-of-the-valley (convallaria), and hostas. Be aware, though, that they are vigorous plants and can soon outgrow allotted space. Remove flower stems as soon as flowering is over. Propagate from root cuttings in winter or by division in the fall. No problems from pests or diseases.

	SPRING	SUMMER	FALL	WINTER	height (ft)	spread (ft)	min temp (°F)	moisture	sun/shade	colors	
Symphytum caucasicum		● ● ●	🌱 🌱 🌱		2	2	1°	🌢🌢	☀	■	Medium-green foliage
S. 'Hidcote Blue'	● ● ●		🌱 🌱 🌱		1½	1½	1°	🌢🌢	☀	■	Very free-flowering
S. 'Hidcote Pink'	● ● ●		🌱 🌱 🌱		1½	1½	1°	🌢🌢	☀	□	Very free-flowering

Tagetes
Marigold

Marigolds are half-hardy annuals with ferny, strongly aromatic foliage and single to fully double flowers in a range of bright colors—shades of yellow, orange, and red—and they vary from dwarf bushy to tall plants. Marigolds are used for summer bedding and patio tubs and window boxes, and flower over a very long period. If you want a really dazzling summer display, there are few other half-hardy annuals to compare with marigolds.

There are four groups of hybrids. African marigolds are noted for their very large, fully double flowers, some cultivars being tall, others shorter, and they have an upright rather than bushy habit. French marigolds are dwarf bushy plants with double or single flowers. Afro-French marigolds are derived from the first two groups and are dwarf and bushy in habit with small single or double flowers. Signet marigolds are dwarf, very bushy plants bearing masses of very small single flowers. African

🌱 planting   ● flower   🌢 well drained   🌢🌢 moist   🌢🌢🌢 wet

marigolds are best suited to very formal bedding schemes and are often used as dot plants in carpets of other bedding plants such as dwarf bedding dahlias or petunias. French, Afro-French, and Signet marigolds can be mass-planted in beds with dot plants of cannas, heliotrope, or *Verbena bonariensis*, for example, or used as an edging for beds and borders. For a really daring display, try mixing

Tagetes 'Safari Tangerine'

Tagetes 'Safari Mixed'

them with yellow argyranthemums, scarlet salvias (*Salvia splendens*), annual rudbeckias, and zinnias. *Nicotiana* 'Lime Green' and *Zinnia elegans* 'Envy', both with green flowers, are more subtle companions for marigolds. Remove dead flower heads regularly to ensure continuous flowering.

The flowers of all marigolds are good for cutting, but especially African marigolds with their long stems. During dry weather, water regularly to keep the plants growing and flowering. Raise plants from seed in early to mid-spring under glass; they are very easy and germinate rapidly. Watch out for gray mold (especially with African marigolds), slugs, and snails.

Flowers

	SPRING	SUMMER	FALL	WINTER	height (in)	spread (in)	min temp (°F)	moisture	sun/shade	colors	
Tagetes Boy Series (French)	🌱🌱🌱	●●●●	●●		6	8	34°	◐	☀	■	Double, crested flowers
T. 'Crackerjack Mixed' (African)	🌱🌱🌱	●●●●	●●		24	18	34°	◐	☀	▯	Produces very large double flowers
T. Gem Series (Signet)	🌱🌱🌱	●●●●	●●		8	12	34°	◐	☀	▦	Produces masses of small single flowers
T. 'Honeycombe' (French)	🌱🌱	●●●●	●●		10	12	34°	◐	☀	▦	Double flowers
T. Inca Series (African)	🌱🌱🌱	●●●●	●●		12	18	34°	◐	☀	▯	Double flowers
T. 'Naughty Marietta' (French)	🌱🌱🌱	●●●●	●●		12	12	34°	◐	☀	▭	Single flowers
T. 'Safari Series' (French)	🌱🌱🌱	●●●●	●●		8	12	34°	◐	☀	▦	Double flowers
T. 'Starfire' (Signet)	🌱🌱🌱	●●●●	●●		8	12	34°	◐	☀	■	Small single flowers
T. 'Tiger Eyes' (French)	🌱🌱🌱	●●●●	●●		8	12	34°	◐	☀	▦	Crested center
T. Zenith Series (Afro-French)	🌱🌱🌱	●●●●	●●		12	12	34°	◐	☀	▦	Double flowers

☀ *sunny*   ◐ *semi-shady*   ● *shady*

Tanacetum

Pyrethrum *or*
Feverfew

Cultivars of *T. coccineum* (pyrethrum) are hardy herbaceous perennials with ferny foliage and daisy-like flowers early in the summer. Grow in a mixed border with other early bloomers such as tall bearded irises, lupines, and oriental poppies (*Papaver orientale*).

Tanacetum parthenium

Cultivars of *T. parthenium* (feverfew) are hardy perennials but short-lived, and are grown as half-hardy annuals. Dwarf mound-forming plants with double, button-like flowers, they are used in summer bedding schemes as an edging where they combine well with most bedding plants, especially scarlet salvias (*S. splendens*). Cut back pyrethrum when flowering is over for another crop of flowers. Support plants with twiggy sticks. Propagate in spring; annuals from seed under glass, perennials by division or from basal stem cuttings. Aphids are the main problem.

	SPRING	SUMMER	FALL	WINTER	height (in)	spread (in)	min temp (°F)	moisture	sun/shade	colors
Tanacetum coccineum 'Brenda'	planting planting planting	flower			30	18	1°	well drained	sun	Bright green foliage
T. coccineum 'Eileen May Robinson'	planting planting planting	flower			30	18	1°	well drained	sun	Bright green foliage
T. parthenium 'Snow Puffs'	planting planting planting	flower flower flower			12	12	1°	well drained	sun	Small button-like flowers
T. parthenium 'White Gem'	planting planting planting	flower flower flower			8	12	1°	well drained	sun	Masses of small double flowers

Thunbergia

Black-eyed
Susan vine

A tender, perennial, evergreen climber, *T. alata*, the best species, is grown outdoors as an annual. With leaves like arrow heads, it produces five-lobed flowers with black eyes (hence the common name).

Combine the black-eyed Susan vine with other annual climbers such as *Tropaeolum peregrinum* (canary creeper) and ipomoea (morning glory), or even with hardy climbers such as clematis. Grow thunbergia in a very warm, sheltered position, and provide supports for it to climb, such as an obelisk, trellis, or pergola. Raise plants from seed in spring under glass. Outdoors there are no problems from pests or diseases.

Thunbergia alata Suzie Hybrids

Flowers

T

🌱 *planting*　　● *flower*　　💧 *well drained*　　💧 *moist*　　💧 *wet*

Thymus
Thyme

Cultivars of _T. serpyllum_ are grown for their flowers. Hardy, mat-forming, evergreen subshrubs, thymes form colorful carpets in summer when they are covered with tiny flowers. The equally tiny leaves are pleasantly aromatic and are gray-green in some cultivars.

Grow in a rock or scree garden, or in gaps in paving. In the latter situation the leaves will release their scent when the plants are trodden on, but do not do this too often or they will become damaged. Thymes are especially suited to chalky soils. The flowers of thyme attract bees. Propagate by division in spring. Not troubled by pests or diseases.

Thymus serpyllum 'Pink Chintz'

	SPRING	SUMMER	FALL	WINTER	height (in)	spread (in)	min temp (°F)	moisture	sun/shade	colors	
Thymus serpyllum 'Annie Hall'	🌱🌱🌱	● ● ●			2	12	1°	💧	☀	⬜	Aromatic foliage
T. serpyllum 'Pink Chintz'	🌱🌱🌱	● ● ●			2	12	1°	💧	☀	⬜	Aromatic, gray-green leaves

Tigridia
Tiger flower

Tigridia pavonia

A tender bulb, the tiger flower produces fans of sword-shaped leaves and highly colorful, multicolored flowers consisting of three large outer and three small inner petals.

The flowers of this plant do not last long, but they are produced in succession. Grow in a mixed border or in patio tubs. The bulbs should be lifted in the fall in frost-prone climates and stored in dry sand in a heated greenhouse or indoors for the winter. Best results in light, sandy soil. Propagate by removing offsets when bulbs are dormant. Few pests and diseases, but watch out for virus and destroy any affected plants.

☀ _sunny_   ◐ _semi-shady_   ● _shady_

Tradescantia

The Andersoniana Group of cultivars are hardy herbaceous perennials with clumps of broad grassy foliage and a long succession of three-petaled flowers. Grow in a mixed border.

Some good effects can be achieved by combining tradescantias with ornamental grasses of similar stature, particularly grasses with white- or cream-variegated foliage. They also associate well with hemerocallis (daylilies) and crocosmias. When flowering is over, cut back the stems to ensure more blooms follow. Propagate by division in spring. Watch out for aphids, slugs, and snails; otherwise there are no problems.

	SPRING	SUMMER	FALL	WINTER	height (ft)	spread (ft)	min temp (°F)	moisture	sun/shade	colors	
Tradescantia Andersoniana Group 'Isis'	planting planting planting	flower flower flower flower	flower		2	1½	1°	moist	sun	■	Large flowers
T. Andersoniana Group 'Karminglut'	planting planting planting	flower flower flower flower	flower		2	1½	1°	moist	sun	■	Distinctive color
T. Andersoniana Group 'Osprey'	planting planting planting	flower flower flower flower	flower		2	1½	1°	moist	sun	□	Blue stamens
T. Andersoniana Group 'Purple Dome'	planting planting planting	flower flower flower flower	flower		2	1½	1°	moist	sun	■	Large flowers

Trollius
Globeflower

The cultivars of *T.* x *cultorum*, the best one to grow, are hardy herbaceous perennials producing clumps of attractive lobed, much-divided leaves and, early in the season, showy globe-shaped flowers. They like very moist conditions, particularly heavy soils, and so are ideal for a bog garden or the side of a pool.

Alternatively, grow these plants in a mixed border if the soil is sufficiently moist. Also good for a moist, long-grass area. Good companions include moisture-loving irises, astilbes, and hostas.

When flowering is over cut back the stems by two-thirds of their length. Propagate by division in spring as soon as growth starts, or immediately after flowering. Watch out for powdery mildew. Otherwise, not troubled by pests and diseases.

	SPRING	SUMMER	FALL	WINTER	height (ft)	spread (ft)	min temp (°F)	moisture	sun/shade	colors	
Trollius x *cultorum* 'Alabaster'	planting flower flower flower	flower			2	1½	1°	wet	sun	□	A restrained grower
T. x *cultorum* 'Earliest of All'	planting flower flower flower	flower			1½	1½	1°	wet	sun	□	Early flowering
T. x *cultorum* 'Goldquelle'	planting planting planting	flower flower			2½	1½	1°	wet	sun	□	Large flowers
T. x *cultorum* 'Lemon Queen'	planting planting flower	flower			2	1½	1°	wet	sun	□	Large flowers
T. x *cultorum* 'Orange Princess'	planting planting flower	flower			3	1½	1°	wet	sun	■	Vigorous grower

planting ● flower   ▲ well drained   ▲ moist   ▲ wet

Tropaeolum

This is a large and varied genus. The most popular are the half-hardy annuals derived from *T. majus*, popularly known as nasturtiums, with either a dwarf bushy or trailing habit. These have large, rounded leaves and large, very showy, five-lobed flowers in a wide range of brilliant or pastel colors. Use them in patio containers and hanging baskets, or at the front of mixed borders.

These plants rarely need companions to enhance the effect, but if you want a contrast mix in some blue *Lobelia erinus*. Nasturtiums flower best in poor soils. *T. peregrinum*, the canary creeper, is a tender annual climber with attractive lobed leaves and masses of small, spurred flowers over a long period. The upper petals are attractively fringed. It is a vigorous grower and can be combined with other annual climbers such as ipomoea (morning glory) and *Thunbergia alata* (black-eyed Susan vine). Provide suitable supports such as an obelisk, trellis, garden arch, or pergola. A good perennial climber is *T. speciosum*, the flame nasturtium. Raise annuals from seed in early spring under glass, or in flowering positions during mid-spring. Pests and diseases include black aphids, caterpillars (of cabbage white butterflies), slugs, snails, and viruses.

Tropaeolum speciosum

	SPRING	SUMMER	FALL	WINTER	height (ft)	spread (ft)	min temp (°F)	moisture	sun/shade	colors	
Tropaeolum Alaska Series (*T. majus*)	🌱🌱🌱	●●●	●●		1	1½	34°	💧	☼	▨	White-variegated foliage
T. 'Empress of India' (*T. majus*)	🌱🌱🌱	●●●	●●		1	1½	34°	💧	☼	■	Leaves flushed purple
T. Gleam Series (*T. majus*)	🌱🌱🌱	●●●	●●		1½	2	34°	💧	☼	▥	Trailing habit
T. peregrinum	🌱🌱🌱	●●●	●●		10	3	37°	💧	☼	□	Pale gray-green foliage
T. speciosum	🌱🌱🌱	●●●	●●		10	3	25°	💧	☼	■	Perennial climber

☼ *sunny*   ☀ *semi-shady*   ● *shady*

Flowers

Tulipa
Tulip

Tulips are hardy spring-flowering bulbs with six-petaled flowers, which are generally produced singly, or in clusters in some species. The cultivars of hybrid tulips have mainly single flowers, although some are double, and most are wine glass- or bowl-shaped. Some of the species have star-shaped flowers. There is a huge range of colors available among tulips, but true blue is not represented.

Tulips are split, according to flower type, into 15 groups and these are included in brackets after the names in the table. Tulips have various uses in the garden. The smaller

Tulipa 'Queen of Night'

Tulipa 'Burgundy Lace'

species like *T. tarda* are suitable for rock gardens or the front of mixed borders. Small hybrids such as the Kaufmanniana and Greigii tulips are excellent in patio tubs or window boxes. The taller hybrid tulips are favorites for formal spring bedding schemes. Traditionally they are planted through carpets of forget-me-nots (*Myosotis sylvatica*), double daisies (*Bellis perennis* cultivars), or wallflowers (erysimum), where color combinations are virtually limitless. However, tulips can also be used informally in mixed borders, planting them in irregular groups or drifts and associating them with spring-flowering shrubs such as forsythia, magnolias including *M.* x *soulangeana* cultivars, *Corylopsis pauciflora*, amelanchiers, ceanothus, exochorda, *Kolkwitzia amabilis*, *Kerria japonica*, *Spiraea* 'Arguta', and *S. thunbergii*. Also plant them around spring-flowering trees such as ornamental cherries (prunus), laburnums, and malus (crab apples). Always grow tulips in a sheltered

Tulipa tarda

🌱 *planting*   ⬤ *flower*   💧 *well drained*   💧 *moist*   💧 *wet*

position. Remove dead flower heads. Species tulips such as *T. tarda* are generally left in the ground for a number of years, but hybrid tulips are lifted every year when the foliage has died down and the bulbs stored for the summer in a dry, airy place after drying off and ripening under glass. Large bulbs can then be planted for flowering again, smaller ones being planted in a nursery bed to grow to a larger size. If you want to plant summer bedding plants before the tulips' leaves have died down, lift the bulbs and heel them in on a spare piece of ground until they die down. Propagate by removing offsets in summer. Pests and diseases include bulb aphids, bulb rot, slugs, and snails. A disease specific to tulips—tulip fire—causes distorted, scorched, or withered leaves covered in gray fungal growth. Remove and burn infected plants. Do not plant tulips again on the same piece of ground for at least three years.

Tulipa 'Apeldoorn'

Tulipa 'Spring Green'

Tulipa 'Clara Butt'

	SPRING	SUMMER	FALL	WINTER	height (in)	spread (in)	min temp (°F)	moisture	sun/shade	colors	
Tulipa 'Angélique' (Double Late Group)	●		🌱🌱🌱		12	5	1°	💧💧	☀		Double flowers
T. 'Apeldoorn' (Darwin Hybrid Group)	●		🌱🌱🌱		24	5	1°	💧💧	☀		Goblet-shaped flowers
T. 'Attila' (Triumph Group)	●		🌱🌱🌱		15	5	1°	💧💧	☀		Cup-shaped flowers
T. 'Blue Parrot' (Parrot Group)		●	🌱🌱		24	5	1°	💧💧	☀		Attractively cut petals
T. 'Burgundy Lace' (Fringed Group)		●	🌱🌱		24	5	1°	💧💧	☀		Fringed, deep-purplish red, cup-shaped
T. 'Carlton' (Double Early Group)	●		🌱🌱🌱		12	5	1°	💧💧	☀		Bowl-shaped, double flowers
T. 'Clara Butt' (Single Late Group)		●	🌱🌱🌱		24	5	1°	💧💧	☀		Cup-shaped flowers
T. 'Flaming Parrot' (Parrot Group)		●	🌱🌱		20	5	1°	💧💧	☀		Attractively cut petals
T. 'Golden Apeldoorn' (Darwin Hybrid)	●		🌱🌱		24	5	1°	💧💧	☀		Goblet-shaped flowers
T. 'Groenland' (Viridiflora Group)		●	🌱🌱		18	5	1°	💧💧	☀		Goblet-shaped, can be green and pink
T. praestans 'Fusilier' (Miscellaneous Group)	●		🌱🌱🌱		12	5	1°	💧💧	☀		Several flowers per stem
T. 'Queen of Night' (Single Late Group)		●	🌱🌱🌱		24	5	1°	💧💧	☀		Cup-shaped flowers
T. 'Red Riding Hood' (Greigii Group)	●		🌱🌱🌱		8	6	1°	💧💧	☀		Leaves marked with purple
T. 'Spring Green' (Viridiflora Group)		●	🌱🌱🌱		15	5	1°	💧💧	☀		Cup-shaped flowers
T. 'Stresa' (Kaufmanniana Group)	●		🌱🌱🌱		8	6	1°	💧💧	☀		Leaves mottled purple
T. tarda (Miscellaneous Group)	●		🌱🌱🌱		6	3	1°	💧💧	☀		Star-shaped flowers

☀ *sunny*   ◐ *semi-shady*   ● *shady*

Verbascum
Mullein

A variable genus, the plants listed here being hardy, semi-evergreen or evergreen perennials, although rather short-lived. From rosettes of large grayish-green leaves (or deep purple-green in some cultivars) bold spikes of saucer-shaped flowers arise.

Used in mixed borders, these plants combine well with old shrub roses, and with perennials such as flat-headed achilleas, artemisias, and ornamental grasses. Mulleins are also suitable for gravel gardens. Best results in chalky soils, which should not be too fertile. Propagate by division in spring or from root cuttings in winter. Regular propagation is advised due to the rather short lives of these plants. Watch out for caterpillars and powdery mildew.

Verbascum 'Helen Johnson'

	SPRING	SUMMER	FALL	WINTER	height (ft)	spread (ft)	min temp (°F)	moisture	sun/shade	colors	
Verbascum 'Cotswold Queen'	planting	flower			4	1½	1°	well drained	sun		Partially evergreen, gray-green foliage
V. 'Gainsburgh'	planting	flower			4	1½	1°	well drained	sun		Partially evergreen, gray-green foliage
V. 'Helen Johnson'	planting	flower			4	1½	1°	well drained	sun		Evergreen, gray-green foliage

Verbena
Vervain

Verbena x hybrida cultivars are half-hardy perennials grown as annuals. Plants may be bushy and upright or spreading in habit, and produce rounded heads of small five-petaled flowers. Mass-plant in beds or grow in containers, including hanging baskets.

Verbena x hybrida

These plants mix well with many other summer bedders, including petunias, salvias, dwarf dahlias, and pelargoniums (zonal and ivy-leafed). *V. bonariensis*, a frost-hardy perennial, can be used as a dot plant in summer bedding schemes and in mixed borders. It looks great with cannas, tall dahlias, or tall ornamental grasses. Raise *V.* x *hybrida* cultivars from seed sown in spring under glass, or buy plug plants. Propagate *V. bonariensis* by division in spring or semi-ripe stem-tip cuttings in summer. Watch out for aphids, powdery mildew, slugs, and snails.

	SPRING	SUMMER	FALL	WINTER	height (in)	spread (in)	min temp (°F)	moisture	sun/shade	colors	
Verbena bonariensis	planting	flower	flower		72	24	25°	well drained	sun		Branching habit
V. x *hybrida* Quartz Series	planting	flower	flower		10	9	34°	well drained	sun		Compact bushy plants
V. x *hybrida* Tapien Series	planting	flower	flower		8	18	34°	well drained	sun		Trailing habit, good for baskets
V. x *hybrida* Temari Series	planting	flower	flower		8	18	34°	well drained	sun		Trailing habit, good for baskets

planting · flower · well drained · moist · wet

Flowers

V

Veronica
Speedwell

This is a large genus of plants, only a few of which are described here. These hardy perennials produce spikes of small saucer- or star-shaped flowers over a long period.

Grow veronicas, such as the ever-popular *V. gentianoides* and the newer *V. kiusiana* from Japan, in a mixed border, using the low-growing kinds at the front. Veronicas combine effectively with many plants, including shrub roses and hardy perennials such as Paeonia, Dianthus (border carnations and pinks), achilleas, alchemilla, geraniums, and sidalceas. *V. peduncularis* 'Georgia Blue' and *V. spicata* subsp. *incana* can also be grown in a rock or scree garden. Propagate by division or from basal stem cuttings in the spring. Veronicas are prone to leaf spot and powdery mildew.

Veronica kiusiana

	SPRING	SUMMER	FALL	WINTER	height (in)	spread (in)	min temp (°F)	moisture	sun/shade	colors	
Veronica kiusiana	🖐🖐🖐	●●●			24	24	1°	💧	☀	⬜	Dome-shaped habit
V. peduncularis 'Georgia Blue'	🖐 ●●●				4	24	1°	💧	☀	⬛	Vigorous grower
V. spicata subsp. *incana*	🖐🖐🖐	●●●			12	12	1°	💧	☀	⬛	Silver foliage

Viola
Pansy *or* Viola

Hardy, short-lived perennials grown as annuals or biennials, pansies and violas have flat, five-petaled flowers held vertically. Pansies have the largest flowers, violas masses of smaller blooms. Pansies are also generally larger plants, violas being smaller and more compact in habit.

Viola 'Sorbet Supreme Mix'

Violas have an incredibly long flowering period and, provided that a suitable selection of cultivars is chosen, they can be found in flower throughout the year. Basically there are summer- and fall-flowering annuals and winter- and spring-flowering biennials. There is a huge range of colors available, some cultivars coming in plain colors, others multicolored, and there are both mixtures and single colors available in many of the series. The "faced" cultivars have dark-colored or black contrasting markings resembling a face.

Pansies and violas are used for bedding and also make excellent container plants, especially for patio tubs and window boxes. They do not really need any other plants to enhance the effect—simply mass-plant them on their own. However, the winter- and spring-flowering kinds are effectively combined with certain spring-flowering bulbs, such as hyacinths, early dwarf tulips, or early Cyclamineus narcissus (daffodils). Pansies and violas also look good planted

☀ *sunny*   ☀ *semi-shady*   ● *shady*

V

Flowers

Veronica kiusiana

149

Viola Penny Series

Flowers

informally in mixed borders, the winter- and spring-flowering kinds around shrubs that flower during these seasons.

Regularly deadhead pansies and violas to ensure continuous flowering. Raise pansies and violas from seed sown under glass in cool conditions. Sow summer-flowering kinds in early to mid-spring and plant out the young plants in late spring.

Biennials for flowering in winter and spring are sown in early summer. Grow on the young plants in a nursery bed and plant them out in the fall.

Pansies and violas have more than their fair share of pests and diseases, and are prone to aphids, foot rot, leaf spot, powdery mildew, rust, slugs, snails, and viruses, particularly mosaic virus.

	SPRING	SUMMER	FALL	WINTER	height (in)	spread (in)	min temp (°F)	moisture	sun/shade	colors	
Viola Clear Crystal Series (Pansy)	planting	flower	flower		8	10	1°				Flowers of medium size
V. Floral Dance Series (Pansy)	flower	planting	planting	flower	8	10	1°				Some blooms bicolored
V. Joker Series (Pansy)	planting	flower	flower		8	10	1°				Bicolored flowers, boldly marked
V. Penny Series (Viola)	flower	planting	planting	flower	6	8	1°				Small flowers
V. Princess Series (Viola)	flower	planting	planting	flower	6	8	1°				Some flowers bicolored
V. Sorbet Series (Viola)	flower	planting	planting	flower	6	6	1°				Masses of tiny flowers
V. 'Super Chalon Giants' (Pansy)	planting	flower	flower		8	8	1°				Very large flowers, heavily blotched
V. Universal Series (Pansy)	flower	planting	planting	flower	8	10	1°				Flowers of medium size
V. Velours Series (Pansy)	flower	flower	planting		6	8	1°				Small flowers, some interesting bicolors

planting   ● flower   well drained   moist   wet

Zantedeschia
Calla lily

Zantedeschia aethiopica **is a frost-hardy perennial. Depending on the climate it may be evergreen or herbaceous, but its best cultivar 'Crowborough' is more or less fully hardy. The calla lily is one of the more exotic-looking plants for the garden with its broad, arrow-shaped leaves and tubular, flaring flowers (correctly called spathes).**

This plant can be grown as an aquatic in a pool in the shallow water at the edge—up to 12in (30cm) in depth. Plant in an aquatic basket filled with heavy loam soil. Otherwise, grow in a border with moist soil well enriched with humus. In this situation a winter mulch of dry straw or leaves will protect the roots in frosty climates. Propagate by division in spring. Prone to aphids and various fungal root rots.

Zantedeschia aethiopica 'Crowborough'

	SPRING	SUMMER	FALL	WINTER	height (ft)	spread (ft)	min temp (°F)	moisture	sun/shade	colors	
Zantedeschia aethiopica	🌱 🌱 ✹	✹ ✹			3	2	25°	💧💧	☀	⬜	Bright green shiny leaves
Z. aethiopica 'Crowborough'	🌱 🌱 ✹	✹ ✹			3	2	25°	💧💧	☀	⬜	Bright green shiny leaves

Zinnia

Half-hardy to frost-tender bushy annuals, zinnias have rounded, daisy-like heads of double or single flowers in a wide range of colors.

Zinnia haageana 'Persian Carpet'

The blooms of zinnias are good for cutting. These plants perform best in hot summers. Grow in a mixed border, particularly with other daisy-flowered plants such as *Rudbeckia hirta* cultivars and tagetes (marigolds) and with ornamental grasses of appropriate stature. Also grow in patio containers, particularly the dwarf *Z. haageana* 'Persian Carpet' (Mexican zinnia).

Remove dead flower heads regularly. Raise plants from seed, under glass in early spring, in flowering positions in late spring. For a long display, sow seeds in succession. Few pests and diseases are troublesome, but watch out for gray mold, particularly with large, double-flowered cultivars.

	SPRING	SUMMER	FALL	WINTER	height (ft)	spread (ft)	min temp (°F)	moisture	sun/shade	colors	
Zinnia elegans 'Dahlia-flowered Mixed'	🌱 🌱 🌱	● ● ●			2	1	41°	💧	☀	▨	Semi-double flowers
Z. elegans 'Envy'	🌱 🌱 🌱	● ● ●			2½	1	41°	💧	☀	⬜	Semi-double flowers
Z. haageana 'Persian Carpet'	🌱 🌱 🌱	● ● ●			1½	1	34°	💧	☀	▦	Small, double, rain-resistant flowers

☀ *sunny*   ☀ *semi-shady*   ✹ *shady*

Troubleshooting

The following diagram is designed to help you diagnose problems with your plants from the symptoms you can observe. Starting with the part of the plant that appears to be most affected—flowers, leaves, or stems—by answering successive questions "yes" [✓] or "no" [✗] you will quickly arrive at a probable cause. Having identified the cause, turn to the relevant entry in the directory of pests and diseases for details of how to treat the condition. Problems specific to flowers grown from bulbs, corms, or tubers are highlighted in a separate diagnostic table below.

FLOWERS

are the flowers distorted or show colored streaks?

VIRUS

have holes been eaten out of the petals?

EARWIGS

are the flowers rotting (i.e. showing a gray down?)

GRAY MOLD

are there brown spots on the petals?

PETAL BLIGHT

LEAVES

are new leaves deformed?

APHIDS

have holes been eaten out of the leaves?

is it a seedling?

WOODLICE

are holes tiny notches?

WEEVILS

also a silvery trail?

SLUGS / SNAILS

only leaves affected?

CATERPILLARS

are the flowers and buds also affected?

EARWIGS

are the markings yellow?

also stunted growth?

VIRUS

are the leaves spotte

are the markings white?

VIRUS

markings only on tops of leaves / is there leaf drop?

RED SPIDER MITE

BULBS, CORMS AND TUBERS		
TYPE	**SYMPTOMS**	**PROBLEM**
bulbs—narcissus, galanthus, scilla	few leaves, no flowers	NARCISSUS BULB FLY
corms and bulbs—crocus, gladiolus, lilium, tulipa	aphids in store; growth deformed	BULB APHIDS
tubers and corms— esp. cyclamen, begonia	plant wilts	VINE WEEVIL
bulbs—tulipa only	withered or scorched leaves; fungal growths on bulbs	TULIP FIRE
bulbs—e.g. narcissus, lilium, tulipa	soft spots in store, especially at base	BULB ROT
corms—e.g. crocus, gladiolus	black or brown spots in store, then corms shrivel or rot	CORM ROT
tubers—esp. dahlia	damp tubers develop soft spots	TUBER ROT

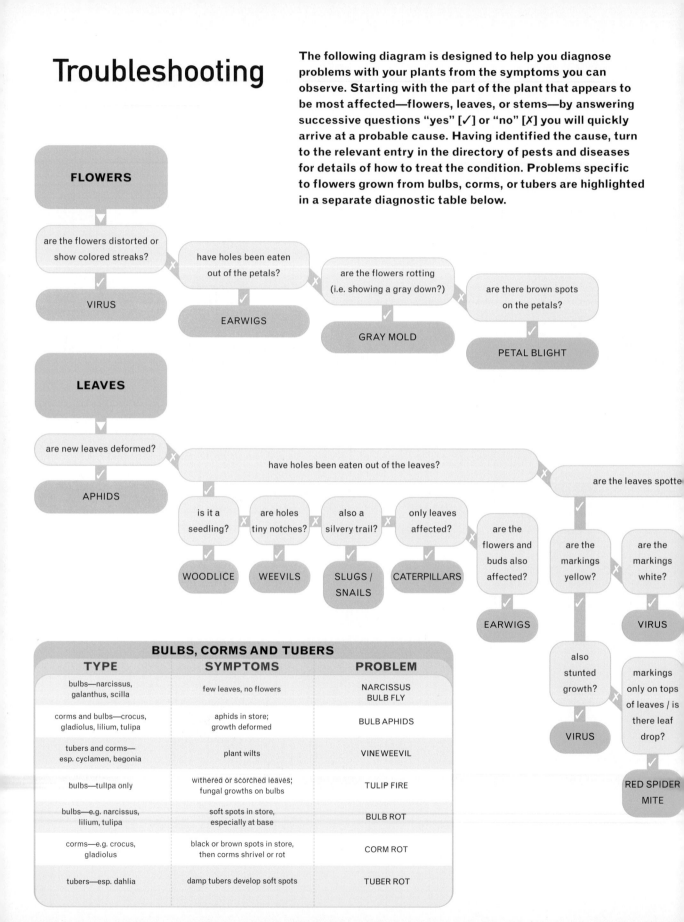

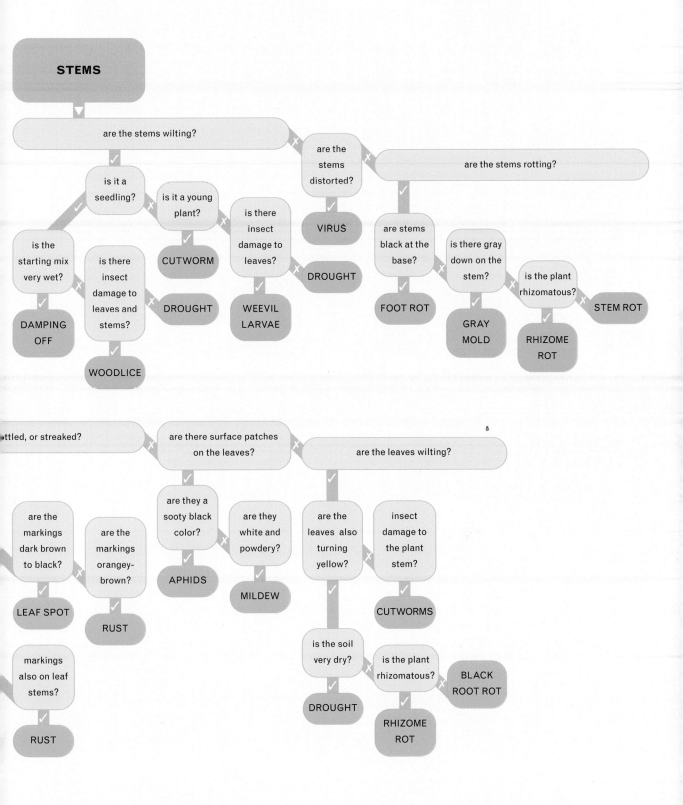

STEMS

are the stems wilting?

is it a seedling?

is the starting mix very wet?

DAMPING OFF

is there insect damage to leaves and stems?

WOODLICE

is it a young plant?

CUTWORM

DROUGHT

is there insect damage to leaves?

WEEVIL LARVAE

are the stems distorted?

VIRUS

DROUGHT

are the stems rotting?

are stems black at the base?

FOOT ROT

is there gray down on the stem?

GRAY MOLD

is the plant rhizomatous?

RHIZOME ROT

STEM ROT

ttled, or streaked?

are the markings dark brown to black?

LEAF SPOT

markings also on leaf stems?

RUST

are the markings orangey-brown?

RUST

are there surface patches on the leaves?

are they a sooty black color?

APHIDS

are they white and powdery?

MILDEW

are the leaves wilting?

are the leaves also turning yellow?

is the soil very dry?

DROUGHT

is the plant rhizomatous?

RHIZOME ROT

BLACK ROOT ROT

insect damage to the plant stem?

CUTWORMS

Pests & Diseases

These are the major pests, diseases, and other problems that affect flowers. Do not be alarmed, though—your plants are unlikely to be troubled by all of these.

Some pests and diseases are very choosy about the plants they attack and go for specific kinds, the narcissus bulb fly that hones in on daffodils being a good example, while others such as certain aphids, particularly greenfly, will go for a wide range of plants. Some symptoms are caused by other factors such as drought, which causes plants to wilt.

There are various ways of controlling pests and diseases: chemical and physical. However, as there is increasing reluctance among home gardeners to use chemical pesticides for environmental reasons, there is strong emphasis here on nonchemical methods of control.

Very safe preparations for pest control based on plant extracts are more acceptable and are becoming more widely available. Biological control—in which a parasite is used to control a specific pest—can also sometimes be used outdoors.

Slugs and snails

Slugs and snails eat the leaves of a wide range of plants and also damage soft young stems and even flowers. They make irregular holes in leaves and can cause severe damage. Slugs and snails are most active during damp weather and they feed at night. Control by placing slug pellets around plants. Alternatively, remove them by hand or, for slugs, use biological control (a nematode). Beer traps—jars sunk to their rims in the ground and half-filled with beer—attract these pests, which fall in and drown.

Petal blight

This disease attacks chrysanthemums, and sometimes other related plants, and anemones, showing as watery lesions or brown spots on the petals. The flowers are eventually destroyed. It is worse during wet weather or if conditions are humid. Remove affected flowers. Spray plants with fungicide containing mancozeb.

Bulb aphids

Certain aphids winter on bulbs and corms in storage. Look out for them on crocuses, gladioli, lilies, and tulips, and simply rub them off, as if left they can cause deformed growth. In the greenhouse, aphids can be controlled by introducing a parasitic wasp, *Aphidus matricariae*, which lays its eggs inside adult aphids.

Woodlice

These gray, "armor-plated" pests feed at night and hide in dark places during the day. Mainly they feed on dead plant material, but they may also damage seedlings by feeding on the bases of the stems or even very young leaves. Physical control is not practical, except to ensure that any plant debris is not left lying around. If seedling damage is a major problem, apply ant powder around the seedlings.

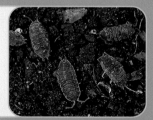

Caterpillars

The caterpillars of various moths and butterflies eat holes in the leaves of numerous perennials and annuals. In a bad attack they can defoliate plants. These grubs are various colors—green, brown, or gray—and are generally hairy. Caterpillars are easily picked off and destroyed, or plants can be sprayed with an insecticide such as rotenone (derris) or pyrethrum.

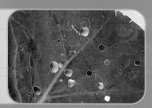

Viruses

Viruses are types of diseases that infect a wide range of plants. The most common symptoms are stunted and distorted plants. The foliage has yellow or white markings such as a mosaic pattern, mottling, ring spots, flecks, or streaking. Flowers may be distorted or show colored streaks. Sap-feeding insects, especially aphids, spread viruses from plant to plant. Viruses may also be spread when handling plants, for example, during propagation from cuttings. There is no cure: pull up and burn affected plants. Keep insect pests under control.

Rust

This fungal disease shows as rust-colored, orange, yellow, or dark brown raised spots on the leaves and stems. The problem is generally worse in damp summers. A debilitating disease, it can cause leaves to die. Numerous perennials and annuals are affected including fuchsias, hollyhocks (Alcea), and irises. Affected leaves should be removed. Spray with a fungicide, such as one containing myclobutanil.

Mildew

The most common is powdery mildew, appearing as white powdery patches on the leaves of many plants. This fungal disease is worse if soil remains dry and if plants are crowded together, which impedes air circulation. Some plants are particularly prone, including bergamot (Monarda), chrysanthemums, and delphiniums. The disease is very debilitating and causes distortion of leaves and shoots. Remove affected leaves. Spray plants with myclobutanil or sulfur fungicide.

Aphids

These are among the most troublesome insect pests, particularly greenfly and blackfly, and they attack a wide range of flowers. The tiny bugs are usually found clustered around flower buds, new shoots, and on the undersides of new leaves. Aphids suck the plant's sap, which has a weakening effect and causes deformed leaves and shoots. They excrete honeydew, a sticky substance on which unsightly sooty mold grows (it looks like soot). Wash off aphids with plain or soapy water, or spray with insecticidal soap.

Rhizome rot

This bacterial disease causes the leaves of rhizomatous irises to turn yellow and wither. Affected leaves develop rot at the base and this soon spreads to the rhizomes. The disease enters the plants through wounds, and is more prevalent during wet weather or in wet soil conditions. Dig up and discard badly affected plants. Avoid damaging plants, as rhizomes that are not badly affected may be saved by cutting out the rot and replanting. Cultivate rhizomatous plants only in well-drained soil to reduce the likelihood of them being afflicted by this debilitating disease.

Narcissus bulb fly

The cream-colored grubs of this fly feed inside daffodil bulbs, which eventually rot. First signs of trouble are few leaves and no flowers. There is no satisfactory control: dig up and discard any bulbs showing symptoms. When daffodils start to die back, mound up soil around the stem bases to prevent adult flies from laying eggs.

Stem rot

Numerous diseases, but particularly sclerotinia, cause the stems of various perennials and annuals to rot. Either the whole stem or part of the stem, and commonly the base, is affected by this condition, and the foliage of the plant wilts. The disease is most prevalent during cool, damp weather, when it can take hold quickly on vulnerable plants. Plants that are badly affected should be removed and discarded immediately, as unfortunately there is no cure.

Leaf spot

Many diseases show up as brown or black spots on the leaves of numerous ornamental plants. The spots vary in size and some are in the form of rings. Plants likely to be affected include carnations (dianthus), pansies (violas), irises, and delphiniums. The best control method is to pick off any leaves showing spots. Spray affected plants with myclobutanil fungicide.

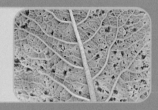

Wilting leaves

Wilting can be caused by a number of diseases although the most common cause is drought. Prolonged dry soil conditions can cause great stress to plants, which react by collapsing their leaves. In severe cases, the stems may also wilt. Even if watering is eventually carried out, young plants may never recover properly—if indeed at all. To prevent wilt, make sure the soil never dries out, ideally by mulching permanent plants and by watering as necessary. Especially keep an eye out in hot weather, when the symptoms can appear suddenly. Cold drying winds can also result in wilting as moisture is rapidly lost from leaves. This applies especially to newly planted subjects, which should be sprayed with water several times a day during windy conditions.

Red spider mite

There are several kinds of these microscopic spider-like creatures that feed by sucking the sap from the leaves of many plants, particularly under glass. Red spider mite is a menace in different ways to several different categories of plant, but in ornamentals its presence results in fine pale yellow mottling on the upper leaf surfaces. A heavy attack can be debilitating and will cause leaves to drop. The problem is worse outdoors during hot, dry summers. Spraying plants regularly with plain water will deter the mites. Under glass, and outdoors during summer, use biological control (a predatory mite), or alternatively, spray plants with insecticidal soap.

Bulb rot

Bulbs of various kinds, including daffodils, lilies, and tulips, are prone to rotting during storage, caused by various diseases. Check for soft spots, particularly at the base of the bulbs (basal rot), which can also make the bulbs feel slimy to the touch. Also, look for brown-colored mold erupting at the sides of the bulb. Remove and discard rotting bulbs. Tulip fire is a serious disease, usually first noticed when young leaves emerge distorted, withered, or "scorched," but stored bulbs may have fungal bodies on them. Dig up and discard affected bulbs, which generally rot eventually.

Weevils

These beetles are easily recognized by their elongated "snout." The most troublesome in gardens is the vine weevil. The dull black adults eat notches out of the leaves of various woody plants but damage is not usually severe. The larvae are much more of a problem. These feed on the roots of numerous plants. Their feeding causes wilting, and invariably death in severe attacks. Grubs are particularly troublesome under glass but are also active outdoors. Use biological control with a pathogenic nematode in late summer.

Gray mold

This major fungal disease, also known as botrytis, can infect all top growth of plants, resulting in rotting. The disease, which shows as a fluffy, gray mold, is particularly troublesome under glass, where scrupulously hygienic conditions should be maintained. Cut off any affected parts of plants, back to healthy tissue.

Cutworms

These caterpillars, the larvae of several different moths and greenish-brown or grayish-brown in color, live in the soil and feed on roots and stem bases of plants, causing young plants to wilt and die. They attack plants just below or at ground level and are particularly troublesome in recently cultivated soil. Remove any found during soil cultivations and use biological control—pathogenic nematodes—during the summer.

Tuber rot

A fungal disease may attack dahlias in store, causing the tubers to rot. Make sure that all moisture is removed from the cut-down stems by standing the plants upside down to drain for a week or two before storing. The tubers also should be dry prior to storage in frost-free but cool conditions. Check stored tubers regularly and if rotting is noticed, cut it away to healthy tissue and treat it with sulfur powder. This condition can normally be checked if it is caught early enough.

Corm rot

Corms such as crocuses and gladioli are prone to several kinds of rot while in store, so check regularly and remove and discard any that show signs of rot. An attack may first show as black or brown spots on the outside of the corm. Later, corms may shrivel or rot. With gladioli, a disease known as core rot causes corms to rot from the inside. Do not plant any suspect corms.

Foot rot

This disease causes the bases of stems to turn black and rot. Various plants are affected, including campanulas, pelargoniums, and pansies or violas. Pull up and discard any plants that show signs of infection. Drench soil around healthy plants with mancozeb fungicide as a preventative. Avoid introducing new plants in the affected area for some time—situate them elsewhere in the garden.

Black root rot

A disease affecting many flowers. The roots become black, but above-ground symptoms are yellowing and wilting leaves. Scrap sickly looking plants and plant something different in the affected site. Use sterilized potting mix when raising plants under glass.

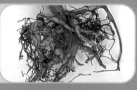

Earwigs

These night-feeding insects, easily recognized by their rear pincers, eat holes in flowers, buds, and leaves, particularly dahlias and chrysanthemums. Set traps among plants at flower height: pots filled with straw and inverted on canes. Check traps daily and remove and destroy any pests.

Damping off

This disease affects seedlings indoors, causing them to suddenly collapse and die. Damping off can spread rapidly and should be prevented by using sterilized seed starting mix and clean containers. Avoid excessively wet starting mix and prolonged very high temperatures. Water containers with copper-based fungicide after sowing and pricking out.

Index of Plants

This index lists the plants mentioned in this book by their common names where applicable and their Latin names in all other instances

General Index

Acknowledgments

The majority of photographs in this book were taken by Tim Sandall. A number of others were kindly contributed by the following individuals and companies and are credited in full below:

John Feltwell/Garden Matters: pp 38(T); 42(B); 46(C); 52(T); 52(B); 59(T); 60(T); 71(B); 72(B); 77(T); 90(B); 94(BR); 95(L;R); 107(B); 110(T); 117(L) (John & Irene Palmer); 117(TR) (John & Irene Palmer); 117(BR); 125(C) (Debi Wager Stock Pics); 126(C) (John & Irene Palmer); 128(B); 130(T); 133(B); 134(TR); 138(T); 140(T); 142(T); 143(T); 144(B)

Unwins Seeds Ltd: pp 50(C); 74(T); 75(C); 76(TR); 76(BL); 79(C); 91(T); 98(T); 98(B); 103(T); 105(T); 108; 110(BL); 116(T); 119; 123(B); 130(B)

Key: T = Top; B = Bottom; L = Left; R = Right; C = Center

The publishers would like to thank Coolings Nurseries for their cooperation and assistance with the photography in this book, including the loan of tools and much specialist equipment. Special thanks go to: Sandra Gratwick; Garry Norris; Ian Hazon; and Brian Archibald. Coolings Nurseries Ltd., Rushmore Hill, Knockholt, Kent, TN14 7NN, England. Tel: 00 44 1959 532269; Email: coolings@coolings.co.uk; Website: www.coolings.co.uk